This highly successful introduction to the world of politics has been fully revised and updated in collaboration with a new co-author, Nigel Jackson of the University of Plymouth. The new edition builds on the reputation for clarity and comprehensive coverage of the previous editions. It explores the varieties of political systems, the main political movements and key issues at the beginning of the twenty-first century.

New to the fourth edition:

- comparison of quantitative and qualitative methods
- more international examples
- greater discussion of non-Western concepts of politics
- the problem of voter apathy and lack of trust in politicians
- more discussion of the 'war on terrorism'
- extended analysis of the role of the Internet in politics including blogs, search engine censorship and e-democracy
- analysis of further key concepts such as genocide and policy networks
- more links to web pages including case studies, further questions to explore and additional learning activities.

Accessible in style and topical in content, this book assumes no prior knowledge of politics. These features make it ideal reading for general readers as well as for those who are just beginning to study politics at undergraduate level.

Stephen D. Tansey has taught Politics at the universities of Ife (Nigeria), Exeter and Bournemouth, for the Open University and the WEA. He is the author of *Business, Information Technology and Society* (also published by Routledge).

Nigel Jackson has worked as a parliamentary agent for a UK political party, for an MP and as a parliamentary lobbyist. Teaching at the University of Plymouth, his research interests are in political communication and political marketing, especially online.

Also available from Routledge

THE ROUTLEDGE DICTIONARY OF POLITICS
DAVID ROBERTSON

FIFTY MAJOR POLITICAL THINKERS
(SECOND EDITION)
IAN ADAMS AND R.W. DYSON

FIFTY KEY FIGURES IN TWENTIETH-CENTURY BRITISH POLITICS
KEITH LAYBOURN

FIFTY KEY THINKERS IN INTERNATIONAL RELATIONS
MARTIN GRIFFITHS

INTERNATIONAL RELATIONS: THE KEY CONCEPTS
MARTIN GRIFFITHS AND TERRY O'CALLAGHAN

THE ROUTLEDGE COMPANION TO FASCISM AND THE FAR RIGHT
PETER DAVIES AND DEREK LYNCH

INTERNATIONAL RELATIONS: THE BASICS
PETER SUTCH AND JUANITA ELIAS

POLITICS

THE BASICS
4TH EDITION

stephen d. tansey and nigel jackson

Routledge
Taylor & Francis Group

LONDON AND NEW YORK

First edition published 1995
Second edition published 2000
Third edition published 2004
Fourth edition, 2008
by Routledge
2 Park Square, Milton Park, Abingdon, Oxon, OX14 4RN

Simultaneously published in the USA and Canada
by Routledge
270 Madison Ave, New York, NY 10016

Routledge is an imprint of the Taylor & Francis Group, an informa

Typeset in Aldus Roman by
Keystroke, 28 High Street, Tettenhall, Wolverhampton

British Library Cataloguing in Publication Data
A catalogue record for this book is available from the British Library

Library of Congress Cataloging in Publication Data
Tansey, Stephen D., 1942–
  Politics : the basics / Stephen D. Tansey and Nigel Jackson. — 4th ed.
      p. cm.
    Includes bibliographical references and index.
  1. Political science. I. Jackson, Nigel A. II. Title.
  JA66.T35 2008
  320—dc22   2007038803

ISBN 10: 0–415–42243–4 (hbk)
ISBN 10: 0–415–42244–2 (pbk)
ISBN 10: 0–203–92919–5 (ebk)

ISBN 13: 978–0–415–42243–7 (hbk)
ISBN 13: 978–0–415–42244–4 (pbk)
ISBN 13: 978–0–203–92919–3 (ebk)

TO THE NEXT GENERATION –
ESPECIALLY ELIOT, TOBY,
FREYA AND JAKE

CONTENTS

ILLUSTRATIONS

FIGURES

BOXES

TABLES

PREFACE

This book is designed as a basic introduction to twenty-first century politics. We do not claim to be able to predict with certainty the political shape of the new century. However, it is already clear that many of the old perspectives of superpower rivalry and class and ideological warfare which dominated the era of the Cold War seem to be of reduced relevance. Issues such as ecology, new technology, Islam, terrorism, feminism and the role of what used to be described as the Third World (referred to as 'the South' in this book) are likely to move to centre stage. An introduction to politics that takes a parochial single-country approach no longer seems sensible in an era of increased international interdependence.

The readers we have in mind are without a systematic knowledge of, or rigid attitudes towards, politics. This book is intended both to enable such readers to make up their minds about politics and to understand more about the academic discipline of politics (or, as it is more grandly described in the United States, 'political science'). In particular, pre-university students, whether or not they have studied politics at school, have found this book a useful indication of the ground covered by university courses. The book has also been found useful for undergraduates beginning courses in politics. It has also formed the basis of short subsidiary courses in politics at under-graduate, postgraduate and extra-mural level. However, we hope that open-minded and intelligent older and younger readers alike will also find much of interest in this approach. Nor would we have any objection to the occasional practising politician quarrying something useful from the work!

We have not taken the view that a 'social scientific' approach requires the assumption of an attitude of detachment from the politics of the day. But neither have we tried to sell a short-term political programme. The approach here is to search for long-term principles that can help guide political actions. 'Politics' has been taken to mean the essential human activity of deciding how to live together in communities. This activity has been put in a long-term and wide geographical context. Frequent reference has been made to both Europe as a whole and the United States as well as to the United Kingdom. The focus is on the relatively prosperous industrialised countries of the 'West', but this cannot be detached from those of the rest of the world. In considering such an ambitious agenda we have drawn extensively on the work of many academics, whose ideas have in many cases already been borrowed (often in caricatured form) by politicians.

In a book designed to help readers make up their own minds about politics, no attempt has been made to hide the authors' liberal and socially progressive point of view. This has inevitably been reflected in such matters as the choice of topics for discussion. But it is hoped to give a fair representation of all other major points of view and to give an indication of where the reader can find accessible versions of alternative perspectives.

HOW THE BOOK IS ORGANISED

The book begins with a discussion of the nature of politics and the variety of academic approaches to its understanding. Chapter 2 illustrates the variety of contexts in which political activity takes place. Chapters 3 and 4 then survey competing ideas about the aims of that political activity.

The final four chapters of the book consider in more detail what and how political decisions are reached. Chapter 5 covers what kinds of decisions are made and how political systems change. Chapter 6 reviews the variety of different states. Chapter 7 focuses on how modern democracies make their decisions. Finally, considering more specifically some particular areas of public policy making, the limitations of public policy-making processes and the role of individuals in politics are discussed in Chapter 8.

The book is not divided up in the same way that many politics courses are into sub-disciplinary areas. But, in these terms, Chapter 1 is about methodology, chapters 3 and 4 are mainly political theory, 2 and 5 mainly political sociology, chapters 6 and 7 are mainly political institutions/comparative government and Chapter 8 public policy and administration.

To assist users of the previous editions of the book, it may be helpful to point out the major innovations in the fourth edition. These are:

- explicit treatment of the need for political theories and comparison of quantitative and qualitative methods in Chapter 1;
- decline in the partisan interpretation of politics is stressed in Chapter 1;
- some more specific definitions of globalisation in Chapter 2;
- continued emphasis on the implicit message that Western democratic politics should not be assumed to be the norm in Chapter 2;
- a discussion of genocide in Chapter 3;
- revision of the discussions of ideology and the Third Way in Chapter 4;
- more discussion of the 'war on terrorism', in Chapter 5;
- linking of the discussion of representative democracy to the ideas of Burke;
- updated discussion of the role of the Internet to refer to blogs and e-democracy;
- analysis of the permanent campaign with more on spin and international politics;
- two new sections in Chapter 8 on changes in the political policy process and the crisis of modern democracy. This has been put in the context of the US/UK axis on the market economy as opposed to the French/German more statist approach;
- Each chapter now ends with a list of useful websites, as well as recommended reading.

This new edition, in addition to obvious changes following such developments as the departure as prime minister of Tony Blair in Britain and developments in the 'war on terror', has also been further amended to strengthen its international references both for the benefit of its many international readers (including readers of editions in Polish and Chinese) and to counter the parochialism of many introductory courses and books in Britain.

At all times the intention is to assist readers to make up their minds about issues, rather than to argue for some predetermined conclusion.

HOW TO USE THIS BOOK

There are many ways to attempt to introduce students to a discipline, and in this book we have chosen to concentrate on introducing some of the major arguments within politics and the concepts associated with them. Logically we have begun with the methodology and boundaries of a discipline. Complete novices to the subject may find this introductory chapter of limited interest at first and can be forgiven for skipping through the second half of the chapter on initial reading.

Students already started on a politics course should find that this broader perspective on their studies stimulates more thought than many more detailed and limited textbooks. It should prove useful especially at the beginning of such courses and by way of revision at the end. It is also intended to help those contemplating such courses to decide if politics is the appropriate subject for them. By encouraging an evaluation of the reader's own political position and evaluating many basic political concepts as part of a sustained argument, we hope to encourage a critical and individual approach which is more valuable than a more 'factual' approach both in the examination room and in practice.

The Appendix on 'Sources on politics' will be found useful in locating additional material in an academic or public library, including the use of newer electronic information sources. Many years of experience teaching at this level have shown that most students greatly underestimate the library resources they have available.

References are organised on the Harvard system so that a date in curved brackets after an author's name indicates a full entry in the References section at the end of the book. Such dates normally indicate the edition used by the author for references but the latest edition for items recommended for further reading. Readers new to the Harvard system should note that the date of the edition used is not necessarily an indication of the date of composition – especially in the case of older and translated works. In addition to the References, each chapter is followed by some recommendations for suitable further reading. Pairs of dates in square brackets after a person's name indicate dates of birth and death – approximate in the case of early figures.

A feature of the book which readers should find particularly useful is the definition of key concepts found in boxes at intervals in the text and indexed in initials at the end. Students will quickly find that any work they submit which does not clearly define its terms will obtain an unfriendly reception, and, conversely, such definitions contribute greatly to clear analysis and communication.

ACKNOWLEDGEMENTS

Finally a word of thanks to students on various politics and public sector management and public relations courses at Plymouth, Exeter and Bournemouth universities, and with the Workers' Educational Association (WEA), for their comments and suggestions on this material.

In addition to the help from colleagues and friends acknowledged in earlier editions, this latest edition has also benefited from useful comments and suggestions from a number of readers, and the work of our editor at Routledge, Craig Fowlie and production editor Abigail Humphries has been much appreciated. The blame for infelicities and errors remains, of course, with us.

POLITICS

THIS CHAPTER . . .

discusses what politics is and the ways in which scholars have attempted to understand it. The first serious professional students and teachers (Greeks such as Plato [427–347 BC] and Aristotle [384–322 BC]) made politics the centre of the curriculum. In the twenty-first century academics are still seeking to explain politics 'scientifically'. This chapter discusses the meaning, importance and problems of such an enterprise.

POLITICS IN EVERYDAY LIFE

Is the study of politics a sensible activity? Any watcher of television news can see that democracies vary in apparent effectiveness, equality and longevity, from peaceful and egalitarian regimes as in Switzerland and Sweden, through the controversial case of the United States of America, to apparently fragile new democracies in Eastern Europe and Latin America. Dictatorships seem to thrive at one time like the former Soviet Union, sending the first satellite into space and dominating half the world, only to crumble away as the result of forces which few seemed able to predict. There are times when it is difficult not to sympathise with the view that such matters are both out of the control and beyond the understanding of ordinary people.

Yet we have seen ordinary people bravely dismantling regimes which seemed immovable, and dying for abstract ideas about politics: thousands of Bosnians and Albanians 'ethnically cleansed' in the name of Serbian national identity in the former Yugoslavia; tens of thousands of ordinary citizens protesting in the Ukraine which led to the Orange Revolution. It seems wrong in the face of such evidence of the capacity of ordinary people to effect, and be affected by, political change not to consider both the nature of political institutions and what action we should take in relation to them.

Leaving aside the dramatic examples of political action and change in faraway places, it is worth examining our own lives and the impact of politics upon them.

Suppose you are an 18-year-old living in the United Kingdom, working at a McDonald's, and hoping for a university place in the autumn. Waking up you may realise that the government (strictly Parliament) has legislated to convert what was a local time of 6:33 or so (depending on the latitude) to 7:30. Turning on the local radio station (whose franchise was granted by a QUANGO (quasi autonomous national (or non-) governmental organisation) you may hear the weather forecast from the government-financed Meteorological Office. After hearing several CD tracks (payment of royalties to the authors and performers must be made by law by the radio station), you drag yourself out of bed (legally mattress materials must be non-flammable), down to your cornflakes (ingredients listed on packet in due form by another law). If you unwisely reach for a cigarette, the government (/European Union) has both insisted on a health warning on the packet and taken a large rake-off in the form of tax.

Without going through every minute of your day, it is clear that government is likely to be affecting almost every one of them in similar ways (air quality, traffic regulations, employment law – fill out the story yourself).

The bigger issues are, of course, affected in the same way. Can you afford to go to university? What bursaries and loans are available, or fees payable, as a result of government policy? How many places has the government financed in universities? How many other students have been educated by the state educational system to university entry level? If, on the other hand, you are unable to make it to university, then your prospects for permanent employment will depend upon the government's management of the economy. Prospects for continued employment with McDonald's are dependent on, among other things, government policy towards foreign companies and the extent and effectiveness of health education campaigns!

So far we have only considered you and the government. Suppose on reaching the kitchen your father snaps at you: 'Can't you clear up the beer glasses and pizza cartons you and your friends littered the place with last night?' Arguably this is a political situation too. Within the family, fathers are sometimes thought to have 'authority' – some sort of legitimate power over children. As an 18-year-old, you might react to the speech as an assertion of authority and react back negatively on the grounds that you are no longer a child to be given orders. Conversely, your father may merely feel that in a community all should play their part and clear up their own mess. But in any case if he wants you to clear up and you do not, this can be seen as a clash of wills in which only one can prevail.

Similarly when you arrive at McDonald's it may well be you have discovered that the assistant manager (who is in charge in the absence of the manager on holiday) is busy establishing in the eyes of the area manager that he can do a better job than his boss. Here we have a struggle for power in which people within the organisation may take sides (form factions as political scientists might say) – in short, organisational politics is being practised.

It soon becomes clear that 'politics' is used in at least two senses, both of which are immediately relevant to everyone's everyday experience. In the narrowest conventional (dictionary) usage – what governments do – politics is affecting us intimately, day by day, and hour by hour. In the wider sense – people exercising power over others – it is part of all sorts of social relationships, be they kinship, occupational, religious or cultural.

WHAT IS POLITICS?

If we try to define 'politics' more formally and precisely, we run into the sort of problems which will be found to recur again and again in this book. It is actually quite tricky to define concepts in scientific disciplines like physics and chemistry, but if you do so, you are not so likely to be accused immediately of failing to understand the problem, of lacking scientific objectivity or of making unwarranted assumptions, as is a writer on politics. One of the problems is associated with whether we are talking about politics as a human activity or politics as an academic activity – or, in American terminology, politics or political science. The search for truth about how human beings exercise power might be thought to be completely separate from actually seeking to exercise that power. But in practice, as we shall see, political ideas are some of the most important weapons in the politician's armoury. Attempts to ignore this are either naive or, quite frequently, a deliberate attempt to present a controversial political ideology as an indisputable political fact.

In this light it is worth considering rather critically the implications of some of the standard academic definitions of politics and of power (Box 1.1).

BOX 1.1   DEFINITIONS OF 'POLITICS' AND 'POWER'

Politics

The science and art of government; the science dealing with the form, organisation and administration of a state or a part of one, and with the regulation of its relations with other states.

(*Shorter Oxford English Dictionary*)

. . . a way of ruling divided societies by a process of free discussion and without undue violence.

(Bernard Crick, 2000)

. . . who gets what, when, how.

(H. Lasswell, 1936)

. . . man moving man.

(Bertrand de Jouvenal, 1963)

. . . the authoritative allocation of value.

(David Easton, 1979)

Power

. . . the production of intended effects.

(Bertrand Russell, 1938)

. . . the probability that one actor within a social relationship will be in a position to carry out his own will despite resistance regardless of the basis on which the probability arises.

(Max Weber, in Gerth and Mills, 1948)

. . . the capacity to mobilize the resources of society for the attainment of goals for which a general public commitment . . . may be made.

(Talcott Parsons, 1957)

. . . the capacity of a social class to realise its specific objective interests.

(Nicos Poulantzas, 1973)

The definitions in Box 1.1 show very considerable differences, reflecting the viewpoint of the author. Most political scientists' definitions of politics are much broader in scope than the first, dictionary, definition which focuses on the state (although admittedly 'part of a state' could be interpreted widely). In effect they largely endorse the view suggested above: that politics is about the social exercise of power, rather than just the state. However, this may reflect the natural 'imperialism' of academics on behalf of their own discipline. Sociologists might argue that 'man moving man' would be more appropriate as a definition of their concerns.

Consider also, though, the unit of analysis, in terms of which these definitions are couched. Weber, Lasswell and de Jouvenal appear to be thinking primarily in terms of individuals exercising power, Crick and Parsons focus upon whole societies, the *Shorter Oxford English Dictionary* talks about governments, whilst Poulantzas views classes as the primary political 'actor'. This reflects a split between individualistic and collectivist theories which will be discussed in greater detail in Chapter 3.

Another contrast in these definitions is that between what has been described as 'zero-sum' and 'non-zero-sum' theories of politics. This terminology is derived from the mathematical theory of games. A zero-sum game is the usual sort of game, such as chess, in which a win by one player is, by definition, a loss on the part of the opposing player or players. There is a fixed amount of 'winnings' which means that the gains of one side are, by definition, losses to the other. Obviously many politicians, and political scientists, see politics this way. Thus Weber and (implicitly) Lasswell both seem to suggest that the political success of one individual may well be at the expense of others who oppose them. It is also a feature of Marxist theories, like that of Poulantzas, that the interests of classes are opposed and are gained at the expense of each other.

However, not all games are of this sort – for instance in collective make-believe children's games, new themes introduced by one player can enrich the enjoyment of the game for everyone – in a game of Cowboys versus Indians, the introduction of Aliens may lead to everyone having a better time. There is not a fixed amount of 'winnings', but by co-operation both sides can achieve more. In a similar way, Parsons explicitly argues that, by co-operation, different groups in society can each obtain greater benefits than would be the case if they work in competition. This view seems to fit well with contemporary emphasis in many parts of the Western world on the practice of mainstream politicians seeking to build coalitions, which involves compromise. Thus different theories place radically different emphasis on consensus (agreement) and conflict in their theories of politics.

There is a growing sense that politics in the established Western democracies is struggling. This unease has been referred to as a democratic deficit, political alienation or civic disillusionment. The possible explanations for such changes are examined by Gerry Stoker (2006), but the argument is that citizens have been increasingly 'turned off' by traditional political behaviour, such as voting in elections. This has manifested itself in a decline in partisanship, or a lessening sense of identifying with key political actors and structures. It has been suggested that increasingly politically active citizens have ignored the coalitions and compromises offered by the existing political elite, and have instead turned to single-issue pressure group activity. But does this apparent decline in traditional partisan electoral politics in some countries necessarily indicate a decline in the importance of politics?

The authors' sympathies lie with Maurice Duverger (1972: 19) who argues, 'The two-faced god, Janus, is the true image of power'. In other words, both conflict and consensus are essential elements to the creation of a political situation. The imposition of one person's or group's interests on another by force and without any element of consent seems far from what most people understand by 'politics', as Crick (2000) argues. On the other hand, a situation (perhaps unlikely) in which a group in total agreement (as to goals and methods), proceeds to achieve more and more of its objectives does not sounds like a political process either.

Thus 'politics' encompasses a broad range of situations in which people's objectives vary, but in which they work together to achieve those aims they have in common as well as competing where aims conflict. Both co-operation and competition may involve bargaining, argument and coercion. Politics may often be more an art than a science, and the art of politics may often be to see the potential for alliances rather than antagonisms amongst differing groups.

APPROACHES TO THE STUDY OF POLITICS

One of the joys, and also one of the frustrations, of the study of politics lies in the variety of approaches adopted by academic writers to the subject. This is a joy in the sense that within one course of study you will be introduced to a rich spectrum of writing ranging from classic philosophers like Plato (1866) and Aristotle (1946), through radical sociologists such as C. Wright Mills (1956) and Pareto (1976), to dedicated modern social scientists wielding statistical tests of significance to analyse huge volumes of computerised data, e.g. Robert Dahl (1971). It is frustrating in that the conclusions of such writers cannot be simply accumulated to form a certain body of knowledge representing the political scientist's view of politics. Students of politics must be ready to live with uncertainty, to sift through varied sources and accept what seems to them to be relevant and valid.

The remainder of this chapter attempts to provide tools to enable students to do their own 'sifting', and to recognise why writers on politics differ so radically. We shall look at three main approaches to the study of politics, and within these various schools of thought. These should be thought of only as a sort of preliminary crude map of the terrain to be covered, not as a rigorous analysis of what kinds of writing on politics is possible, or as a series of watertight divisions. However, it will be found that two writers within a 'school' generally have more in common, and are more likely to agree on what has already been established, and perhaps to refer to each other, than two writers in different schools.

The three main contemporary academic approaches to the study of politics can be described as 'traditional scholarship', 'social science' and 'radical criticism'. With an element of exaggeration they might also be thought of as the British, the American and the French approaches (although the 'American' approach has gained much ground in Britain and internationally in recent years).

'Traditional scholars' often approach matters on a rather piecemeal basis looking at one specific country, political institution, theoretical concept or writer in depth, often with the tools and preconceptions of another academic discipline – especially history or philosophy. Thus the core of the politics curriculum in Britain, at least until recently, has been the study of individual British political institutions in their historical context; the great political philosophers; and what was misleadingly titled 'comparative government'. The latter was, in practice, largely the study of American, French and Soviet government and politics separately. Often British courses have been part of a humanities-oriented programme such as the Oxford PPE (Philosophy, Politics, Economics) programme. A comparison of the leading UK and US journals showed that the leading UK journal, *Political Studies*, had 91 per cent of its articles focusing on institutional, descriptive, conceptual or philosophical topics (including history of political thought), whilst the *American Political Science Review* had 74 per cent of its articles in the behavioural/empirical or deductive/ rational choice categories (Norris, 1994: 15). In continental Europe politics has often been a subsidiary part of departments of faculties of law, sociology or history.

'Social scientists' would denounce the traditional approach as 'idiographic' (a word derived from 'ideogram' – a personal mark or signature), espousing instead a 'nomothetic' or generalising approach in which the endeavour of scholars of politics must be ultimately to derive general theories or laws about the nature of political behaviour. Thus a typical American-style curriculum presents political science as one of a group of related social science disciplines, including sociology and economics, all using modern quantitative/computer-oriented methods of 'analysing data' scientifically.

'Radical critics', whilst not denying the need to produce useful generalisations from the study of politics, have denounced the conservative bias of US-dominated political science. Often their primary allegiance has appeared not be to an academic discipline but to a general doctrine calling for the radical change of existing (Western) societies – most frequently some variety of Marxism, but similar criticism can be produced from an ecological, theological or feminist perspective.

The basis of the distinction being drawn is mainly in terms of what writers see their task to be, the methods they employ, the level and type of their analysis, and the values they espouse, rather than the details of specific theories advanced. In addition, though, a comparison of the specific theories advanced by different schools and approaches does show a concentration on different areas of human experience, broad patterns of difference in their content, and a tendency to draw upon similar models and to use the same concepts within schools. On examination it will often be found that where writers from different approaches and schools deal with what is apparently the same topic (e.g. 'democracy', 'elections', 'society') their concerns and assumptions are often so different that no real dialogue can be said to have occurred. Table 1.1 offers an overview of these major approaches and schools.

TRADITIONAL SCHOLARSHIP

The first academic writers on politics – Plato and Aristotle – whose works are still studied in detail in most British universities – were unaccustomed to the modern practice of compartmentalising knowledge into separate disciplines. Hence they combined insights from history and current affairs with discussions on the big moral issues such as 'What is the best form of government?' or 'What is justice?' This somewhat 'eclectic' approach (combining insights from various different sources) was also adopted by some of the more readable classic writers in the nineteenth century such as John Stuart Mill [1806–1873], Bryce [1838–1922] and De Tocqueville [1805–1859].

Table 1.1 Major contemporary approaches to politics

	Traditional	*Social science*	*Radical*
Task	Piecemeal explanation	Science of politics	Radical social change
Methods	Descriptive, historical, philosophical analysis	Quantitative or theorising illustrated	Ideological criticism
Values	Liberal democratic	Pro-US democracy and 'development'	Anti-establishment
Level of analysis	Political, philosophical, psychological	Political and social	Multi-level
Scope	Individual institutions or countries	USA or area studies	Global and historical
Content	Constitutional consensus disturbed by cataclysmic events	Pluralism	Class/gender/species conflict
Schools	(a) Liberal-institutional (b) Historical (c) Philosophical	(a) Functionalist (b) Economic (c) Systems	(a) Marxist (b) Feminist (c) Ecologist (d) Religious fundamentalist (e) Postmodernist
Typical concepts	Constitutional convention, great man	Political culture, market, feedback	Contradiction, patriarchy, jihad

Source: Adapted from Tansey (1973)

These writers saw the rise of democracy as the major political development of their time and sought to analyse not only the idea, but also its contemporary manifestations in different countries, and to suggest improvements and accommodations with the emerging reality of democratic government.

Serious writers on politics now tend to be university lecturers, who have to have specialist interests and lists of articles in professional journals and/or monographs published by respectable academic publishers. They tend now to adopt a much more limited conception of their role, with philosophically trained writers exploring concepts and the history of ideas, historians limiting themselves frequently to small periods of time and limited geographical areas, and students of political institutions specialising in electoral systems, UK parliamentary select committees or the politics of privatisation. There is no doubt that such academic specialisation may reap benefits in terms of specific discoveries (and in terms of obtaining rapid publication in academic journals). But this gain is also undoubtedly at the cost of some loss of perspective and the loss of a non-academic audience – who often fail to see the relevance of much of this work to current policy issues.

Within British university politics departments much admirable scholarly work continues to be produced on political theory and 'political institutions' without any systematic attempt to relate findings to general theories of political behaviour or 'social science'. A few holders of professorial chairs may still describe themselves as historians or philosophers rather than 'political scientists'.

Students of 'political theory' in this mode have tended to divide roughly into two main camps. One group are the philosophers who see their main task as the elucidation of political concepts (such as justice and democracy) with at least an eye to their relevance to contemporary concerns. A second group are the historians of ideas who have been concerned to trace the evolution of writings on politics, the intent of the writers of these texts and their influence on events.

Those who have written on 'political institutions' have often been less explicit in their theoretical intent, but writers such as Ridley (1975) and Rhodes (1997) have articulated the rationale and assumptions of much of this writing. In established and relatively stable democracies like Britain and the United States, it is evident that much of what we call politics centres around important governmental institutions like parliaments, elections, government departments, local authorities and the like. The study of how these institutions have evolved, the rules and practices surrounding them, and consideration of how they may be improved, is clearly of the utmost importance. As citizens, and possibly future public employees or even politicians, we may feel that such activities scarcely need elaborate justification.

However, the sceptical and the ambitious may combine to throw doubt upon the academic credentials of such activities. Is the result

really 'knowledge' which can legitimately be examined in universities – or merely pragmatic common sense which can be used by
those who agree with its (conservative and liberal?) assumptions? To
meet such objections there has been a development of more methodo-
logically aware 'new institutionalism' of which Peters (1999) discerns
no fewer than seven varieties. The sceptical will continue to argue
that the operations of representative institutions are merely a
deceptive mask for the real politics of exploitation below (see the
section on Radical criticism, p. 19), whilst the ambitious see only
scientifically established theories as the acceptable basis of knowledge
in the twenty-first century.

SOCIAL SCIENCE AND POLITICS

The proposition that our knowledge of politics should be scientifically
derived seems, at first sight, undeniable. The application of scientific method in many other spheres (e.g. physics, biochemistry,
astronomy) has yielded not only a broad consensus on the truth of
various scientific 'laws', but also practical results in the shape of space
travel and 'miracle' drugs. If the application of systematic observation, computerised analysis of data, the testing of hypotheses
through experiment and the painstaking building of small bricks of
fact into enormous edifices of knowledge can work in one sphere, why
not in another? Since human beings are currently at such logger-
heads over the nature of politics, it might be thought, indeed, that the
construction of a science of politics is the most urgent intellectual task
of our time.

The problems of creating a valid science of politics seem, however,
to be so enormous as to place the whole project in some doubt. They
include problems of value conflict, of complexity, of method and of
philosophy.

It is tempting to dismiss conflicts of value as irrelevant to scientific
investigation. The conventional argument is that science is morally
neutral ('value-free'), but can be used for good or evil. Thus the structure of the atom is the same everywhere, whether our knowledge of
this structure is used to destroy civilisations, to fuel them or merely
to understand their most basic constituents.

It is easier to apply a knowledge of biochemistry to creating
individual health than it is to use a knowledge of politics to create a

healthy society. But that is because there is more agreement on what an ill person looks like than on what is an ill society. However, such ethical problems of objectives are seen as separate from scientific problems as to how things work. In principle the authors would accept this proposition, although this then drastically reduces the likelihood of increasing social consensus by creating a science of politics because scientific analysis cannot resolve the problem of conflicting human objectives.

In social analysis, however, it has been impractical to create a 'value-free' vocabulary acceptable alike to social democrats, neo-conservative free-marketeers, Marxists and feminists. Suppose we try to describe a university staff meeting. A social democrat might observe academic democracy at work. A neo-conservative may see only a series of individuals asserting their interests. A Marxist may see wage-slaves ideologically dominated by the imperatives of the capitalist system. Meanwhile a feminist sees a series of males exerting patriarchal domination.

Another example is the Internet, whose creators wanted information to be freely available online, a value in its own right, but now increasingly it is being challenged by a different value of those who want to control and use such access to information. Thus the concepts we use to observe social reality have values 'built-in' to them which make 'objective' analysis difficult if not impossible.

An additional problem in applying scientific analysis to the social/political arena is the complexity of the phenomena being studied. Scientific method has so far been most successfully applied to physical systems, less successfully to biological systems composed of physical systems, and with only limited success to human psychological systems composed of biological systems. So that it should be no surprise that social systems comprising a still higher and more complex level of system are most resistant to analysis.

Typically science is seen as characterised by the testing of hypotheses, through experiment. The experimental method is largely closed to political scientists since they do not possess the power to dictate to whole human societies how they should behave. In any case experiments require identical control groups for comparison which, it is arguable, cannot be created. Some small-scale laboratory simulations of human power situations have been attempted with interesting results (e.g. Milgram, 1965), but the applicability of the results of these to whole societies is disputable. Statistical manipulation of existing sets of data about human societies may be a partial substitute for experimental techniques, but it could be argued that few convincing data sets exist. Some attempts at marshalling these include the *World Handbook of Political and Social Indicators* (Taylor and Jodice, 1983), and the Country Indicators for Foreign Policy Project at Carleton University, Canada (www.carleton.ca/cifp). One very basic problem for international data sets is that many countries do not have reliable population figures, for example Nigerian census figures have been politically contested because of their influence on the ethnic balance of power. It is also difficult to compare financial values in different currencies because of artificial exchange rates and differences in purchasing power.

Scholars committed to a scientific approach to politics have sought to overcome this problem by collecting quantitative data about political behaviour. Classically this has been done through social surveys which may be carried out on a large scale by market research firms, or on a smaller scale by researchers themselves. These tend to be focused upon voting behaviour and mass attitudes to political systems. However, legislative voting patterns and the texts of newspapers, political speeches, expenditures by governments and a wide variety of other observations can also be treated as quantitative data to be subjected to statistical analysis.

Modern statistical analysis is a very sophisticated discipline which enables the researcher to make judgements on the existence, or not, of significant associations between variables. These are commonly assessed as being 95 per cent or 99 per cent unlikely to have occurred by chance. However such questions as what proposition to investigate, what variables to examine, whether to treat variables as dependent or independent require an explicit or implicit theory of what is happening to be tested. There is a logical gap between a statistical association and a causal relationship which is what such researchers generally aspire to (see John, 2002).

On a philosophical level it has been argued that the sort of causal explanation that would be perfectly satisfactory in physical science would be unsatisfactory in explaining social phenomena – social explanations need to explain the motives of the persons involved, not just predict successfully what will happen (Runciman, 1969). Additionally, if we accept that human knowledge and motivation are an important part of every political system, every advance in political knowledge is potentially available to the members of the systems we study. The knowledge we produce by analysing political systems becomes potentially a part of those systems and may, of course, upset any predictions we make about them (Popper, 1960, and see Chapter 5).

Such considerations often lead to an emphasis on more qualitative methods of investigation, for example participant observation, in-depth interviews, case studies, textual deconstruction and focus groups. The emphasis in such investigations is often on contextualising and understanding the meaning of events to participants (see Devine, 2002). Such methods are more frequently applied by traditional or radical scholars – especially postmodernists.

SCHOOLS OF POLITICAL SCIENCE

Some of the problems of establishing a social science of politics become evident if we examine the writings of some of those most committed to the enterprise. It quickly becomes evident that there is no consensus on the concepts and methods to be employed, or the theories which can be assumed to have been already established.

Perhaps the most influential group of 'political scientists' are those stemming from Gabriel Almond and the deliberations of the Committee on Comparative Politics of the American Political Science Association in the 1960s. Although much criticised on theoretical grounds, the terminology and approach adopted by these 'functionalist' writers is still widely prevalent in empirical studies of American, British and comparative politics.

In a vastly influential early work, Almond and Coleman (1960) argued that we should speak of:

> 'Political System' instead of 'State'
> 'Functions' instead of 'Powers'
> 'Roles' instead of 'Offices'
> 'Structures' instead of 'Institutions'
> 'Political Culture' instead of 'Public Opinion'
> 'Political Socialization' instead of 'Citizenship Structure'.

Their argument was that by studying the processes necessary to maintain any political system in a variety of environments, rather than focusing on conventional liberal democratic institutions, they were creating the basis for a scientific approach:

> This is not only a matter of conceptual vocabulary [sic]; it is an intimation of a major step forward in the nature of political science as science . . . towards a probabalistic science of politics.
>
> (Almond and Coleman, 1960)

This attempt has been very successful in that thousands of writers have employed the vocabulary suggested, virtually every modern country has been described in these terms, and a vocabulary separated from that of everyday political discourse has been widely adopted by professional political scientists. Unfortunately there is little evidence that the vocabulary is used any more precisely than its 'old-fashioned' predecessors (Sartori, 1970), or that the assumptions implicit in the approach are any less arguable than (or, indeed, very different from) the liberal institutional approach. For instance, there has been no substantial agreement on what functions are necessary to maintain a political system (Dowse, 1972) or on the desirability of understanding politics in terms of the maintenance of the stability of existing sovereign states. Luard (1990) argues for a global perspective – see Chapter 2.

A good illustration of some of the problems of employing this newer vocabulary is to consider the concept of 'political system'. This is used rather loosely by most of the functionalists to indicate that politics is not merely limited to traditional constitutional institutions but that they are influenced by social and economic conditions within a country. As Nettl (1966) has pointed out, this usage often *assumes* that the system is an entity that exists and carries out some defined role – such as 'the allocation of value'. Alternatively the idea of system may be used more as a conscious analogy with engineering systems as with Deutsch (1963) who sees the political system as a steering mechanism for society – a flow of information through decision-making mechanisms which can be improved.

Systematic sociological thinkers such as Talcott Parsons (1957) see that 'functions' are highly theoretical processes analytically distinguished from a messy empirical reality. The problem then becomes to see what predictions such a theory is making. The 'emptiness' of system theory is perhaps most clearly seen if the writings of David

Easton (1979) are considered. He states that 'political system' is a purely analytical concept which can be applied to any collection of entities the theorist finds convenient. He then suggests the possibility of the system responding to 'input' from the outside 'environment' by 'outputs' which in turn may affect the environment so as to stabilise it. In such a case a stable 'homeostatic' system has been achieved. However, such an outcome is by no means inevitable – the problem then is to know when such an analysis is appropriate, and when a breakdown of the system might occur.

Thus many writers now claim to be adopting a 'system' approach, but it is often unclear whether they believe that political systems are observable entities, analytical frameworks, useful analogies or a problem-solving device.

By way of contrast, let us consider a more recent and perhaps trendier group of political scientists – the 'rational choice' theorists (or as we will usually refer to them, the 'economists'). They have adopted an alternative approach which, instead of starting with the behaviour of whole societies, focuses on the behaviour of individual political 'actors'. Mainstream economists have analysed markets starting with the behaviour of individual consumers and entrepreneurs who are assumed to rationally pursue their own interests (maximise utility or profit). The behaviour of individual voters, bureaucrats or legislators can be considered in the same way (Downs, 1957; Tullock, 1965; Himmelweit *et al.*, 1985). As with economics, it is not asserted that all actors are rational. The assumption is only that the system functions on the basis that most actors will be rational, and that irrational actors will cancel each other out/go 'bankrupt', etc. (Nor does maximising utility exclude the proposition that some actors will derive utility from altruistic actions.)

As an example of this approach, the behaviour of bureaucrats is not seen in constitutional terms as giving impartial policy advice to minister's, or in functional terms as part of both the interest-aggregation and rule-enforcement functions. Their behaviour is described as seeking to maximise their agency budgets in order to maximise their own power, salary and prestige. An alternative example is voters who vote in their own self-interest, rather than what they might objectively think is best for the country as a whole. Both examples stress the importance of 'economics'.

THEORIES, MODELS, PARADIGMS

Faced with a thicket of rival approaches and theories, readers may be tempted to demand who is right and who is wrong, or despairingly conclude that they will return to the subject in thirty years' time when the 'experts' have made up their minds. Alas neither tactic is likely to succeed, since no omniscient oracle is available to answer the question and thirty years of waiting will probably increase the complexity of the choice. What perhaps may help to clarify matters is to try to separate out a number of activities that are frequently confused in the effort to generate a science of politics. To do so, we need to consider how scientists normally work.

Popper (1960) has convincingly argued that scientific laws are useful general predictive propositions, which have been extensively tested and not disproved. Few of the propositions advanced by political scientists seem to meet this test. As we have already seen, many of the propositions advanced by 'empirical political theorists' are difficult to apply to the real world of politics, do not make unequivocal predictions, and certainly have not yet been extensively tested. Some more limited propositions might be regarded as testable hypotheses, the production of which constitutes a preliminary to the creation of usable theories.

It used to be thought that scientists derived their hypotheses for testing from the observation of as many 'facts' as possible (the 'positivist' view of science). More recent historians of science have observed that in fact most innovative hypotheses come from a combination of acute observation and the application of 'models' of reality often derived from another area of science. Observers need to have an idea of what they are looking for! A 'model' is a simplification of reality that enables us to suggest relationships between the things we observe.

In politics numerous different models have been, and still are, applied. For instance, as we shall discuss at greater length later on, one of the dominating models in early modern (liberal) thought was the legal model of a contract applied to relationships between citizens and rulers or the state. Medieval thinkers tended to prefer an organic model of the state – e.g. seeing the parts of a state as being like the parts of the human anatomy. Easton/Deutsch's application of a cybernetic (information system) model in the age of the computer thus becomes unsurprising in the 'postmodern' age.

Clearly, as Deutsch (1963) points out, models are not in themselves right or wrong, merely, helpful or unhelpful. Choice of models will depend on their relevance, economy and predictive power – the latter encompassing ideas of rigour (do theories based upon it give unique answers?), combinatorial richness (the number of patterns that can be generated from it) and organising power (can a model be applied in many different circumstances?).

Really successful models can be at the heart of what Kuhn (1970) terms a scientific paradigm. Thus the Newtonian model of matter as a series of particles whose relationships could be described in terms of a series of simple mathematical equations dominated physics for several centuries. Evolutionary development proposed by Darwin continues as the dominant paradigm in modern biology. Despite the positivist view of scientific development referred to above, Kuhn argues that most scientific endeavour ('normal science') consists in the further application of existing models to new areas, or the explanation of apparent deviations from the dominant model in terms derived from it. Nor should this be despised; a great deal of modern technological and scientific progress has rested upon this process of 'pygmies standing on the shoulders of giants' – ordinary knowledge workers amassing detailed information within the dominant paradigm.

In these terms, political studies can be seen as an academic discipline in the pre-scientific stage in which no dominant paradigm has yet emerged. What are described here as 'schools' can be seen as aspirant paradigms. The main question that has to be asked is how useful a source they are of models applicable to new situations, of testable hypotheses and of concepts for helpfully describing and analysing events. Absolute truths cannot be found.

RADICAL AND POSTMODERNIST CRITICISM

One characteristic of a scientific theory is that it should be value-free – there is no left-wing physics and right-wing physics, just good physics and bad physics. It is not that 'ideological' (see section on Ideology in Chapter 4) distortions are impossible or unlikely – theological and political considerations have hindered the acceptance of the Darwinian paradigm in biology for instance. But, in the long term, the insistence on observational, statistical, and above all experimental verification of theories, and probably the existence of a relatively united world professional organisation of scholars in particular subject areas, has enabled a consensus on paradigms, theories and concepts to emerge.

Consideration of many approaches put forward by political scientists reveals that the models upon which they are based, the concepts they employ and the theories they espouse frequently imply a clear set of values which others might well wish to dispute. If we consider Almond's functionalist model for instance, it seems clearly to view politics as a matter of maintaining political stability by enabling political interests in a system to be conciliated ('interest articulation and aggregation'). This is done by a state that functions through a traditional liberal pattern of legal rules ('rule making, rule enforcement and rule adjudication'). This model then stresses values of 'pluralism' (see section on Elites, classes and political pluralism in Chapter 5) and consensus which may be uncontroversial in the United States (where most political scientists live) but were clearly not acceptable in the old Soviet Union, amongst left-wing thinkers in Paris or in Tehran. Moreover, it creates a set of interesting challenges for China's political elite. Similarly, a glance at the individualistic model put forward by the 'economists' reminds one of the famous Margaret Thatcher remark that 'there is no such thing as society – only individuals'. Such theories clearly imply a fashionable suspicion of big government and stress on the 'profit motive' in the broad sense.

The obvious rival approach to political analysis stressing individualism and consensus is to consider the collectivist and conflict-oriented view of politics put forward by Marxists. There are, in fact, as we shall see later in Chapter 4, as many varieties of Marxism as there are of political science. But the basic model, stemming back to Marx and Engels's *Communist Manifesto* (1848), is of a society divided into large collectivities (classes) whose interests are in basic conflict. The only long-term resolution of such conflicts which stem from the basic relationship of exploitation between the capitalist bourgeoisie (the owners of the 'means of production') and the proletariat ('wage-slaves') is through a socialist revolution.

Although to readers in the Western world such an approach seems biased, is this judgement any more than taking-for-granted the values of our own society? Many Soviet citizens took these assumptions for granted in the same way that most British or American citizens assume that 'democracy' means a society in which everyone can vote at periodic elections where the rich can buy unlimited media exposure for their views.

A number of writers (Milliband, 1969; Gramsci, 1969) have approached the analysis of modern politics through a variety of Marxist models with, in some cases, enlightening results. Conventional assumptions have been questioned, and further economic and political dimensions to problems exposed. In the Western world, for instance, the cultural and media influence of capitalism has been emphasised, whilst in the 'third' world the Marxist emphasis on the international economic environmental influences (Williams, 1976) seems much more realistic than analysis of political parties that are liable to disappear overnight in a military coup (Sklar, 1963; Weiner, 1962).

As with conventional political scientists, the work of Marxist writers is of variable quality and interest to the ordinary reader. Here too a tendency to mistake assumptions for conclusions, or to jump to conclusions favourable to the initial model adopted can be discerned. In addition, perhaps, there may be a greater tendency to engage in 'theological' disputes within the school about the proper use of concepts and to take explicit policy positions. It is not always clear how academic (in accord with the canons of conventional scholarship) some books are intended to be. Conversely, of course, some Marxist works – particularly the *Communist Manifesto* itself – have been subjected to an orgy of academic criticism despite their explicitly polemical role.

More recently a number of radical feminist writers have emerged, who have questioned the assumptions implicit in conventional political analysis. They too have seen society primarily in terms of an exploitative relationship ('patriarchy') between collectivities (adult heterosexual males versus the rest). (It should be emphasised that this is a discussion of radical feminist writers – many feminists adopt a more liberal, moderate, stance.) Like later Marxists they have stressed cultural and media aspects of political relationships, but also stressed the political aspects of personal relationships. Whereas conventional analysis has looked at explicit political conflicts reflected in conventional party divisions, these writers have seen potential (seismic) splits repressed by conventional politics. Some writers on animal liberation and ecology could also be seen in the same methodological light as the Marxist and feminist critics discussed here. However, for convenience, they are discussed in a later chapter.

Lest the idea of repressed political divisions be dismissed out of hand it is worth considering the case of African-Americans in the United States. As recently as the 1950s in many parts of the USA, they were deprived of basic human rights and discriminated against. Living in a 'democracy' and resenting their condition, sometimes even in a majority in their local community, African-American concerns still did not even feature on the political agenda. Starting from this situation, Bachrach and Baratz (1970) put forward an interesting model of political activity, combining insights from both the pluralist and Marxist models. They suggest that an apparently free play of political interests in a 'democratic' system may coexist with suppressed conflicts in which the interests of certain groups often fail to reach the political agenda. Policies favouring suppressed groups, even if nominally adopted by governments, will not be fully implemented by the machinery of government. In short, what Schattschneider (1960: 71) calls a 'mobilization of bias' is built into the system against them. Whilst Bachrach and Baratz are mainly concerned with racial biases, clearly these biases can equally well be those of gender, ethnicity, religion or economy.

The radical writers discussed do not necessarily dismiss the enterprise of a science of politics – old-style Marxists frequently claimed that 'scientific' socialism gave them a superior insight into contemporary economy and society. They merely question the assumptions upon which contemporary analysts work. Postmodernist critics, influenced by philosophers such as Wittgenstein and Foucault, however, throw doubt upon the possibility of an impartial analysis of political behaviour. They stress that the very language used to describe political events is the product of struggles between different users of language and is 'internally complex, open, appraisive and fought over' (Gibbins and Reiner, 1999: 7). A good illustration of this is the contemporary concept of 'a war on terrorism'. There are no absolute foundations for morality and knowledge so that knowledge and judgements are inevitably subjective. Traditionally political science uses a vocabulary that assumes the primacy of the nation state and political conflicts based upon producer interests. Postmodernist critics often stress the impact of globalisation and consumerism in undermining these assumptions (Gibbins and Reiner, 1999: 120–133).

Finally, it has been argued that modernist writing on politics ('political science') has been dominated by a male North American professional elite committed to predominantly quantitative methods. A postmodern approach would abandon the idea of a unitary study with a consensus on methods and encourage greater use of writing by a global network of excluded and non-professional groups (Gibbins and Reiner, 1999: 167–178).

CONCLUSION

In looking at work by writers on politics, the important question is not so much if they employ some methodological orthodoxy, but whether their methodology is appropriate, consistently applied and helpful (Box 1.2).

BOX 1.2 ASSESSING THE USE OF METHODOLOGY IN POLITICS

Is the approach employed appropriate to the problem in hand?

Are theories, concepts and models clearly defined and consistently applied?

Are theoretical assumptions distinguished from empirically established conclusions?

Is ALL the evidence on the issues examined?

There is good work published by writers of all persuasions. Conversely some authors seem only to look for evidence supportive of their theoretical assumptions. In the present state of knowledge, it will often be found that a combination of insights derived from different approaches often throws the most light on an issue.

RECOMMENDED READING

Crick, Bernard, 2000, *In Defence of Politics*, 5th edn, London, Continuum International.

A stimulating and readable essay that defends Crick's own concept of politics against totalitarians, experts, nationalists and other false friends.

Leftwich, Adrian, 1983, *Redefining Politics*, London, Methuen
Interesting for the breadth of examples employed from the Aztecs to the World Bank.

Marsh, David and Stoker, Gerry (eds), 2002, *Theory and Methods in Political Science*, 2nd edn, Basingstoke, Palgrave
A useful, more advanced collection of contributions which cover approaches to politics, methodological differences (quantitative, qualitative, comparative methods, etc.) and theories of the state.

Stoker, Gerry, 2006, *Why Politics Matters*, Basingstoke, Palgrave Macmillan
Considers the causes of contemporary disenchantment with politics and makes the case for democratic politics.

Zuckerman, Alan S., 1991, *Doing Political Science: An Introduction to Political Analysis*, Oxford, Westview Press
A US view which stresses the study of politics as an academic social science.

WEBSITES

(See Appendix for more on websites as a resource for students of politics.)
http://www.vts.rdn.ac.uk/tutorial/politician
Internet Politician: online tutorial with many useful links.

http://www.HaveYourSayOnline.net
UK political system for citizenship education.

http://www.apsanet.org
American Political Science Association, includes an explanation of what is political science.

http://www.psr.keele.ac.uk
Richard Kimber's excellent Political Science Resources web page.

http://www.psa.ac.uk/www/default.htm
Political Studies Association (UK) WWW gateway.

http://ipsaportal.unina.it

International Political Science Association portal gives access to, describes and assesses for accessibility and usefulness 'the top 300' international sources on politics.

2

SYSTEMS

THIS CHAPTER . . .

elaborates upon a point raised in the introduction: that politics is not an activity confined to modern liberal democratic national governments. Chapter 1 argued that politics can be seen in personal and organisational activity – a point to be developed further in relation to our later discussions of feminism, anarchism and ecology. This chapter analyses the politics of societies without formal governments and the systems of government in kingdoms and empires before considering the focus of modern politics: the nation state. It considers the extent to which developments at a supranational level constitute a threat to the dominance of such states. Political 'system' is being used here in a loose sense to denote a complex of interconnecting political activities in a society or societies – it does not imply the adoption of any particular system model.

STATES AND SOCIETIES

For a graphic illustration of the thesis that politics is not just about how states are run, let us consider the case of societies without a state and see if we can identify anything resembling what we would normally think of as 'politics'.

This raises the issue of what is meant by a state. At this stage, let us ignore some complicated academic arguments and settle upon a working definition (Box 2.1) from Max Weber [1864–1920], a liberal German sociologist.

BOX 2.1   DEFINITION OF 'STATE'

Power

An organisation 'that (successfully) claims the monopoly of the legitimate use of physical force within a given territory'.
(Weber, in Gerth and Mills, 1948: 78)

This reflects the way most people probably see the world today. The globe is seen as divided into a series of exclusive geographical areas (countries or nations), each of which has a government whose people recognise its authority to maintain order amongst them, by force in the last resort if necessary. This government may, of course, be divided into central, regional and local levels and executive, legislative and judicial arms, but all these bodies are seen as a system for taking decisions on behalf of the nation (or society) and maintaining law and order.

POLITICS WITHOUT THE STATE: TRIBAL SOCIETIES

This is a picture we shall be questioning later. For now let us point out that until very recently 'tribal' groups have been 'discovered' in the forests of Papua New Guinea and Brazil living apparently undisturbed by the governments which purport to represent them at the United Nations. Of course such tribal groups may be thought of merely as traditional 'mini-states' and as only a minor deviation from Weber's model. However, social anthropologists who study such groups in detail have shown convincingly that tribal societies may differ radically from the state model of government.

Social anthropologists often avoid the use of 'tribal' in this context as implying a condescending view of the peoples concerned as primitive – this is not the authors' intention. Many of the groups concerned have sophisticated cultures, high levels of artistic achievement and admirable ways of life. 'Tribal' is used here as an easily intelligible synonym for what anthropologists frequently term 'simple societies' – those having common cultures (e.g. one religion and language), undifferentiated role structures (most people do a small range of similar jobs), with strong emphasis on kinship and custom (Mitchell, 1959). Following Weber, the defining characteristic of such societies may be taken to be a claim to common ancestry.

One way in which these groups differ from the state model of government is in terms of territory. Whilst many such groups do have what they regard as their own territory, some are so nomadic that they can make no such claim. Groups like the Fulani of northern Nigeria herd cattle through lands partially cultivated by others. The Kalahari Bushmen and similar groups range broadly over deserts or forests which may also be used by other groups. Such groups think of government as a property of what sociologists describe as the kin group – all those people descended from a common ancestor or married to such persons. Hence the idea of the 'blood brother' – to become a member of the group it is necessary either to marry into it or to be adopted as a member of a particular small family group.

Still more startling to the modern Western citizen than such groups' relative indifference to the idea of a territory being subject to a particular code of law, is the absence in some of them of anything resembling a fixed governmental organisation. Whilst the absence of a chief or council might not be regarded as so strange in tiny groups such as the !Kung bushmen of the Kalahari desert (Marshall, 1961), it seems almost incredible in groups numbering as many as a million or more such as the pre-colonial Tiv of Nigeria (Bohannan, 1965).

How can centralised political institutions be avoided in such societies? One explanation lies in the attitude to law found in most tribal societies. Western societies (following the nineteenth-century English jurist, Austin) tend to see law as the creation of a sovereign representative legislature. Tribal societies see law as a part of the way of life inherited from their ancestors. Thus living human beings only interpret and enforce the authority of the ancestors and no legislature is necessary. Such a view is clearly only tenable in relatively stable societies – although, as Gluckman (1965) points out, rebellion against those interpreting the law is perfectly possible in such a system.

What is unthinkable is the revolutionary process of replacing existing laws with new ones. The inflexibility of such a system can easily be exaggerated since in practice, as with English common law, old laws can be reinterpreted in new circumstances or quietly ignored as being no longer appropriate.

But does not the enforcement of law and the defence of the group require centralised government? The example of the Tiv suggests one way round this problem. They operated what the social anthropologists term a 'segmentary lineage system'. This means basically that every Tiv's place in society is governed by the lineage to which they belong – i.e. how they are descended from the ancestor of the group, 'Tiv'. It is not that the more closely related you are to the founder of the tribe the more important you are – there is no royal family since all are held to descend from the same source. Thus every Tiv is equal and a fierce egalitarianism reigns. Instead, in any dispute people claiming descent in the same line are expected to take sides together. Naturally should non-Tiv attack a Tiv, all members of the group would be expected to assist if need be. If fighting or quarrelling takes place between Tiv, however, support would be due to people in 'your' lineage.

Such a system seems merely to encourage conflict and disorder. If everyone can rely on a host of supporters in a dispute with others, will not disputes be the order of the day? Especially in a situation where there are no established permanent tribal chiefs or headmen (in the sense this is usually understood). In fact, though, the system seems to have worked well in practice. One reason for this was the existence of a considerable consensus on the customs (laws) to be applied. Disputes were not automatically the subject of violence or warfare but settled through meetings (or 'moots') of those concerned in the broad, Tiv, sense. After a certain amount of more or less violent posturing, the form was for all to have their say on the rights and wrongs of the dispute with relatives helping the aggrieved sides to present their case. Then a resolution of the dispute was attempted by mediation between the two lineages. If a solution could not be found the two groups would remain 'at daggers drawn' until a solution could be found.

In such a situation a premium was placed on bargaining and reconciliation rather than mechanical law enforcement. Many of those on either side might not feel too deeply affronted by (say) an alleged case of adultery, failure to pay up on a dowry payment or words said in a drunken brawl. But everyone would be severely inconvenienced if the other lineage in the village was not prepared to co-operate in the next hunt or harvest. An additional subtlety, which modified any tendency to take disputes too far, was the consideration that your opponents in this dispute might be needed in a larger dispute with more distantly related Tiv at some time in the future!

The Tiv are only one example of numerous tribal societies that have existed without centralised governmental institutions. Many have used some variation of the combination of 'feuding' and informal reconciliation systems practised by them. Additionally though, disputes might be settled by resort to oracles like the famous classical Greek oracle at Delphi, in which disputes were arbitrated upon using magical signs resulting from sacrifices. The ambiguity of some of these pronouncements may well have been a sensible political device on the part of the oracle, or medicine man, to avoid identification with either side and promote a negotiated settlement.

Other societies practised a division of functions on an 'age grade' basis in which, for instance, the oldest men might collectively manage relationships with the gods, another male age group constitute the leaders of the hunt, the oldest women practise medicine, and so on. In some groups important functions connected with warfare, law and order, or magic might be vested in secret or title societies, membership of which had to be earned by giving feasts to existing members, undergoing initiation ceremonies and performing subordinate roles in a trainee grade. In such societies skill in magic or warfare might be rewarded by promotion 'on merit', or promotion might depend upon seniority.

Authority in such societies might rest upon a variety of foundations – a reputation for wisdom in settling disputes, knowledge of traditional remedies for illness, ability as a war leader or merely being the grandparent of a very large (polygamous) family. Such authority figures might well be known by a title which translates into English as 'chief' – but their powers were often far from the absolute despotisms imagined by many early Western writers on these subjects. (Of course, chiefs in some tribal societies did have what we might regard as 'despotic' authority, e.g. Shaka the nineteenth-century Zulu chief who ordered whole battalions of his men to commit suicide as a demonstration of his absolute authority.)

In these tribal 'stateless societies', then, there is law rather than anarchy (in the everyday sense of no guarantees of law and order); equally, collective decisions on self-defence and economic co-operation are also made – but in a decentralised fashion. Many members of these societies would also emphasise that collective activities also occur on a spiritual level. In short, life continues and even apparently prospers without the state with its accompanying mechanisms of professional armies, bureaucrats, prisons and the like.

It is not surprising that, consequently, some modern thinkers – anarchists in the technical sense – have argued that the same is possible in a modern context. We shall examine their views at more length in Chapter 3. First, however, it is interesting to look at another example of what might be described as 'politics without the state', although this is perhaps a slightly more arguable case.

FEUDALISM

This second example is the feudal system – particularly as it was practised in Europe in the eleventh and twelfth centuries – though it has also applied in other parts of the world, such as in pre-modern Japan (Reischaur, 1956; Prawer and Eisenstadt, 1968). European feudalism is of interest as being perhaps 'nearer to home' for contemporary European readers, and as showing the state as we understand it to be a more recent innovation than some may have imagined. It may also suggest some lessons for the future of Europe.

At first sight, feudal Europe was full of states and mini-states, rather than stateless. Did not England, France, Poland and other familiar states already exist in this period – admittedly accompanied by extra 'players' on the international scene like Burgundy, Saxony and Venice? The appearance of kings, dukes and doges on the scene would seem to indicate the presence of strong centralized decision-making institutions for these territories. The similarity of names with institutions and territories of later periods may well, however, be quite misleading. Outside of England and France, particularly, it soon becomes clear that the idea of a number of territories each with its own legal jurisdiction is quite inappropriate.

This is clearest in the area round about what is now Germany in what was misleadingly called the Holy Roman Empire (accurately described as neither 'Holy', 'Roman' nor an 'Empire' by Voltaire [1694–1778] (1756: Ch. LXX). The empire masked a confusing array of jurisdictions. The 'Holy Roman Emperor' was the nominal supreme ruler of a hotchpotch of kingdoms, dukedoms, sovereign bishoprics, independent or federated cities and the like. His powers over each were different and ill-defined. The heads of some of these territories had the power to elect the emperor's successor. The Catholic Church, in the shape of the pope, claimed powers over the emperor and his 'vassals' (those who had sworn allegiance to him), which in later times were felt to be 'sovereign' prerogatives. Equally the Church claimed exclusive jurisdiction over all the clergy and many matters of family law – as well as rights to censorship and the levying of separate clerical 'taxes'. In some cases incumbents of independent kingdoms such as France and Spain held territory within the Empire as nominal vassals of the emperor or some other 'ruler'. Similar confusions were to be seen in relationships between the King of England in his capacity as Duke of Normandy and the King of France.

Law enforcement and defence were the subject of a patchwork of rights and privileges, the consequence of a pyramid of personal relationships between lords and vassals. Each vassal, in turn, was lord to an inferior group of aristocrats, until one descends to the level of the ordinary knight in his manor. At the aristocratic level the possession of land entailed not only something like the modern idea of ownership, but, perhaps more, the notion of government. In principle, in the early feudal period, land could only be held by those prepared to administer and, most importantly, defend it. Hence only adult fighting men could hold land. If, for instance, the king gave land to a duke, the only way the duke could hope to hold it was by sub-contracting the administration and defence of much of it to a group of earls or counts. Each earl or count, in turn, would obtain the allegiance of knights to hold particular manors, or fortified villages.

One consequence of this is, logically, an overlapping of jurisdictions in that the same area would be under the control of (in our example) a king, a duke, a count and a knight. Undoubtedly, also, the Church would also claim jurisdiction in some cases. For that matter it was common for hard-up lords to grant jurisdiction in commercial matters to town councils through charters – the terms of which some councils in Britain still preserve and attempt to enforce.

In practice lords were interested primarily in matters relating to their feudal dues – the equivalent of modern taxation and rents originally primarily payable in labour services. The lord might quite frequently originate from a different part of Europe, linguistically and culturally isolated from his serfs – so that they would often prefer to seek justice through informal community channels. Amongst lords, appeals to judgement by legalistic tribunals were often avoided in favour of trial by combat or through the pursuit of feuds or vendettas which could operate in very similar ways to the system described earlier in relation to the Tiv (Bloch, 1961).

Thus it is clear that in the feudal period, as in tribal stateless societies, conflicts over the allocation of resources could be resolved; communities could make decisions about their defence and economic welfare; but no effective and centralised state machinery existed to carry this out.

STATES WITHOUT NATIONS: KINGDOMS

At a later stage in European history, some individual feudal territories evolved over several centuries into something much more like a modern state. Kingdoms emerged with distinct boundaries within which central authorities claimed exclusive jurisdiction, sophisticated judicial systems with rights of appeal from local courts up to the centre, a taxation system divorced from the rents payable to the owners of land, and, in some cases, representative legislative assemblies. Part of the attraction of the Protestant Reformation for princes was the opportunity both to assert legal control over matters such as family law which had previously been Church matters and to reassign extensive Church property holdings to themselves and their supporters. Henry VIII's example in these matters was accompanied by similar phenomena in countries such as Sweden, whilst even Catholic monarchs such as Louis XIV began to assert control over religious orders, and to negotiate greater influence over the Church in their territory.

In essence similar political institutions to these kingdoms were also found in many other parts of the world. For instance, in what is now Nigeria at about the same period it seems likely that sizeable kingdoms existed in Benin, Yorubaland (Oyo) and in Hausaland

(Kano, etc.), whilst much earlier such kingdoms were to be found in India and Central America.

By definition, a kingdom can be regarded an example of dynastic politics. That is, they are not so much governments by individuals as by families. In the European examples this usually meant that the state was regarded as all the possessions of a single family regardless of geographical sense or the ethnic or national origins. Thus the modern United Kingdom includes Scotland, Wales and parts of Ireland, as well as the Channel Isles, because the kings of England inherited these areas from the Duchy of Normandy, succeeded to the separate throne of Scotland, or conquered adjacent lands. The kingdom was not united by linguistic, cultural or religious similarities. Other members of the family were frequently expected to take a major role in government – queens ruling in the absence of kings, the eldest son of the Crown of England being designated Prince of Wales. Similarly, Belgium and Holland could be regarded as possessions of the Spanish royal family. Within a royal family, rival claims to the succession could arise, and conflict between young supporters of the heir to the throne and established counsellors of the king was virtually the norm.

In the African examples mentioned, the family's role took very different shapes. Within the context of polygamy, there was more scope for dispute as to succession. Such disputes taking the most drastic form were in Zululand where it was usual for the king to execute any brothers who failed to go into hasty voluntary exile (Lemarchand, 1977). In the Yoruba kingdoms a version of the succession crisis involved 'king-makers' selecting the heir from the ranks of a number of princely families who each provided a king in turn.

These monarchic political systems shared a 'court' style of politics in which the administration of the royal household and its estates were inseparable from the business of the kingdom as a whole. Power in such systems might well reside primarily with those who most frequently had the ear of the monarch regardless of official position. This might include the king's mistress, confessor or hairdresser. The politics of such a system is primarily conducted within a consensus on fundamental values (those of the tribe or ruling aristocracy). There is emphasis on individual advancement through patronage; a powerful patron rewards his supporters and followers with benefits derived from his control or influence over government that might well be regarded as corruption in a contemporary democracy.

The assumption may often be made that a monarchic state is a 'despotic' one in which the monarch's will is final. This seems to be far from the case in practice. First the monarch's position is usually a traditional one. The same tradition that places the king in power frequently sets distinct limits upon the exercise of it. The king may be seen as divinely sanctioned and protected, but this implies that he respects the religious feelings of his people. These may be expressed by religious authorities – archbishops, high priests or synods – who are regarded as equally legitimate within their spheres as the monarch is in his. A good example of the sort of limit that might apply is to consider the important area of taxation. In the African kingdoms mentioned, Hausa kings were traditionally entitled to levy taxes, but the Yoruba kings could only rely upon a traditional level of offerings on specified occasions. Even the strongest English monarchs required the approval of the Houses of Parliament, particularly the House of Commons, to levy taxes – although they might be able to manipulate a favourable majority by the use of patronage.

The limits on the exercise of royal power also include the lack of any strongly developed administrative machinery, particularly at local level, so that the king might effectively have to persuade nobles/gentry and municipalities to co-operate. The political capacity of the occupant of the throne was also a vital consideration. When minors succeeded to the throne, such a system might, in effect, become government by a committee of prominent court members, whilst the chief minister of a foolish or lazy king might easily have effective power. In the Japanese case, the shogun or prime minister became the effective power for centuries, becoming, in turn, a hereditary office.

Although kingdoms of the type described are now rare, they are not extinct (for instance Kuwait, Nepal and Saudi Arabia) and the dominance of this type of political organisation for centuries in many parts of the world is a caution against assuming contemporary state forms are inevitable. Furthermore many of the concepts we have introduced here, such as political patronage and court politics, can still be applied in contemporary political systems; consider the Reagan White House in which the chief executive's wife's astrologer is alleged to have been vitally influential.

STATES WITHOUT NATIONS: EMPIRES

Perhaps still more remote from contemporary experience is the concept of empire. Yet this is a form of rule that has dominated large parts of the globe for millennia. The most notable examples upon which we shall concentrate at first are the ancient empires of China and Rome. But similar structures were to be found in India (e.g. the Moghul Empire), in Africa (Egypt and Mali) and in Central and South America (e.g. the Aztecs). Nor should it be forgotten that, more recently, each of the European nations sought to create colonial empires in Africa, Asia and the Americas, whilst the USA and the former USSR could both be accused of having colonial possessions by other names.

It is tempting, and not totally misleading, to attribute the longevity of many empires to the military advantage of a large and powerful state surrounded by much smaller states, or tribal territories. Whilst empires may be briefly built on military advantage alone as, perhaps, was that of Alexander the Great, the longer-lasting examples can be attributed not only to size, but also to the advantages of a 'civilised' culture in the literal sense of a society centred upon relatively large urban centres containing specialised personnel who contributed technical and organisational advantages to the empire. The prestige and self-esteem associated with such systems may well help them to survive. Certainly the ruling groups of the Chinese, Roman and British empires were all firmly convinced of the superiority of their cultural inheritance, and successfully imparted this ideology to many of their subjects and neighbours. However this conviction did not prevent such systems from adopting and adapting to useful features of surrounding societies.

The history of China is particularly noteworthy for the way in which the empire was militarily subdued on a number of occasions by warlike tribes from the periphery of the empire. However the conquerors on each occasion came to be merely a new ruling group operating a very similar political system to the one they had defeated (Eberhard, 1977). The adaptability of the Romans is well illustrated by their reactions to Greek culture in the early period and the transformation from the Classical Empire based on Rome into the Byzantine Christian Empire based on Constantinople. One vital feature of such systems is the way the rulers must be prepared to tolerate linguistic, cultural and religious diversity, provided that subjects are prepared to make the necessary political compromises with the primary needs of the empire.

Such empires have generally been characterised by the development of an extensive cash economy, permitting complex economic exchanges over long distances. These same distances have required efficient means of communication amongst the 'civil servants' of the empire, who must also be capable of working together in a co-ordinated fashion. The empire can only survive militarily by deploying its military resources over long distances to optimum effect. Thus literacy and bureaucracy as well as good roads (or a navy) and professional soldiers become a necessity.

The Chinese mandarinate is a good illustration of many of these themes (Gerth and Mills, 1948: Chs. VIII and XVIII). China was unified for centuries by an administrative pyramid of mandarins, linking the court and the rural districts, who were required to pass examinations in a common core of knowledge. This centred upon literary and historical texts and was mostly concerned with developing an educated gentleman with a good knowledge of ritual. Good government was mainly seen in terms of political stability rather than social and economic progress. Despite this, some writers stress the role of the Chinese bureaucracy in regulating the drainage and waterway system of China just as the Egyptian priesthood served the pharaoh, sacrificed to the gods, and controlled the waters of the Nile through an elaborate drainage system (Wittfogel, 1957: 17–18, 26–27). Whatever the usefulness of the services they performed, it is clear the cohesion of the system was vastly assisted by the common origins, knowledge and attitudes of these administrators who were amongst the first who could reasonably be described as 'bureaucrats' (see Chapter 8).

One final point worth emphasising is the contrast between the ancient empires and the nineteenth- and twentieth-century European colonial empires in their attitudes towards their subjects. Basically this may be encapsulated in one rather nasty word – racism. The European empires increasingly were based upon a core metropolitan state that claimed to be a nation and often a democracy. The empire was a separate area of colonies whose dependence on the metropolitan area could only be easily justified by an allegation of the incapacity of their inhabitants to rule themselves. Nineteenth-century anthropologists' findings were used and abused to justify a doctrine of the racial or cultural inferiority of 'coloured' people compared with the 'white' race. In theory official attitudes might not quite go so far as to allege permanent inferiority on the part of the governed. British policy in principle was based on grooming colonies for self-governing 'dominion' status (like the white ex-colonies of Australia, New Zealand and Canada), whilst the French, for instance, were much more prepared to accord equal rights to 'natives' if they assimilated French culture and behaved as black Frenchmen. However the Nazi view of the permanent inferiority of 'non-Aryan' races probably reflected the practice of European colonial residents more accurately for most of the nineteenth and early twentieth centuries. The near extermination of the aboriginal inhabitants of Tasmania, and the South African colonists' doctrine of apartheid are extreme examples of these attitudes at work.

In contrast to this, the Chinese restricted their empire mainly to groups who could be assimilated into the Chinese way of life, though viewing groups outside the empire as racially and culturally inferior. The Romans extended Roman citizenship to a number of other urban centres and made no systematic discrimination between Italian, Greek or African subjects of the empire.

NATIONS AND STATES

Earlier we took the state to be, in Weber's words, an organisation 'that (successfully) claims the monopoly of the legitimate use of physical force within a given territory'. We suggested that the model of government and the state which this may suggest – of a world dominated by sovereign 'nation states' – is a relatively arguable and new one. Europe did not look much like this until about 1919, after the Treaty of Versailles. Africa only came near to the model from the 1960s. Countries like the United Kingdom (as we saw earlier) and the former Soviet Union and Yugoslavia are (or were) clearly multinational. The Antarctic remains the subject of (frozen!) conflicting claims to jurisdiction.

We shall examine questions of national and ethnic identity at greater length in Chapter 5, but it is worth stating here that states with a one-to-one relationship with an unambiguous 'nationality' are difficult, or impossible, to find. Thus even France, one of the originators of the doctrine, is still faced with regional identities such as Breton and Basque, some of whom would prefer an independent existence. Conversely Switzerland, Belgium and Canada all contain considerable French minorities to complicate their national identities. Nor are these isolated examples – virtually every African country is the product of the more or less arbitrary drawing of lines on the map in the nineteenth century. For example, modern Nigeria contains three major – and many minor – population groups, with two of the major groups – the Yoruba and the Hausa – being found in substantial numbers in neighbouring states.

THE NATION STATE AND SOVEREIGNTY

Although nation states are difficult to come by in practice, the predominant theory of the state today, as incorporated in the concept of the United Nations and in international law, is that of the 'sovereign state'. States' legitimacy is based mainly on the idea that each nation has a right of self-determination. The people of a nation thus are seen to consent to the establishment of a government over them which supports a system of law appropriate to their culture and traditions. This idea came clearly to the fore in human history only with the French and American revolutions at the end of the eighteenth century.

The model of government in which a nation makes decisions through the state machinery may be helpful in justifying the establishment of self-governing democratic systems in opposition to alien or autocratic rule. Arguably it becomes an obstacle to understanding the working of a modern sophisticated liberal democratic state, which is usually divided into executive, legislative, and judicial arms, and central, local and regional levels of government. The outcome of the constitutional working of these specific institutions of government can be regarded as the 'nation's' decision. An oversimplification that is, however, often put forward is that some individual element in the constitutional structure is the body which incorporates the national will. In the French tradition there has been a tendency to see the National Assembly as that body. The Soviet tradition was to see the Communist Party in an analogous position. In the liberal tradition, however, the distinction between the government of the day and the state – between opposition and treason – is a clear and vital one.

POLITICS BETWEEN STATES

If we conceive of the world in terms of the nation-state model already described, then international politics looks much more like the politics of stateless societies than the internal politics of states. That is, there is something called international law, but there is no final authority to enforce, interpret or change it. Although the United Nations can be seen as a potential world legislature/government, it is at present based on the theory that individual states possess 'sovereignty' and are the final arbiters of what goes on within their territories. All powers of international organisations, including the United Nations, are held to depend upon the agreement of states to treaties authorising such powers.

Thus politics at international level can be seen to depend on compromise and negotiation, rather than upon authoritative decision making by representative organs. In legal theory Monaco is as sovereign as the United States, and both are equally free to resort to force in the last resort to defend their national interests and to go back upon their international treaty obligations. In political practice it is clear that smaller states, with less in the way of military and economic resources to back up their bargaining, are more dependent on the perhaps insubstantial ground of international respect for law and treaty obligations. From the point of view of the study of politics, international relations offers a particular challenge, since the processes of decision making are often even more obscure than at national level, and the consequences potentially more profound. Traditionally historians tended to describe international relations in terms of the decisions of individual statesmen pursuing, more or less intelligently, 'the national interest', which was often related to the 'balance of power' between nations. Thus international relations can be seen as a game played between more or less rational players, largely of what we previously termed a 'zero-sum' variety – more power for one nation being gained at the expense of less for another, with skilful players achieving goals by forming winning coalitions.

Seeing international relations as a competitive spectator sport neglects the importance of consensual, non-zero-sum goals in international relations. It is more important to ordinary citizens that everyone stays alive and continues in mutually beneficial economic and trading activities, than that they belong to a state which is more powerful than the others.

This in turn relates to the question of the 'national interest'. We have seen the difficulty in defining a nation – e.g. can it be assumed that the English have the same interests as the Welsh? Similarly professional politicians may experience much more satisfaction from being part of a powerful state than a simple peasant might. Again if, say, in the nineteenth century, British investors' rights in some Latin American country are safeguarded at the loss of a number of sailors' lives, does the safeguarding of one group's (relatively large) income justify the loss of several poor men's lives? The 'national interest', then, may obscure domestic conflicts of interest by wrapping them in the national flag.

To describe national policy making in terms of individuals making choices may be a vast oversimplification, as Allison's (1987) work makes clear. He analysed the Cuban missile crisis, in which the United States was faced by a Soviet attempt to install ballistic missiles in sites in Cuba. He showed how not only the president and the secretary of state were involved in the decision-making process, but also the perceptions of the Central Intelligence Agency (CIA), the professional military, the US representative at the UN and others. Assumptions about the motives of the other 'side' and the reactions of potential allies, and the electorate, were also seen to be crucial. Allison argues that for a full picture of the foreign policy process, decision making must be seen as part of processes of organisational decision making and of political bargaining. More recently, similar arguments could be applied to the Bush administration's decision to invade Iraq in 2003.

POLITICS BEYOND THE STATE: INTERNATIONAL INSTITUTIONS

The United Nations General Assembly is in many ways an unconvincing 'world parliament' since it is based on the equal representation of giant countries (in population terms) like Brazil and Russia with mini-states like the Gambia and Luxembourg. Nor can a body which allowed dictators like 'Papa Doc' Duvalier of Haiti or General Amin of Uganda to misrepresent the populations they terrorised be seen to possess great legitimacy. The Security Council can be seen as a potential world 'government'. Its inclusion of Permanent Members (USA, China, Russia, Britain and France – each with a veto over any decision by the Council) may have the merit of political realism, in that the UN cannot be expected to act effectively without Great Power agreement. Alas, until the 1990s, the Cold War meant virtually all effective action by the UN was stillborn. Even now with apparently greater international consensus, whilst humanitarian action in the former Yugoslavia, Liberia and the Congo has been possible, the UN is handicapped by the lack of effective executive apparatus and in 2003 splits in the Security Council once more prevented effective action against Iraq. Long delays in taking humanitarian action in the Darfur region of the Sudan were accounted for partly by UN weakness against any recalcitrant sovereign state and partly by Chinese oil interests.

However, focusing on major political decisions at the summit level of international organisations may well be a misleading guide to their importance and potential. The examples of NATO, the European Union (EU) and OPEC (Organisation of Petroleum Exporting Countries) suggest that, when international organisations serve what is seen as a clear and necessary purpose, genuine and effective multinational co-operation is possible. These organisations are of considerable interest in that they have exercised powers that are commonly seen as fundamental activities of 'sovereign states' on a collective basis.

Another example of the way international bodies are working effectively in the modern world is to consider such obscure bodies as the International Standards Organisation (ISO) or the International Telecommunications Union (ITU). Bodies like these hammer out essential technical agreements which enable telephones across the world to operate as one vast international network, enable computer manufacturers on opposite sides of the globe to manufacture equipment that will work together, and agree on common scientific units in which new discoveries can be expressed.

MULTINATIONAL ENTERPRISES AND 'GLOBALISATION'

The importance of multinational enterprises in the modern world is difficult to overestimate. Some of these firms have a greater financial turnover than the gross national income (GNI) of a medium-size state (see Table 2.1). Thus Malaysia has roughly the same size 'economy' as the major German insurance company Allianz, whilst the small Central American country of Belize has less than 1 per cent of the revenue of Toyota. Such figures are greatly affected by international currency and market fluctuations as a comparison with previous editions of this book will demonstrate.

In addition many of these corporations control vital economic resources such as oil (the 'Seven Sisters': Exxon, Texaco, BP, etc.), banking (Bank of America, HSBC, ING) and computing (Microsoft, Intel and IBM). In some cases the world price of an entire commodity may be under the control of a multinational enterprise (e.g. De Beers and diamonds).

Virtually all multinational enterprises are clearly based in one host country, with the majority of shareholders and senior personnel from

Table 2.1   Multinationals and countries compared

State or company	Revenue or GNI ($ billion)	Company national headquarters
USA	12,913	
Japan	4,976	
Germany	2,876	
UK	2,273	
China	2,169	
Brazil	662	
Wal-Mart	349	USA
Royal Dutch Shell	319	Netherlands
Indonesia	282	
BP	265	UK
Portugal	181	
Toyota	179	Japan
Malaysia	126	
Allianz	125	Germany
UBS	105	Switzerland
Colombia	105	
PetroChina	68	China
Bangladesh	67	
Guatemala	30	
Jamaica	9	

Sources: Compiled by the authors from World Development Indicators Database, World Bank, April 2007 and the Forbes Global 2000, February 2007
GNI = Gross National Income

that country. (The few exceptions include Anglo-Dutch operations such as Unilever and Royal Dutch Shell.) Operations in specific countries may, however, be minority-owned and largely staffed by local personnel. Most significant multinational enterprises are owned in the USA with Japan and European countries (including Britain) some way behind. Nine out of the twenty biggest multinationals in 2007 were of US origin, whilst the US companies on Forbes list had a combined market capitalisation of 13.9 trillion dollars.

In bargaining with governments in the 'South' a multinational enterprise is a sophisticated and richer organisation bargaining with a poorer and less skilled and well-informed one. This can be illustrated by the problems even large Southern countries such as South Africa and India have had in their relations with multinational pharmaceutical companies over drugs to treat HIV/AIDS (Seckinelgin, 2007).

Even in bargaining with a middle-rank power like the UK, a large Japanese or American corporation has very considerable negotiating power since it has the alternative of setting up elsewhere within the EU and exporting to the UK from there. Even a US corporation dealing with its own government can channel its funds and development projects 'off-shore' to lower labour cost countries or tax havens.

In the past, multinational enterprises often ran virtually independent operations in separate countries (e.g. Ford in the USA, UK, Germany, Australia). But they are now increasingly pursuing integrated global strategies in which financial resources can be swapped around the globe, production is planned centrally, resources coming from the cheapest country relevant to the market in mind whilst profits are channelled to the most tax-efficient point. (Thus Ford has implemented a 'world car' strategy in which all models will have interchangeable parts and components can be shipped all over the world to be assembled in models appropriate to the market in question.) This is only possible as a result of a sophisticated global use of information technology including the Internet (see Tansey, 2002: Ch. 3).

Marshall McLuhan (1964) has familiarised many people with the concept of the 'global village' in which rapid satellite reporting and transmission of electronic images of events, from the invasion of Baghdad to the Olympic Games, familiarise everyone instantly with the same version of events all over the world. A shared repertoire of pop videos, international sporting events and Hollywood films characterises the mass media in many parts of the world. A shared consumption of similar goods such as Nintendo games, Reebok trainers and Coca-Cola is thought to have helped create an international popular (youth) culture. Internet developments such as YouTube and MySpace have enabled the creation of interactive global youth networks sharing music, chat and video clips.

Unprecedented levels of international travel – both for holidays and business, and even for education and spiritual enlightenment – have been made possible by modern technological developments. In addition television documentaries, advertisements and films have all familiarised people all over the globe with something of the way of life of people in faraway places – especially that of affluent America.

On a perhaps more serious level, international publishing operations and the growing practice of international professional communication through journals and conferences have made professionals in all spheres more rapidly aware of the new achievements and standards of international colleagues.

The social and political implications of all this is immensely controversial. In countries as varied as France and Iran many of these developments have been denounced as 'creeping Americanisation'. There seems little doubt that a growing awareness of standards of living and freedom in the rest of the world was immensely influential in bringing about the end of communism in Eastern Europe.

It is increasingly difficult for national governments to cut their people off from knowledge of developments elsewhere in the globe and this knowledge can be political dynamite. In the USA in the 1960s a series of urban riots were said to have been incited by the greater knowledge of the urban poor of the extent of their deprivation as a result of television. As singer Gil Scott-Heron once satirically announced, 'The Revolution will not be televised'. It is not beyond the scope of possibility that one of the greatest forces for instability and change in the next century will be a similar awareness of deprivation on behalf of the millions of inhabitants of the South.

Many of the themes introduced so far are encapsulated in the concept of 'globalisation' (Luard, 1990; McGrew and Lewis, 1992; Baylis and Smith, 2005). Definitions of globalisation, and attitudes towards the idea differ radically from writer to writer (see Box 2.2).

BOX 2.2   DEFINITIONS OF GLOBALISATION

> . . . the removal of barriers to free trade and the closer integration of national economies.
>
> (Stiglitz, 2002: ix)
>
> A historical process involving a fundamental shift or transformation in the spatial scale of human social organization that links distant communities and expands the reach of power relations across regions and continents.
>
> (McGrew, in Baylis and Smith, 2005: 24)
>
> De-territorilization – or . . . the growth of super-territorial relations between people.
>
> (Scholte, 2000: 46)

The authors define globalisation as the thesis that the increasing global interdependence of states, individuals and social and economic organisations is reducing the autonomy of individual states. Box 2.3 summarises some of the factors at work.

BOX 2.3   GLOBALISATION – CHALLENGES TO THE NATION STATE

Internal instability	from mini-nationalisms, ethnicity, etc.
External instability	need for regional/global security
Economic dependence	on global economic and financial organisations
Social integration	development of world standards for human rights, professional behaviour
Technical integration	dependence on world communication networks and leading-edge technical developments increases vulnerability
Ecological interdependence	threats of pollution, global warming, etc. insoluble within state boundaries.

With the disintegration of the Soviet Bloc and the increasing integration of China into a world capitalist trading system, the political power of multinational companies in a globalised world has become increasingly central and controversial. The rules governing economic relationships between states are increasingly decided through international organisations such as the World Trade Organisation (WTO), the World Bank and the International Monetary Fund. These in turn are often dominated by the United States and to some extent the EU, both of which are sympathetic to the interests of multinational companies (Baylis and Smith, 2005: Ch. 14 by Woods).

For instance, Sell (2003) argues that the heads of twelve multinationals successfully lobbied the WTO to mould the Agreement on Trade-Related Aspects of Intellectual Property Rights (TRIPS) in the interests of their companies. This technical-sounding victory has been important in making it difficult for countries in the South to make available generic drugs to treat AIDS or to resist the import of genetically modified plant species. Multinational companies have also lobbied hard, via the WTO, to ensure that they are entitled to tender for the provision of privatised government services across the globe.

POLITICS AS A UNIVERSAL ACTIVITY

The more international relations is analysed, the less important the differences between international and domestic politics seem to be. As we shall see in a later chapter, it can be argued that explaining relationships between member states and the EU is very like explaining relationships between the states and the federal government in the USA. Equally, insights from domestic politics, and even the politics of stateless societies, can be of relevance to international politics.

To return to the theme introduced at the beginning of this chapter, the evidence presented suggests that politics in the broad sense we defined it in Chapter 1 is a more or less universal aspect of life in human societies. Strictly speaking we have not established this – only produced evidence that politics is widespread in many human societies (for further discussion see Human nature and politics in Chapter 3). But we have established that centralised national governments – although a dominating feature of modern Western societies – are by no means inevitable.

RECOMMENDED READING

Anderson, Benedict, 1991, *Imagined Communities: Reflections on the Origin and Spread of Nationalism*, 2nd edn, London, Verso
   A highly regarded analysis of a key aspect of the modern world – nationalism.

Baylis, John and Smith, Steve (eds), 2005, *The Globalization of World Politics*, 3rd edn, Oxford, Oxford University Press
   A very accessible introduction to international relations.

Finer, S. E., 1997, *A History of Government*, 3 vols, Oxford, Oxford University Press
   A treasure trove of information on the historical development of political systems – no doubt too long for most beginners to read from end to end.

Fortes, M. and Evans-Pritchard, E. E., 1961, *African Political Systems*, Oxford, Oxford University Press
   Fascinating series of case studies of tribal politics.

Prawer, J. and Eisenstadt, S. N., 1968, 'Feudalism', in Sills, David L. (ed.), *International Encyclopaedia of Social Sciences*, New York, Macmillan, Vol. 5: 393–403
   Excellent short introduction, many other useful articles in the same publication.

Scholte, J. A., 2000, *Globalization: A Critical Introduction*, London, Macmillan
   A good overview of 'globalisation'.

WEBSITES

http://www.fordham.edu/halsall/sbook.html
   Internet Medieval Sourcebook of Fordham University Center for Medieval Studies (for feudalism).

http://www.worldbank.org
   Useful source of global statistics on economy and governance.

http://www.fride.org/eng/Publications/publication.aspx?item=787
   Factual information on the political systems and governments of specific Arab countries.

http://pdba.georgetown.edu
Political database of the Americas provides information on the political systems of the Caribbean, Latin and South America.

http://www.forbes.com/lists
Forbes Global 2000 database of multinational enterprises, the rich, etc.

http://www.polity.co.uk/global
Globalisation debate and good links.

http://www.cfr.org
Influential US Council on Foreign Relations.

http://www.isn.ch
Security and global politics from a Swiss/European perspective, with excellent links pages.

http://www.globalpolicy.org
Monitors United Nations policy making with good resources and links on globalisation, etc.

http://www.theglobalsite.ac.uk
British academic site with critical articles on globalisation.

www.globalisation.eu
From a European free-market think tank.

3

CONCEPTS

THIS CHAPTER . . .

explores some of the fundamental debates which have occurred about the nature of politics and of the state. It examines the controversies surrounding the interpretation of key concepts such as authority, justice, rights, equality and freedom. Although we approach these issues here in a somewhat abstract and academic manner, it should not be forgotten that in many cases disagreements about these issues have been rooted in historical conflicts of great practical importance. Thus it is no coincidence that many of the key English writers on such matters – for example Hobbes [1588–1679] and Locke [1632–1704] – wrote around the time of the English Civil War when the nature of state authority was central to political events. Similarly the major contributors to debates on the nature of revolution or nationalism – e.g. Lenin [1870–1924], Machiavelli [1469–1527] – themselves played important roles in the political events of their own times.

HUMAN NATURE AND POLITICS

One of the major divisions in politics is the relationship between human nature and politics. Philosophers, theologians and psychologists as well as political scientists have argued as to the inevitability of conflict and aggression amongst human beings (in this context perhaps significantly usually referred to as 'Man'!). On the right, Hobbes, De Maistre [1754–1821], Nietzsche [1844–1900] and others have seen conflict, violence and a struggle for dominance as intrinsic to human nature with a consequent need for a strong state to enforce peace. On the left, the potential for consensus and co-operation among human beings has been emphasised by writers such as Thomas More [1478–1535], Locke, Rousseau [1712–1788] and Tolstoy [1828–1910]. On the right, conflict and aggression are seen as 'natural', whilst on the left such behaviour is seen as learned.

Evidence on this key issue of 'nature versus nurture' is both plentiful and inconclusive and the reader is referred to standard texts on social psychology and anthropology for details. However, if we examine evidence from studies of genetically identical individuals it is found that they do differ in such characteristics as intelligence (and, presumably, aggressive temperament) when brought up in different families within the same society, although not so much as genetically different individuals do. Thus there appears to be both a genetic and a social component to 'human nature' (Eysenck and Kamin, 1981; Rutter and Madge, 1976). An examination of the expectations about human nature to be found in different societies shows that they do seem to differ quite radically – especially in simple or tribal societies. There are groups, such as the Zuni Indians of New Mexico, which place a premium on co-operation and consensus and expect and obtain a very low level of aggression from their members. Other groups, such as the Dobu of New Guinea, base their whole social structure on the assumption of mutual competition and aggression. Benedict (1935) suggests that both societies show a range of temperament within individuals, but that range is around a socially defined norm that differs greatly between the two.

Many of the classical sixteenth- and seventeenth-century writers on political theory attempted to argue the case for the need to have a state, from the assumed inconveniences of an original 'state of nature' in which there was no state to mediate between individuals. Hobbes suggested that in such a state there would be a war of every man against every man and the gains in security associated with any state were thus infinitely greater than the loss of freedom involved in obeying its authorities. Early Libertarians such as Locke and

Rousseau argued against this partly by suggesting that, even without the state, Men were social animals who would co-operate (although Locke concedes such co-operation might generate disputes for which an impartial arbitrator would be useful).

IS THE STATE NECESSARY?

As we saw in an earlier chapter, there is evidence for Locke and Rousseau's view if we understand the debate to be a literal one. Societies like the Tiv, Zuni or Dobu do not have a centralised decision-making apparatus claiming authority over a given territorial area. Thus the state may be desirable, but it is not, strictly speaking, necessary. However, it is difficult to envisage a modern industrial large-scale society functioning without some such mechanism; difficult but not impossible since a small minority – anarchists – advocates precisely this.

First it may be necessary to clarify the term 'Anarchism' (Box 3.1). Our first definition represents the colloquial definition of anarchism – supported by few, or no, political theorists, but dreaded by conservative politicians as the consequence of illegal popular political action. Arguably it might be more correctly given as a definition of 'anarchy' rather than 'anarchism'.

BOX 3.1 DEFINITIONS OF ANARCHISM

1 Absence of government; a state of lawlessness due to the absence or inefficiency of supreme power; political disorder.

(*Shorter Oxford English Dictionary*)

2 The Philosophy of a new social order based on liberty unrestricted by man-made law; the theory that all forms of government rest on violence and are therefore wrong and harmful, as well as unnecessary.

(Goldman, 1915)

3 A doctrine which poses a criticism of existing society, a view of a desirable future society; and a means of passing from one to the other.

(Woodcock, 1975)

Emma Goldman's [1869–1940] definition highlights the anarchist's opposing view that order need not be imposed by authority but should stem from free agreements between free individuals. Writers such as Tolstoy [1828–1910] and Kropotkin [1842–1921] would argue that existing states incorporate the systematic use of violence against the population through the police, prison system and the armed forces. The concept of 'justice' is caricatured by imprisoning the poor and defenceless. The concept of 'defence' is caricatured by destroying the lives of millions to defend the interests of the propertied minority. Most anarchists argue that our present wasteful urban industrialised lifestyle should be replaced by a more ascetic and healthy one. Kropotkin argued that five hours labour a week from everyone could yield a middle-class lifestyle for all. Autonomous communes and voluntary literary, educational, artistic and sporting associations would freely exchange goods and services on a non-profit basis (perhaps basing exchanges on Proudhon's idea of the hours of labour involved in each product or service).

As Woodcock's definition suggests, a crucial problem for anarchists is how to make the transition to the new state of affairs. Most would advocate simply withdrawing consent from current ways of doing things and practising a new libertarian lifestyle immediately. Hence a number of anarchists have sought to set up 'communes' independent of current states, whilst Proudhon [1809–1865] advocated the setting up of an independent banking system based on labour-hours. As Howard Zim puts it:

> The anarchist sees revolutionary change as something immediate, something we must do now, where we live, where we work. It means starting this moment to do away with authoritarian relationships – between men and women, between children and parents, between one kind of worker and another kind. Such revolutionary spirit cannot be crushed like an armed uprising.
>
> (Quoted in Pennock and Chapman, 1978)

A minority of anarchists urge that the state machinery needs to be smashed by armed insurrection, or have taken to terrorist violence. Anarchist terrorism has mostly been in response to unjustified state campaigns against tiny minorities of rather theoretical anarchists. This violent tendency is well illustrated by the following quotation:

In giving dynamite to the down-trodden millions of the globe, science has done its best work . . . a pound of this good stuff beats a bushel of ballots all hollow.

> (Johann Most, *Science of Revolutionary Warfare – a Manual of Instruction in the Uses and Preparation of Nitro-glycerine, Dynamite, Gun-Cotton, Fulminating Mercury, Bombs, Fuses, Poisons, etc., etc.*, 1885; quoted in Horowitz, 1964: 41–42)

Anarchism as a political movement has had only a small direct practical impact. Perhaps the most influential avowedly anarchist groupings were those in 1930s Spain. Anarchist thinking, however, influenced Gandhi and the Indian Independence movement, the student movements of the 1960s and many other left-wing protest movements, and contemporary feminist and ecological groups (see Chapter 4, Ideologies).

WHY SHOULD I OBEY THE STATE?

The example of the anarchist who declares that we should secede from the authority of the state prompts the question of why we should obey the state. Of course part of the answer to this may be merely prudential. If we do not obey the state (pay our taxes, enrol in the armed forces when required, wear clothes in public places, etc.), its agencies may detect our violation of its laws and punish them. However, if we look for a moral justification for obedience we must look in two main directions. First, we need to consider arguments based on the moral need to preserve an essential or desirable social institution and second, arguments based on the idea of our consent to the authority of a specific form of state (probably a liberal democratic one). Conservative theorists (like Burke) have tended to emphasise the first line of argument, liberal theorists (like Locke) the second.

To the extent that the state represents a safeguard against the chaos, crime and confusion resulting from the acts of selfish and conflicting individuals, it may be seen as having a claim upon our obedience. As the institutionalisation of law it may be seen as worthy of respect and obedience. Theologians, following St Augustine's [354–430] *City of God*, have often seen the state as an institution ordained by God to discipline sinful humanity. Classical Greek writers such as Aristotle and Plato regarded man as a naturally social animal who should abide by the rules of the 'polity' (a community organised politically) which created the civilised conditions within which they flourished. Both schools of thought, therefore, considered obedience to the state as a normal part of the moral duty of all thinking men and women. Disobedience is therefore to be censured not only for the immediate harm it might do, but also for the example it sets to others.

The democratic view stresses that it is the duty of the good citizen to respect the products of the decision-making processes established in their name and surviving only with their consent. Even a bad law should be obeyed until it can be amended by democratic processes since the evil of undermining the democratic system is assumed to be greater than that for which the law is responsible. However a law enforcing genocide or slavery or other major breach of 'human rights' would not be covered by this argument. Here the evil done by the law is unarguable and that done by setting an example in conscientious refusal to accept a 'democratic' enactment much less so. Because the government reflects the interests of the majority of the community, minorities should respect its decisions whilst reserving the right to seek to reverse them. Thus obedience to the state should reflect a rational act of choice on the part of an educated citizenry (Singer, 1973).

In terms of the classical theorists, the contrast is neatly illustrated by that between Hobbes and Locke. Both used the metaphor of a legal contract adopted in a 'state of nature'. In Locke's case the establishment of a trust between the governors and the governed was envisaged as well as a contract to set up a civil society. Thus obedience to the government remains conditional upon it carrying out its part of the compact. But in Hobbes's case, the contract simply empowered a third party – the government – to enforce the peace:

> I authorize and give up my right of governing myself, to this man, or this assembly of men, on this condition, that thou give up thy right to him, and authorize all his actions in like manner. . . . This is the generation of the great Leviathan, or rather (to speak more reverently) of that mortal God, to which we owe under the Immortal God, our peace and defence.
> (*Leviathan*, Ch. XVII, 176)

THE NATURE OF AUTHORITY

In this section we attempt to clarify the concept of authority by distinguishing it from power, by distinguishing political authority from other kinds of authority and, finally, exploring Weber's analysis of the different types of political authority.

The definitions of power quoted in Chapter 1 all included the idea of achieving results by a variety of means. Authority can be seen as a particular kind of power relationship in which the legitimacy (literally 'lawfulness') of the exercise of power is accepted, to some degree, by the other actors in the situation. As we saw in Chapter 1, other power relationships may be based not on the acceptance of authority but on force, persuasion or manipulation.

In most political situations legitimacy implies an appeal to an established system of law, but it may take on the broader meaning of 'in accord with moral law'. Weber (Gerth and Mills, 1948: Ch. X) distinguishes between 'traditional authority' and 'rational legal authority'. Both of these will normally refer to an appeal to an established system of law. Thus in a tribal society the customary law gives authority to chiefs, whilst in a modern liberal democracy a rationally organised system of statute law gives authority to political and bureaucratic office holders. Both of these arrangements will be reinforced by moral doctrines – e.g. that the gods/ancestors have bequeathed their way of life to the tribe or the sanctity of majority votes. In stable societies, ideally, there is no conflict between moral and political obligation.

On occasion, however, rival claims to authority may conflict, particularly in societies in transition or crisis. Thus in South Africa before its transition to full democracy, the traditional authority of the King of the Zulus on occasion conflicted with the rational–legal authority of President Botha (head of the apartheid regime). Both, in the end, had to defer to the authority of the leader of the largest popular movement – Nelson Mandela. Weber suggests the description 'charismatic' for the authority of leaders, such as Mandela, who are followed because of their personal qualities rather than any legal position they may hold. Literally this terminology derives from the Greek root 'a favour specially vouchsafed by God – especially a gift or talent' (*Shorter Oxford English Dictionary*) and emphasises, at first sight, the exceptional qualities of those exercising such authority. But, as Weber points out, such divine gifts are not always recognised;

only in moments of crisis when normal claims to leadership are losing their authority is such authority likely to appeal. Equally such leaders usually claim to represent new potential sources of moral authority – be they God (Mohammed), the nation (Hitler) or the people (Mandela). As the examples quoted suggest, such authority may be exercised in many different times or places, for good or for evil. These categories of authority were intended by Weber as morally neutral.

WHAT IS JUSTICE?

If authority is power exercised in accordance with the law, we might reasonably ask: what is so special about the law? As we have seen, followers of Hobbes might be quick to assert that the alternative is violence and chaos and that almost any law is better than no law at all. Many people, however, would tend to associate law not only with order, but also with justice. For many people law must have a moral dimension to be acceptable; the 'order' enforced by the law must be of a morally defensible character. What, then, characterises such a just society? This is one of the oldest questions in political theory addressed directly by the first major classic text – Plato's *Republic*. To give some idea of the debates surrounding the term we shall examine not only Plato's somewhat conservative answer to this question but two later approaches: that of the utilitarian theorist Jeremy Bentham [1748–1832] and that of the liberal writer John Rawls [1921–2002] (see Box 3.2).

Plato's answer is presented as a dialogue between his teacher Socrates and some of his friends and colleagues. One friend quotes a rival teacher, Simonides, to the effect that justice consists in giving everyone their due. This is interpreted as doing good to our friends and harm to our enemies. This is easily dismissed since, if our enemies are good men, this would clearly be immoral. Further reformulations of this idea also seem to be logically untenable. At this point, another colleague, Thrasymachus, advances what he sees as the realistic view that justice is 'the interest of the stronger'. He defends this apparently paradoxical point of view by identifying justice with carrying out the law and asserting that the strongest will dominate the government of any country and rule in their own interests. (A version of what we shall later describe as elite theory.)

The discussion starts on the level of individual morality – will justice lead to individual happiness and injustice to unhappiness? Socrates, however, argues that justice can be most clearly understood on a state level. In the ideal state, there are three kinds of role to be played. The guidance of the state must be through the exercise of wisdom by the best citizens – the Guardians. The defence of the state must be in the hands of the bravest and most spirited – the Auxiliaries. The production of necessities will be carried out by the rest – the Producers.

Justice resides in the harmony between the parts of society, achieved by each fulfilling the role for which they are most fitted. Thus Simonides's concept of justice as giving each his due is returned to, but with a clearer idea of what this entails.

This theory may be interpreted as very conservative – as support-ing a hierarchical and authoritarian society in which class divisions reflect natural divisions of talent amongst the population and in which propaganda and censorship are employed (Popper, 1962: Vol. 1). There are implicit in Plato's account some more radical strands. For instance, he explicitly endorses equal educational opportunities for women and the selection of Philosopher rulers on merit, not on the basis of birth.

In contrast, Bentham's views on the realisation of justice in the state were based on different assumptions. His sole criterion for the establishment of a just legal order was that the legislators should seek 'the greatest good of the greatest number'. Furthermore he made the radical and democratic assumption that it was not up to philosophers to decide on the values the state should pursue. Instead the just state would reflect its citizens' own moral, economic and aesthetic choices. It was in this context that he put forward the, sometimes mis-represented, thesis that 'Pushpin [read nowadays 'computer games'?] is as good as Poetry'. The best way to ensure that legislators reflected the views of the inhabitants of the state, he argued, was to have them elected by universal suffrage. Justice is therefore to be found in a democratic society, which respects the moral equality of the individuals composing it (Bentham, 1948).

Rawls's (1971) *Theory of Justice* is the most prominent work to criticise Bentham's view which, it can be argued, has dominated discussion in the nineteenth and twentieth centuries (Gorovitz, 1976: 273–276). Rawls puts forward a view of justice that deals with some of the apparent inadequacies of utilitarianism. Thus it might be shown that embarrassing a few unlucky individuals on a TV show might make millions of viewers happy – thus achieving the happiness of the greatest number – but few would feel sure that this was a 'just' proceeding. Nor is it easy (possible?) to compare people's subjective experience of 'utility'. His method is to consider what principles rational policy makers would adopt if they knew a great deal about human nature and society, but had no idea of the role they themselves played in it, or what goals they wished to pursue – what he calls 'a veil of ignorance'.

His conclusion is that two fundamental principles of justice would emerge. First, each person is to have an equal right to the most extensive total system of equal basic liberties compatible with a similar system of liberty for all. Second, social and economic liberties are to be arranged so that they are both (a) to the greatest advantage of the least advantaged and (b) attached to offices and positions open to all under conditions of fair equality of opportunity. The first principle has an absolute priority over the second. The logic of this is that if we did not know what social positions we held, or what objectives we were seeking to pursue, we would want to ensure that any goals could be pursued by anyone and that none would be victimised for the sake of the rest.

Rawls argues that this notion of justice accords with the common intuitions that people have on the matter and offers a logical basis for evaluating actual social orders. Gorovitz (1976: 286) argues that:

> Such a view is plainly at odds with the rugged individualism of the unconstrained free enterprise economy, and is equally at odds with the highly controlled communist or socialist state that submerges individuals' autonomy in the quest for social welfare.

BOX 3.2 JUSTICE

the harmony between the parts of society achieved by each fulfilling the role for which they are most fitted: '. . . adherence to their own business on the part of the industrious, the military and the guardian classes, each of these doing its own work in the state is justice.'

(Plato, 1866: Book IV, para. 434)

> it is the greatest happiness of the greatest number that is the measure
> of right and wrong.
>
> > (Bentham, 1948: Preface, 3, para. 3)
>
> Justice as fairness – principles (a) 'equality in the assignment of basic
> rights and duties'; (b) 'social and economic inequalities . . . are only
> just if they result in compensating benefits for everyone and in
> particular the least advantaged members of society.'
>
> > (Rawls, 1971: 14–15)

INDIVIDUALISM VERSUS COLLECTIVISM

In discussing concepts of power in Chapter 1 we saw that some
writers tend to focus upon collective entities such as societies or
classes in their analysis of politics, whilst others were more prone to
focus upon the activities of individuals. Our earlier discussions in this
chapter suggest that this type of difference may be more than a mere
difference of focus in the method of analysis, but that it may also
reflect a fundamental difference of values. For Bentham and Rawls,
both writing in the liberal tradition, the starting point for political
reflection is the individual. Not only are individuals seen as the
fundamental building blocks from which societies are composed.
More importantly, political arrangements are seen as devices to be
judged by the extent to which they recognise the moral equality of
individuals and allow them to make decisions about their own lives in
an 'autonomous' (self-governing) fashion.

Classical and medieval writers tended to see the focus of political
enquiry as the creation of good societies in which, as a consequence of
the wisdom of constitution makers and princes, good men would
flourish. This can be seen in Plato's assumption that a just society is
one in which there is a correct distribution of functions between its
constituent social groups and that the just individual is the just
society in microcosm. Similarly some medieval writers fondly
compared the just state to a hive of bees or colony of ants in which all
did their appropriate part without a thought for the boredom and toil
implicit in the ordinary 'worker' role in such societies. More recently,
as we shall see in the next chapter, fascists have subordinated the

good of individuals to that of race or nation, whilst some communists have similarly exalted the interests of party or class over that of their constituent individuals.

RIGHTS: NATURAL, HUMAN, LEGAL

Like 'authority' and 'justice', 'rights' are frequently referred to in political discussion without much attempt at definition. 'Rights' are generally associated with individuals and are thus part of the broad liberal tradition dominant in modern political thought. By definition a right may be thought of not only as an authority to act possessed by an individual but as universally possessed by individuals (in the same situation), or by individuals within a specific legal system. This is so by definition because the term 'privilege' would apply if only some individuals have power to do something in a given situation.

The doctrine that all men possessed 'natural' rights started to come to prominence in the seventeenth century as part of the debate, of which Hobbes and Locke were a part, on the limitations on the power of the British Crown. In the eighteenth century the revolutionary potential of these ideas was dramatically realised in the American and French revolutions. Such ideas were associated with deism – a rational reformulation of Christian ideas – which stressed that the Creator had instituted not only natural laws which governed the motions of the planets and all other natural objects, but similar moral laws governing human relationships. Man had been given the power to discover all these laws by reason. By examining how men lived together in existing societies we can see that there are certain pre-requisites for civilised co-operative living which all men should recognise. Thus the American Declaration of Independence proclaimed inalienable and God-given rights to the pursuit of life, liberty and the pursuit of happiness. These were elaborated in the French Declaration of the Rights of Man.

Much of modern history could be read as the broadening of the concept of rights from a narrow legalistic application of the idea only to 'civilised' white men, to a broader concept of social and cultural rights applicable to women, non-whites and children as well (some readers may wish to add animals to the list). The concept of human rights as expressed in the United Nations Universal Declaration of Human Rights (1948) is thus a modern development of the earlier theory of natural rights. It, too, represents a moral claim to equal political treatment on behalf of those for whom it speaks.

Such natural, human or universal rights that are largely a moral claim for equal and just treatment should be distinguished from legal rights that are enforceable in the courts of a specific legal system. These can be subdivided into the rights given by any specific piece of legislation and rights that are guaranteed by a constitution.

In many systems, such as the United States, rights guaranteed by the constitution (e.g. that in the Fifth Amendment to remain silent under legal interrogation) supersede any contrary statement in ordinary legislation.

EQUALITY

Equality is a politically emotive word that has played a key role in modern politics from the French Revolution of 1789 to the present day. 'Equality' in politics clearly does not mean everyone, regardless of circumstances, should be treated equally – e.g. the blind and sighted to be equally entitled to free white sticks! 'Equality' in this sense would mean inequity (unfairness, injustice). Most modern commentators and the UN Universal Declaration of Human Rights endorse equality of rights and of dignity. But how far does equality of rights go?

Equality before the law is important but in a capitalist economy does not in itself guarantee education, health or a pension in old age (the law may merely give everyone an equal right to buy these things but not establish any sources of income to enable this to be done). Article 25 of the Universal Declaration (1948) does envisage 'the right to security in the event of unemployment, sickness, disability, widowhood, old age or other lack of livelihood in circumstances beyond his control' and Article 26 talks of a right to a free universal system of education. Maurice Cranston (1962), however, argued against placing these 'social' rights on a par with older 'civic' rights on the grounds that they *cannot* be achieved for all in some poor countries and that such thinking encourages the idea that civic rights may be legitimately 'traded' for social rights, or are also only a long-term aspiration.

'Equality before the Law' does imply freedom from sexual and racial discrimination. A modern issue is the legitimacy of positive discrimination in favour of disadvantaged groups such as women and ethnic minorities such as 'untouchables' in India.

'Equal rights' are normally interpreted as relating to some *minimum* standard – e.g. a house, a job, etc. – not that all have the same standard of housing or equal pay.

Another related but separate issue is the extent to which social policy can and should be directed toward reversing social inequalities (LeGrand, 1982). The short answer would seem to be that most of these rest much more upon the nature of the fiscal, economic and legal systems than on social policies in a narrow sense. Distinctions should also be drawn between social inequalities that are the result of *economic differences*, and those that result from attempts to maintain *social distance* between different status groups. For instance British social class or Indian caste differences may not reflect the economic circumstances of those concerned. A British national lottery winner might still be refused admission to a golf club on the grounds of an uncouth accent or unconventional appearance, whilst an Indian untouchable (even if a well-paid professional) could still be rejected as a dining companion by those of Brahmin caste.

BOX 3.3   CONCEPTS OF EQUALITY: SUMMARY

Treating everyone the same.

Treating everyone appropriately.

Equality before the law – 'Equal subjection of all classes to the ordinary law of the land administered by the ordinary courts' (Dicey, 1941: 202–203).

Political equality – equal political rights (e.g. voting, citizenship) to all.

Equality of opportunity – 'success or failure [in careers] must be made to depend only upon the capacity or character of the persons concerned, not on the accidents of wealth' (Benn and Peters, 1959: 128).

Social equality – reducing or eliminating the 'social distance' (attitudes of superiority/inferiority) between social groups (e.g. classes or ethnic groups) (see Benn and Peters, 1959: Ch. 5).

POSITIVE AND NEGATIVE FREEDOM

One of the most used and controversial words in the political vocabulary is liberty or freedom. Because it has such a good emotive ring to it (i.e. it is what Weldon (1953) calls a 'hurrah!' word), no one can appear to be against it. Therefore philosophers and politicians redefine freedom as that of which they approve. The result is that a wonderful confusion of definitions of freedom has been produced by political philosophers (Box 3.4).

BOX 3.4   DEFINITIONS OF FREEDOM

consists in having of Government, and those laws by which their Life and Goods may be most their own. It is not having a share in Government.

(Charles I, 'Speech from the Scaffold', in *Works*, 1662: 454)

The assurance that every man shall be protected in doing what he believes to be his duty against the influences of authority and majorities, custom and opinion.

(Lord Acton, *History of Freedom*, 3)

the mere impulse of appetite is slavery, whilst obedience to the law which we prescribe ourselves is liberty.

(Rousseau, *Social Contract*, Book I, Ch. 8: 16)

the absence of opposition.

(Hobbes, *Leviathan*, Ch. XXI: 204)

the power a man has to do or forbear any particular action.

(Locke, *Essay*, II, Ch. XXI: 15)

necessity transfigured.

(Hegel, *Logik*, §158)

a participation in the revelation of what-is-as-such.

(Heidegger, *Existence and Being*, 334)

control over ourselves and over external nature which is founded on knowledge of natural necessity.

(Engels, *Anti-Duhring*, Ch. XI)

(From Cranston, 1954: 8, 12, 23–24)

By way of a heroic simplification which may help to get an initial grasp of the differences at stake, we may adopt Berlin's terminology of 'positive' and 'negative' concepts of freedom (Berlin, 1958). Berlin himself went on to elaborate four concepts of freedom (Berlin, 1969). The 'negative' view is that of the classic English writers that 'I am normally said to be free to the degree to which no human being interferes with my activity' (Berlin, 1958: 7). The positive view is one which defines freedom as 'being one's own master' (Berlin, 1958: 16). To put the matter more baldly, negative freedom is freedom *from*, whilst positive freedom is freedom *to*.

At first sight such distinctions appear trivial and unimportant. However, one important consequence of the positive view may be that paradoxically it may be used to argue that, as Rousseau (1913: 15) puts it, one can be 'forced to be free'.

If one is forced to obey a morally justified law that conflicts with one's immediate inclinations – 'the impulse of appetite' – then one's 'real' self is said to be realised. Conversely opponents of the 'negative' view of freedom would argue that those legal freedoms of speech, assembly, equality before the law and so on are of little benefit to Indian peasants with insufficient means to maintain themselves.

ANALYSING POLITICAL CONCEPTS

Our discussion of political ideas in this chapter has illustrated that political terms which may be taken for granted in everyday conversation or argument conceal depths of meaning and room for divergent interpretations which have led to centuries of argument. It is clear that there is a need in academic and everyday discussion to clarify the way in which a term is intended if it is to be understood. Plato saw philosophical enquiry as essentially about discovering the 'pure form' of each concept. Other writers, similarly, have thought of concepts as having an essential or root meaning. Most modern scholars, however, would concede that it is foolish to waste too much time attempting to establish the 'real' meaning of words. Since words have been, and are, used in different ways even in the same society, let alone over centuries of use in a host of different ones.

Academic linguists and some contemporary philosophers tend to concentrate on the 'descriptive' definition of words – examining how they are used in common practice and perhaps offering some rules for ensuring that you are unlikely to be misunderstood by adopting an unusual or deviant use of the word. Contemporary linguists have abandoned the practice of old-style grammarians of attempting to prescribe rules for the 'correct' use of words. It would be very foolish to attempt to legislate that, for instance, a word in English must always be interpreted via its Greek, Latin or German origins – language being a living and changing vehicle for communication rather than an ancient monument.

In order to communicate clearly, however, it may on occasion be useful to adopt a 'stipulative' definition and say 'This is what I will always mean by this term.' This is frequently a legitimate and useful academic device. It may also sometimes be permissible to coin a new word for use as a technical term to avoid the emotive and vague commonly used one. The problem, as we saw in Chapter 1, is that such neologisms may well come to be used as imprecisely as the terms they seek to replace.

In politics the practice of 'persuasive' definition of words is commonplace. By this the writer or speaker tries to persuade their audience that their definition of the word in question is the superior usage. We have seen this illustrated already in this chapter (especially in our discussion of freedom). As we have seen, such attempts are more frequently an attempt to persuade the audience about the value judgements they should make, than a technical exercise in clarifying vocabulary.

Very often political debate, in practice, is an attempt to label your opponents' ideas with what Weldon (1953) calls a 'boo!' word and your own with a 'hurrah!' one. Thus Conservatives will wish to label Labour measures as 'nationalisation' and their own as 'freedom' whilst New Labour speakers now frequently denounce their opponents' proposals as sacrificing 'caring' to 'ideology'. In the USA doctors' representatives consistently speak of 'socialised medicine' (boo!), thus identifying the measure with communism, rather than a national health service. Roy Hattersley tells the tale of how, as an apprentice (old) Labour politician, he was once advised that, if in doubt on an issue at a party meeting, to roundly declare 'What is needed on this issue is a truly Socialist policy', wait for the applause (hurrah!), and then to change the subject!

RECOMMENDED READING

Benn, Stanley I. and Peters, Richard S., 1959, *Social Principles and the Democratic State*, London, George Allen and Unwin
    An analysis of key concepts in political theory which still repays careful reading.

Gerth, H. and Mills, C. Wright (eds), 1948, *From Max Weber: Essays in Sociology*, London, Routledge & Kegan Paul
    One of the classic texts of political sociology which is more readable than some more modern writing – for authority, bureaucracy, Chinese mandarinate, etc.

Raphael, D. D., 1990, *Problems of Political Philosophy*, 2nd edn, Basingstoke, Macmillan
    Useful standard introductory text – focused on basic concepts.

Thiele, Leslie Paul, 1997, *Thinking Politically: Perspectives in Ancient, Modern and Postmodern Political Theory*, Chatham, NJ, Chatham House
    An original and stimulating discussion of the nature of political theory – a good follow-up to more conventional texts such as Raphael.

Woodcock, George, 1975, *Anarchism*, Harmondsworth, Middlesex, Penguin
    Raises some very fundamental questions about the state and politics.

Woolff, Jonathon, 1996, *An Introduction to Political Philosophy*, Oxford, Oxford University Press
    An excellent follow-up to this and the next chapter.

WEBSITES

http://www.psa.ac.uk/www/default.htm
Political Studies Association (UK) WWW gateway see under Resources for particular political philosophers.

http://www.constitution.org/liberlib.htm
Liberty Library of Government Classics includes full texts of many political theorists.

http://flag.blackened.net/daver/anarchism/index.html
The Anarchist Library.

http://www.yale.edu/lawweb/avalon/diana
Online human rights archive of Yale Law School.

www.un.org/rights
United Nations' view on rights.

www.amnesty.org
Leading international rights campaign organisation.

4

IDEOLOGIES

THIS CHAPTER . . .

is about the 'isms' of politics: conservatism, liberalism, socialism, Marxism, fascism and so on. It considers not only the general nature of these broad currents of political thinking, but also gives some idea of the relationship these have had with political regimes and parties. It considers some ideologies that have only recently come to prominence in the West – communitarianism, feminism, 'ecologism' and Islamic 'fundamentalism'. The chapter begins with the concept of 'ideology' itself and how useful that may be. It then considers how ideologies may be classified and then looks at what might be broadly regarded as the right, continuing with the left and ending with the centre.

Because this chapter covers so much ground, the ideas of individual political thinkers do not get the space they deserve. It is hoped that the reader will be inspired to examine some of these thinkers in their own words. A good starting point is a reader such as Morgan (1992).

IDEOLOGY

'Ideology' itself is a difficult term to interpret though it is widely used and abused. One school of thought led by Karl Popper (1962) interprets 'ideology' as a way of political thinking typical of totalitarian movements. To Popper an ideology is an all-encompassing and closed system of thought. Not only does such a system have something to say about virtually all political, social and moral issues, but it is virtually impossible to disprove because there is always an explanation, within the terms of the ideology, for any apparent deviation from its predictions. Thus for some (perhaps crude) Marxists the revolution is always 'imminent' – but when it fails to come it is because the revolution was betrayed by its leaders, objective social conditions were misinterpreted, or capitalism found new outlets for its surpluses.

For Popper, then, ideological thinking should be opposed to scientific theorising which always produces *falsifiable* hypotheses. A scientific approach to social matters consists in developing piecemeal explanations about how things work and testing them out – not in having a grand theory that explains everything. The validity of scientific propositions (which are falsifiable) can be agreed upon by any two persons of good will in the light of the current evidence and are subject to modification in the light of new evidence. To make political judgements, however, people must also employ judgements about values, which are specific to them and cannot be resolved by looking at evidence. Political innovation therefore depends upon building consensus about values between the people concerned as well as correctly interpreting cause and effect. Consequently rather than building some grand Utopia on the basis of first principles, social change should proceed by means of 'piece-meal social engineering' (Popper, 1960: 64).

From this point of view the political doctrines of the centre – democratic socialism, liberalism and conservatism – are all non-ideological since they accept the need to base social policy upon as scientific as possible a review of its effects, and upon the value judgements of the members of the community affected.

However it is quite common to use the word 'ideology' in a much looser way to mean any more or less cohesive set of political principles. In this sense, liberalism, socialism and conservatism can also be described as 'ideologies', and this is the sense in which we have used the word as the title for this chapter. Marxists tend to use the word to suggest the dominant ideas of a society, which they see as reflecting its means of production, and therefore the exercise of power. Thus from many points of view liberalism may fairly be described as the ideology of the capitalist era. As with many political terms no definitive use of the concept can be prescribed – McClellan (1986) notes 27 different interpretations of the concept – what is important is that the sense in which it is used is clearly understood. Box 4.1 summarises three major views.

BOX 4.1   IDEOLOGY AS A POLITICAL CONCEPT

Popper: an all-encompassing and closed system of thought (the opposite of scientific thinking).

Broad sense: any more or less coherent set of political principles.

Marxist: the dominant ideas of a society seen as reflecting its means of production.

'RIGHT' VERSUS 'LEFT'

It is conventional to classify political movements and thinkers as right wing or left wing. This apparently derives from the first French National Assembly when the pro-monarchist conservatives sat on the right and the revolutionary republicans sat on the left of a semicircular assembly. The European and modern French parliaments adopt a similar seating pattern to this day. Such a classification can be controversial – the European Parliament groups have often asserted they are to the left of the position that others see them in. Clearly, too, what is radical and left wing in one context (e.g. republicanism in British colonial North America) can become conservatism in another time or place (e.g. republicanism in the modern United States).

Generally speaking, however, the right is seen as against political, economic and social change, the left in favour of it. The right tends to be monarchist, clerical and favours the interests of the established propertied classes, whilst the left is identified with republicanism, anti-clericalism and the interests of the masses (workers or peasants). This picture derives from French nineteenth-century politics.

In contemporary liberal democracies it may be helpful to supplement this picture by emphasising the existence of a large democratic centre committed to the existing constitutional system, but accepting the legitimacy of gradual social and economic change. Both the far right and the far left are (usually) minorities who wish to drastically modify the existing constitutional and social system – the left in an anti-capitalist, the right in an ultra-nationalist (perhaps racist) direction.

The 'left'/'right' distinction is a shaky one indeed. It conflates three different distinctions in attitudes. The first distinction turns on the *degree* of change from the 'status quo' – in favour or against change from the present situation (which in turn is affected by which status quo one is considering). A second distinguishes the *direction* of change – in favour of or against capitalism, clericalism or some other key political value. A third considers the *method* of change – constitutional or revolutionary.

In terms of the conventional linear distinction, fascism and communism may be seen as occupying opposite extremes with liberal democrats at the centre. From a 'centre' point of view constitutional individualism constitutes one alternative whilst totalitarian collectivism (whether of the 'right' or the 'left') is the opposite extreme. Some anarchists might go one stage further seeing non-violent individualistic anarchism as the real left, with Leninists and fascists as the extreme right since both are prepared to mould individuals to a blueprint by force.

An alternative to the traditional linear model is a circular model. Here the extremes of fascism and communism are not at opposite ends, but actually next to one another in the circle, because they share similar totalitarian traits.

THE OLD RIGHT: MONARCHISM

Monarchism might be seen in a medieval European context as a centrist rather than a right-wing ideology. Certainly conventional Catholic thought has been happy to acknowledge the legitimacy of princes. The gospel urges Christians to 'render therefore unto Caesar the things which are Caesar's' (Matthew 22: 21). The normal situation in medieval Europe was of secular government by kings or emperors who were crowned by the pope or by archbishops authorised by him.

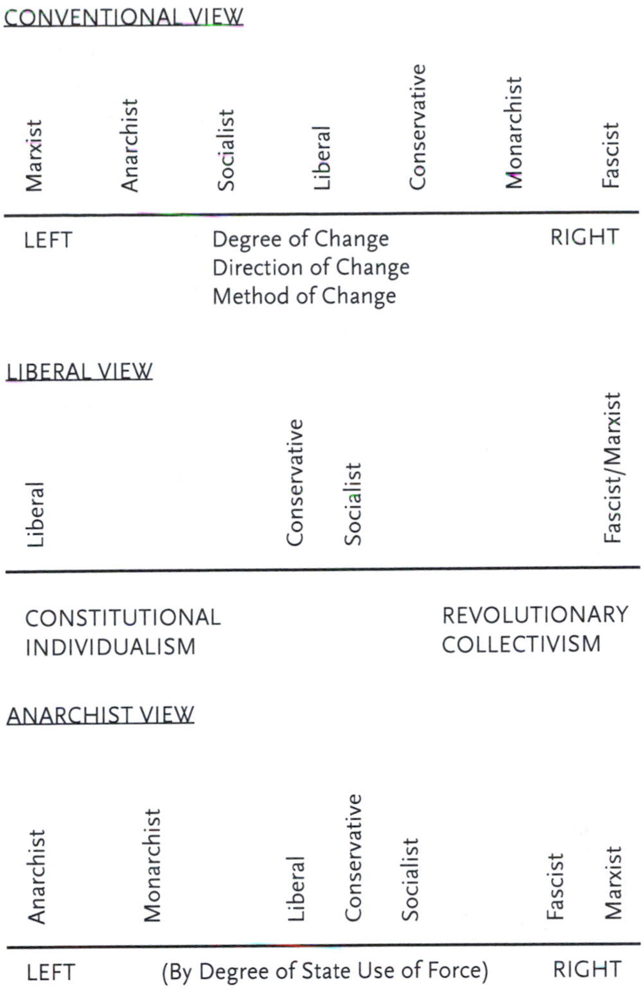

CONVENTIONAL VIEW

Marxist	Anarchist	Socialist	Liberal	Conservative	Monarchist	Fascist

LEFT		Degree of Change				RIGHT
		Direction of Change				
		Method of Change				

LIBERAL VIEW

Liberal		Conservative	Socialist			Fascist/Marxist

| CONSTITUTIONAL | | | | REVOLUTIONARY | |
| INDIVIDUALISM | | | | COLLECTIVISM | |

ANARCHIST VIEW

Anarchist	Monarchist		Liberal	Conservative	Socialist		Fascist	Marxist

| LEFT | | (By Degree of State Use of Force) | | | | | RIGHT | |

Figure 4.1 Classifying ideologies

This was formalised in the theological and political doctrine of the 'two swords' – secular and clerical authority supporting each other and respecting each other's spheres of influence. In effect there was a division of powers with, as we have seen, the Church administering areas of family and property law and having its own taxes (tithes).

There was royal influence over Church appointments and churchmen often manned the royal administration. However, the power of the Church to place a kingdom under an interdict (preventing the faithful from taking part in the full range of religious observances) constituted in many ways a more powerful weapon than the armies of kings, or the emperor.

It was only after the development of the modern idea of state sovereignty (e.g. as by Bodin in his *Republic* of 1576) and especially after the assumption of leadership over the Christian Church in their countries by Protestant kings (starting with Henry VIII) that the more radical idea of the divine right of kings became established. As parliamentary forces in seventeenth-century England increasingly stressed the idea of popular sovereignty, the Stuart kings were increasingly attracted to the idea that countries could only have one sovereign and that he held authority from God not man. In countries like France in which republics were founded, the restoration of the power of an executive, rather than figurehead, monarchy became increasingly the trademark of anti-democratic and ultra-conservative forces.

In other countries that retained a monarchy, a pro-monarchist position might be combined with a more moderate stance (as in nineteenth-century Germany where Bismarck combined social reformism and nationalism in a politically powerful combination with monarchism). Paradoxically, in recent years in Spain the monarch has used his appeal to the right to help engineer a return to constitutional democracy.

THE RADICAL RIGHT: NAZISM AND FASCISM

In contemporary circumstances, however, the forces which are generally seen as furthest to the right are not those of monarchism but those of fascism or Nazism. In many ways such movements are the furthest removed from the democratic centre since they deny the legitimacy of the idea of democracy and of universal human rights, whilst the extreme left – in the shape of communists – have generally claimed the symbolism of democracy and frequently claimed to be more democratic than liberal democrats.

Hitler's 'National Socialist' Party was not without a populist strand in that the 'Führer' (leader) was seen as representing the true interests of the German 'Volk' (people) more completely than any democratic process could do. It was also, in rhetoric at least, anti-capitalist – with capitalism seen as a Jewish conspiracy to rob the Volk of its birthright. The state was seen as the embodiment of the public good and clearly had the responsibility to organise the economy, the educational system and the whole of social and cultural life. A major emphasis of the movement was on the mobilisation of the German people through a single party using the modern technology of mass communication.

In practice Nazism was dominated by the urge for power of its elite and their commitment to xenophobia, racism and nationalism. The urge to right the perceived wrong of the Versailles settlement of 1919 and strong nationalist feelings (shared by many Germans) was elaborated into a nightmare doctrine. The right of an 'Aryan' master race to 'living space' to the East and to cleanse itself of 'alien' elements such as Gypsies and Jews as well as to eliminate any mentally or physically defective specimens of their own race was asserted. The attempt to implement a state based on these doctrines resulted in the deaths of millions across the whole planet (the Holocaust).

Hitler's views, articulated in *Mein Kampf* ('My Struggle'), built in many ways upon more orthodox conservative German political theorists and philosophers. Hegel [1770–1831], for instance, had stressed the importance of a strong state, its role in defining culture and the existence of a logic (or dialectic) of history which justified war by superior states upon inferior ones. Schopenhauer [1780–1860] glorified Will over Reason. Nietzsche [1844–1900] believed in the creation of a race of superior individuals. Views like these were combined with carefully selected 'scientific' findings about natural selection and the nature of human racial divisions to create an ideology which had a powerful appeal in the politically volatile atmosphere of an economically depressed Germany in the 1930s.

Italian fascism, by contrast, although drawing upon many of the same causes of social and political discontent and using many of the same methods to achieve power – street warfare and mass rallies for instance – placed much less emphasis on racism. As an alternative to democracy the appeal of the leader was combined with an attempt to create a corporatist structure of representation in which bodies such as the Church, the army and employers' associations and even workers' syndicates could be represented. Spanish and Argentinian fascists have developed similar ideas and institutions.

With the defeat of Hitler, explicit endorsement of Nazi or fascist ideas has, on the whole, become rather unfashionable. On the extreme right in Europe even those who express a qualified admiration for Hitler have tended to deny that the wholesale slaughter of Jews in the Holocaust took place, rather than enthusiastically endorse it. The swastika is more prized as an icon for rebellious youth to embarrass parents with, than a serious political symbol. But racist and extreme nationalist sentiments remain the mark of the extreme right together with an anti-communist/labour rhetoric.

It is interesting that the most recent large-scale use of near-Nazi symbolism (admittedly a three-, rather than a four-legged 'swastika') has been by the South African AWB movement seeking to defend apartheid in its dying days. The South African apartheid regime could be seen as the last contemporary fascist state with an ideology based on racialism and supported by an apparatus of torture and repression. The Milosovich Serbian regime in the former Yugoslavia might also be interpreted in a similar way, although here, too, the ideology is nominally one of nationalism rather than racialism.

MARXISM

At the opposite end of the left/right political spectrum it is conventional to place the followers of Karl Marx [1818–1883]. In practice it is clear Marxists vary enormously in their radicalism and in their beliefs.

We have already seen (Chapter 1, p. 20], that Marx and Engels adopt a collectivist and conflict-oriented view of politics. It is worth stressing that this is part of both a theory of history and a programme of political action. As Marx says 'The philosophers have only *interpreted* the world differently – the point is to *change* it' (*11th Thesis on Fuerbach*, Marx and Engels, 1962, Vol. II: 403). Both the theoretical and the practical parts of their writing are impressive in their scope and depth. Marx and Engels published extensively not only on the nature of contemporary capitalism, but also on the transition from feudalism to capitalism and on ancient and oriental societies (Marx and Engels, 1962, *passim*).

In the more theoretical writings of Marx and Engels 'the dialectic of Hegel is turned upon its head' (Engels, *Fuerbach and the End of Classical German Philosophy*, Marx and Engels, 1962, Vol. II: 387). By placing nineteenth-century capitalism in perspective as one of several stages of history which inevitably lead on to new, higher, stages, Hegel's idea of a logic of history is adopted. But instead of the Ideal manifesting itself progressively through history, ideas (ideology) are seen as reflecting the underlying material 'means of production'. As Engels puts it:

> *all* past history with the exception of its primitive stages was the history of class struggles; that these warring classes of society are always the products of the modes of production and exchange – in a word, of the *economic* conditions of their time; that the economic structure of society always furnishes the real basis from which we can alone work out the ultimate explanation of the whole superstructure of juridical and political institutions as well as of the religious, philosophical, and other ideas of a given historical period.
>
> (*Socialism, Utopian and Scientific*, Marx and Engels, 1962: 134–135)

Class warfare will only cease to be the dynamic of history with the abolition of class in the future communist society.

Much of their work was also seeking to build up a socialist movement (the International Working Men's Association) which shared their moral rejection of the exploitative nature of capitalism. As the *Communist Manifesto* shows, the theory can be impressively marshalled as rhetoric to buttress an appeal to political action. The feeling of being on the side of history, having a 'scientific' insight into social processes, and being morally in the right, is a heady brew which still appeals – especially to the young and politically idealistic.

LENINISM AND STALINISM

In the twentieth century the most obvious heirs to Marx have been the leaders of the former Soviet Union. The most ideologically creative and politically influential of these were Vladimir Illich Lenin (born V. I. Ulyanov) [1870–1924] and Joseph Stalin (born Joseph Vissarionovich Dzhugashvili) [1879–1953]. They led this successor state to the Russian Empire in their capacities as secretaries of the

Russian Social Democrat Party (Bolshevik – 'majority' – faction) and later the Communist Party of the Soviet Union.

Marx and Engels envisaged socialist revolution taking place in the most developed capitalist countries through mass action by trade unions and democratic socialist organisations. Lenin and Stalin adapted the theory to suit the needs of a conspiratorial revolutionary organisation fighting an autocratic empire in which the majority of the population were still peasants. The adoption of representative democracy would have meant the loss of power by the Bolsheviks (who, at best, were firmly supported by the relatively small group of urban workers). In order to justify permanent control of a monopoly single-party hierarchy over the Soviet Union the doctrines of 'the dictatorship of the proletariat' and 'democratic centralism' were developed. The party leadership was seen as representing the emergent majority – the working class – that would be the majority as industrialisation proceeded. Lenin developed Marx's concept of the dictatorship of the proletariat to mean 'the organization of the advanced guard of the oppressed as the ruling class, for the purpose of crushing the oppressors' (Lenin, 1917: 225). True democracy could only be created by eliminating the exploitative bourgeois minority. Within the party the dominance of the leadership was defended by appealing to their greater knowledge of the 'scientific' doctrine and the prevalence of infiltrating 'counter-revolutionary' forces. 'Democratic centralism' was defined by the 1961 Communist Party Constitution as including the election of all party organs, strict party discipline, subordination of minorities to majorities and lower organs to higher organs. In practice unwelcome criticism from below was denounced as 'factionalism' and 'unbusinesslike' discussion if not downright treason (Schapiro, 1965: 63–65). Similarly Russian dominance in the former empire was effectively protected by a doctrine of the existence of a new 'Soviet' nationality which superseded both 'Great Russian Chauvinism' and 'Bourgeois [i.e. non-Russian] Nationalism'.

The apparent success of the Soviet regime in building a strong industrialised state capable of defeating Nazi Germany from a previously underdeveloped peasant economy led to the imitation of the regime in numerous East European countries, China, the Far East and Cuba. In many cases the 'cult of personality' developed around Stalin in the Soviet Union was imitated in relation to indigenous leaders such as Mao Zedong, Ho Chi Minh, Hoxha and Castro. Most of these claimed, with varying degrees of justification, to have produced ideologically improved versions of Marxism of their own.

OTHER MARXISMS

As George Orwell (1949, 1968) observed, the language employed in the totalitarian Marxist–Leninist regimes became increasingly divorced from reality. Dictatorship was described as democracy. Enormous differences in lifestyle were characterised as equality. The repression of national movements (as in Hungary in 1956) was described as maintaining peace and freedom and so on. Regimes which were nominally revolutionary, were actually characterised by bureaucratic conservatism and were increasingly seen as inefficient as well as hypocritical.

In the inter-war period, and during the Second World War, many European socialists tended to identify with 'communism'. The positive role of the Leninists in opposing fascism, and the achievements of the Soviet Union in terms of apparent economic growth and positive welfare measures, impressed intellectuals. A degree of direct financial subsidy to sympathetic West European parties and unions was also influential. The major socialist movements in such countries as France and Italy remained aligned with Moscow and continued to describe themselves as communist even through the Cold War period. Writers such as Jean-Paul Sartre in France continued to describe themselves as communists despite increasing problems of conscience in identifying with regimes which ruthlessly persecuted their own dissenting intellectuals.

However, increasingly, Western Marxists began to take independent intellectual stands apart from the rather stultifying orthodoxy of Marxist-Leninism as well as distancing themselves from the Soviet regime. In particular the idea of rigid economic determinism in history came in for re-evaluation. In Italy Gramsci (1969) stressed the humanistic strands in Marx's early writings and the role of ideology in influencing the functioning of the modern state.

The British writer Ralph Miliband stressed the role of the state in exercising a semi-autonomous role in history. He continued to take a pessimistic view of the likelihood of a capitalist economic system 'primarily geared to the private purposes of those who own and control its material resources' satisfying the needs of ordinary people

(Miliband, 1969: 268). But he conceded that 'the British political system does incorporate a number of democratic features which makes it possible for "ordinary people" to make themselves heard'. The system of 'capitalist democracy' is one of competition between capital and labour with a strong bias in favour of the former. There is 'permanent and fundamental contradiction or tension between the promise of popular power enshrined in universal suffrage, and the curbing or denying of that promise in practice' (Miliband, 1984: 1). Miliband was pessimistic about the potential of social democrats to empower ordinary people whilst regarding orthodox communists as too authoritarian. In practice he appears to anticipate a great danger of a drift from capitalist democracy to 'capitalist authoritarianism' (Miliband, 1984: 154).

A radical break with Stalinism is represented by a number of minor Marxist groups that were influenced by the writings of Leon Trotsky (born Lev Davidovich Bronstein) [1879–1940]. Trotsky had been a major colleague of Lenin's in the revolutionary period – acting as military Chief of Staff during the revolution and actually espousing the possibility of an independent Russian revolution before the Bolshevik Party in the pre-revolutionary era. After his expulsion by Stalin from the USSR, and before his assassination on Stalin's orders in Mexico in 1940, Trotsky denounced the way in which Communist Party rule had created a new class of exploiters in the Soviet Union – the party 'Apparatachiks' (Trotsky, 1945). This theme was elaborated by other critics such as Milovan Djilas (1966) who aligned himself with the revisionist Yugoslav regime. Under Tito the Yugoslavs attempted to develop a more humane and participative version of communism in which workplace democracy and multinational participation played a greater role than in the USSR.

The events in Paris of 1968 are a vivid illustration of the diversity of the modern left (Seale and McConville, 1968). A student protest against the Gaullist government's somewhat inept attempts to ban politics from university campuses mushroomed into larger demands for university reform, the end of the Vietnam war and finally the replacement of the de Gaulle regime by a true 'participative' democracy. The occupation of factories by strikers, the erection of barricades in Paris and a general strike were felt to lay the ground for a revolution by the student-led Trotskyist and Maoist 'groupuscules' who led many of the protests. The orthodox Communist Party, however, was more concerned to preserve its control over the bulk of the trade union movement and with its parliamentary electability than to identify itself with immediate and radical political and social change.

RADICALISM

Another slippery political term is 'radical'. The authors are happy to follow the *Shorter Oxford English Dictionary* on this. In adjectival use radical is said to mean going to the root, origin or foundation. Politically in English it refers to 'an advocate of "radical reform"; one who holds the most advanced views of political reform on democratic lines and thus belongs to the extreme section of the [English] liberal party (1802)'. In France, radicals are particularly identified with republicanism and anti-clericalism. More generally radicalism can be used to characterise a style of politics that frequently returns to one set of theoretical first principles in seeking solutions to all sorts of problems. This may be contrasted with 'pragmatism', which emphasises the practical consequences of a decision rather than its theoretical roots. A radical might then tend in a number of different directions but always to an extreme degree.

Radicals in politics were thus once extreme democrats; more recently the term has often been applied to far left socialists, but increasingly it has been on other dimensions that radicalism can be measured. Islamic fundamentalists, radical feminists, Greenpeace, even Thatcherite Conservatives in Britain could all be described as 'radicals'. But the principles to which these groups appeal are very different from each other and from earlier generations of political activists. The similarity that these theorists share is a tendency to solve all sorts of different problems from their own rather limited repertoire of concepts. Everything comes down to the Koran, patriarchal domination, ecological crisis or the market, as the case may be.

RADICAL THEISM – CATHOLIC, PROTESTANT AND ISLAMIC

> When Adam delved and Eve span,
> Who was then the gentleman?

> (John Ball)

John Ball, the priest who led the Peasants' Revolt in 1381, was one of many popular leaders who placed a more radical interpretation on the Bible than did official church leaders. The radical possibilities of the gospel message that the poor would inherit the earth and the protestant stress on the sovereignty of the individual conscience have strongly influenced the left of the British political tradition. The Diggers and Levellers in the Civil War period threw doubt not only upon the position of the established Church, but upon the existing basis of property and political representation (Greenleaf, 1983: 351).

In the New World, in colonies such as seventeenth-century Massachusetts and Connecticut, membership of the dominant Christian sect was virtually the same as citizenship (Morison and Commager, 1962, Vol. I: 57–65). Similarly, in such continental cities as Calvin's Geneva, the processes of government and the interpretation of God's word were virtually indistinguishable (Tawney, 1938: 132). At a later stage in American history (1847), the Mormon leader Brigham Young led his people out of the United States to found Salt Lake City. There they could practise their own religion (including polygamy) in accordance with Young's interpretation of the Book of Mormon (Morison and Commager, 1962, Vol. I: 590–593).

Thus it is clear that Christian fundamentalism can be a considerable political force – as it remains to this day in the United States where the backing of the Evangelicals may have proved decisive in securing victories for both Reagan and George W. Bush. 'Fundamentalism' – a literal approach to the interpretation of the Bible – is, strictly speaking, a purely theological doctrine and not equivalent to a belief in the political supremacy of the Church. Some fundamentalists would endorse a strict separation of secular and religious matters, but where they are in a majority this distinction has often ceased to be of practical importance.

None the less it is Islamic fundamentalism which appears in many ways the most dynamic political–religious movement of the early twenty-first century. Islamic 'fundamentalism' is something of a misnomer since virtually all Muslims take the same sort of literal approach to the status and interpretation of the Koran that Protestant evangelicals take to the Bible. Because of a historic legacy deriving from European conflict with Islam during the crusades and as a part of colonialism, there is a tendency in the West to identify Islamic 'fundamentalism' with intolerance, fanaticism, terrorism and the like (Said, 1987). Historically there is little evidence for such an identification – Islamic doctrine being explicitly a tolerant one – at least in relation to 'The People of the Book' – Jews and Christians. As the body count in Bosnia suggests, intolerance between Muslims and Christians has often been the other way around.

What is clear is the attraction of Islam in the South as a sophisticated and 'civilised' religion that permits polygamy and is not identified, as is Christianity, with the former colonial powers (Gbadamosi, 1978). Hence in areas such as southern Nigeria, where tribal religions formerly predominated, Islam has often grown much faster than Christianity, whilst in areas which have been historically Muslim, such as Egypt, the reassertion of Islamic identity is a part of the rejection of Western colonialism.

Islam has the great advantage of offering not only a religious doctrine, but a social and cultural tradition separate from, and equal or superior in many respects to, that of Christian Europe. Centuries of theological and artistic achievement can be drawn upon. Pilgrims making the journey to Mecca (usually by jet airliner rather than camel train) will be greeted by the spectacle of vast assemblies of the faithful from all over the world with whom to exchange experiences. The doctrine of Islam has always been one not only of common religious observance, but the assertion of a social and political unity of all the faithful – the Umma (Islamic community). Consider the Koranic verse 'this your nation is a single nation, and I am your Lord so worship me' (Surah 21: verse 92).

The political appeal of Islam can be seen in the way in which pragmatic politicians, like Saddam Hussein in Iraq, turned to it as a way of generating political support. The Ayatollah Khomenei, in Iran, was immensely effective in denouncing the Shah as an agent of the American 'Satan' in allowing alcohol, Coca-Cola and mini-skirts and discouraging polygamy and hashish. Khomenei described Islamic government as the government of the 'oppressed upon earth' in a reference to the Koranic verse 'And we wish to show favour to those who have been oppressed upon earth, and to make them leaders and inheritors' (Surah 28, v. 5).

The problems of applying Islam to contemporary political situations and structures are considerable and are discussed further in Chapter 6. Perhaps the major difficulty is its strict incompatibility with ideas with which it is often, in practice, confused. Thus, in the Middle East, nationalism, pan-Arabism and Islam are often identified – yet Syrian or Egyptian nationalism may conflict with a sense of Arab identity; whilst many Muslims are Iranian (Persian), African, Indian or Indonesian rather than Arab. The contemporary Western tendency to identify Islamic fundamentalism with terrorism owes much to the use of force by Palestinian nationalists and their sympathisers. The adoption of titles like 'the International Front for Holy War Against Jews and Crusaders' may disguise, in many cases, much more concern with opposing the policies of the ('imperialist') USA and of the state of Israel than with theology. In opposition to Western influences such distinctions may not matter very much – but in constructing alternative political institutions or alliances they do.

ECOLOGY AS POLITICAL RADICALISM

As early as the beginning of the nineteenth century, Wordsworth opposed the coming of the steam train to the Lake District as fatal to its character and Blake denounced the 'dark Satanic mills' of the industrial revolution. The conservation of the natural environment did not, however, become a major element in practical politics until relatively recently. Conservationism did figure quite largely in the late nineteenth-century US Progressive movement. But only in recent years have Ecology or Green parties been represented in European legislatures and presented a comprehensive political pro-gramme. Before this, pressure groups pioneered environmental causes such as rural planning, national parks, and smoke and noise abatement which have now become mainstream public policies.

Governments have been involved with environmental issues from almost the earliest times. In England royal forests like the New Forest were protected for a variety of reasons including recreation (hunting), as an economic and strategic resource (timber for the navy) and are now increasingly seen as rare habitats to be protected for the sake of the rare species within them as well. In the United States the 'unsettled' lands of the west were viewed as federal property to be allocated in the public interest.

The green movement is unusual, however, in deriving an overall coherent philosophy from a scientific discipline. Ecology is the science that studies the relationship between organisms and their physical environment. As scientific study has proceeded, the multiple inter-dependencies between the different organic species on the planet and the crucial impact of climatic and geological influences have become clear to us in a way that was not obvious to earlier generations.

With the development of an industrial urban civilisation dependent upon the consumption of fossil fuels, and our own increasing knowledge, it has become clear that the environment is being moulded in potentially dangerous ways by human beings as never before. The Rio Earth Summit of June 1992 found political leaders from all over the globe discussing seriously the depletion of world resources (especially non-renewable energy sources); the phenomenon of global warming; the dangers of chemical, biological and radiation pollution in the atmosphere and oceans; the destruction of animal and plant species through the destruction of valuable habitats such as the rain forest. Non-governmental groups at the same summit stressed the human population explosion and the unequal distribution of resources between North and South as contributors to a single problem result-ing essentially from uncontrolled industrial growth.

The various wings of the green movement are inclined to unite in seeing these problems as the dominant political agenda for humanity in the early twenty-first century. Ecology or green campaigners usually suggest that both capitalist and communist ideologies are part of the problem. Resources are being used up at an exponential (ever-increasing) rate, whilst the healthy complexity of the ecology of the planet is being continually reduced by commercial agriculture and industrial pollution. Thus virtually all issues from human repro-duction, through patterns of industrial investment and domestic consumption to tourism can be viewed in an ecological light.

Divisions within the movement can be observed – particularly between what one might call the romantics and the scientists. On the 'romantic' side, the stress is on back-to-nature ideas such as homeopathy, vegetarianism, naturism and developing folk-music-playing rural communities. On the 'scientific' side, the stress is on projections of economic and ecological disaster if present trends in industrialisation and consumption continue. A different division has also been observed between what is sometimes called the 'light anthropocentric' and the 'deep ecology' wings (Vincent, 1992: 217). The first group stress the practical problems for human beings and may concentrate on individual problems pragmatically. Deep ecologists call for a total change of attitude by humans to recognise the intrinsic value of all other species.

An interesting example of the 'deep ecology' approach is James Lovelock's 'Gaia hypothesis'. This sees the earth as a single self-regulating organism. He stresses that living things created the atmosphere, the fertility of the soil, the temperature of the atmosphere, the oxygen we breathe, etc. and are, in turn, crucially dependent upon these things (Lovelock, 1979). It would seem to be a matter of some debate whether, despite the scientific terminology, this is a scientific, moral or spiritual doctrine. One implication of this would seem to be that if necessary Gaia will wipe out any species – including humanity – which seeks to upset the natural harmony of the ecosphere.

As a political doctrine for intellectuals 'ecologism' has great advantages – it has something to say on almost every issue, is opposed to many contemporary orthodoxies (especially the desirability of economic growth), has a variety of esoteric insights to offer and has appealing emotional undertones. In this sense, then, ecologism can be seen as a rather radical and oppositional doctrine. On the other hand, in asserting the rights of succeeding generations against the present, there are echoes of the conservative sentiments expressed by Burke. He wrote: 'I attest the retiring, I attest the advancing generations, between which, as a link in the great chain of eternal order we stand' (quoted in Sabine, 1951: 519).

On the level of practical politics, Greens can identify themselves with a variety of appealing local movements – especially of the NIMBY (Not In My Back Yard) variety. There may, however, be major problems in educating large electorates in the need for measures which run directly counter to the consumerist trends of the times and in achieving the necessary international co-ordination to attain green objectives (see Chapter 5). As a result a lot of green political activism is to be found in pressure group activity, rather than political parties.

FEMINISM AS POLITICAL RADICALISM

A consciousness of the need for political action to secure equal rights for women is scarcely new. As we saw in an earlier chapter, Plato envisaged women participating on an equal basis in government in classical times. As early as 1792 Mary Wollstonecraft was arguing the case for female emancipation (Wollstonecraft, 1985). By the beginning of the twentieth century women had achieved the franchise in some American states and the Women's Suffrage movement had become a major political issue in Britain with radicals prepared to use violence against property and even suicide as a political weapon. Despite the achieving of universal suffrage in virtually all Western democracies, feminism remains a live political issue for many and the overwhelming passion of a few.

The vote has not brought equality of pay, status or opportunity for women. Attitudes to this fact may be roughly summarised in Table 4.1. 'Radical' feminists have tended to see feminism as an all-embracing matter which should determine attitudes to a wide variety of issues – including the nature of work, authority structures and careers, education, taxation and personal relationships. Western society has been warped by the aggressive and acquisitive elderly males of the species dominating and exploiting the young and the female.

Possibly as a result of media overreaction and misrepresentation of the views of a minority of radical feminists (customarily caricatured as bra-burning lesbians in the tabloid press), many people of moderate views would now hesitate to describe themselves as 'feminists'. However, moderates are now found endorsing what most people of the older generation of feminists would have regarded as a feminist stand. Thus they take for granted the desirability of equal political rights for women, freedom to pursue any career without discrimination, and equal pay for equal work.

Even amongst conservatives on the issue, few can be found to argue for the inferiority of women. In many cases the ostensibly flattering line is taken that women have quite rightly preferred not to get involved in male power games and should not compromise their essential nature by doing so (compare comments on racial apartheid in Chapter 5).

Radical feminists would argue that their more moderate sisters mistake the size of the problem in asserting equal status in a male-dominated society. Their analysis of the problem and suggested strategy and tactics vary greatly from one group to another.

Table 4.1 Attitudes to gender differences

	Radical feminist	Moderate feminist	Conservative
Problem	**Patriarchy: government by men.** Domination and exploitation of women by older men. Ideology dominates many women's thoughts as well as social institutions and socialisation	**Under-representation of women; sexual discrimination**	**None** – apparent inequalities reflect *different* role women play in society – caring for others. Beauty, gentleness, more important than power, etc.
Causes	**Sexist power structure.** Rowbotham: sexual division of labour. Firestone: male control of female reproduction. Marxist (Engels): reserve army of labour	**Prejudice, ignorance – tradition, socialisation**	**Biology.** Evolution or God has given females genetic tendency to passivity; caring, conscientious disposition
Solution	**Revolution.** Marxist, personal or lesbian? Society must be remade: assumptions *re* family, carers, careers, politics, etc. reversed	**Integration.** Women to play full part in existing society	**Apartheid.** Women to remain separate but equal
Action	**Women's liberation.** Remove male structures of domination and ideology. Personal – take control of own life. Marxist – as part of proletarian revolution	**Female participation.** Education Piecemeal legal action Use legal rights to full, e.g. political nominations or educational opportunities	**Legal action inappropriate.** Safeguard family values

Thus Marxist feminists tend to follow Engels in seeing the exploitation of women as being part of the capitalist phenomena of a 'reserve army of labour'. Capitalists exploit an under-trained, under-paid and often part-time female workforce in order to keep the more organised and militant male workforce in order, allowing women to come somewhere near to potential only in the absence of men at the war-front. True emancipation can only come with the triumph of a proletarian revolution – which will wipe away these repressive mechanisms (together with the bourgeois view of the family as male property). Other writers are less convinced that male domination is associated with capitalism, pointing to the recurrence of a sexual division of labour in many non-capitalist societies (Rowbotham, 1972) and the power accruing to males until recently from their control of female reproduction (Firestone, 1971).

Most radical feminists have taken a line similar to the anarchists (indeed Emma Goldman (1915) is a pioneer in both movements) that revolution must begin in the private lives of those who are convinced of its desirability. 'The personal is the political' is the slogan of many radical feminists who argue that the centralised and authoritarian imposition of a way of life is a male style of politics. A tiny minority go one step further and argue that males will never voluntarily give up their power – no ruling class does – so that only in separatist lesbian communities can women achieve equality and freedom.

Feminist ideas can be seen as an application of liberal ideas on the rights of all to self-development. Some feminists have been influenced by Marxist doctrines about exploitation and ideology. The mainstream of the women's movement, however, has been very much a series of autonomous self-help groups responding to the personal and political situation of their members.

LIBERALISM

Liberalism may be understood in a broad or in a narrower sense. In the broad sense, one can argue that liberal ideas of individualism and constitutionalism form the basis of a constitutional consensus shared by most of the mainstream parties in the states of the European Union, the United States and many other 'liberal democracies'.

In the narrower sense, liberalism is a doctrine professed by a number of democratic parties distinguished from more conservative/

Christian democrat parties on the right and socialist parties on the left. The Liberal International is a formal expression of this and includes the US (mainly New York) Liberal Party and the UK Liberal Democrats. An intermediate use of the term is common in the United States, where people on the left of the two main parties are frequently described as liberals with the expectation that they favour such causes as internationalism, civil rights and increased government intervention and spending for social welfare. Many of these ideas are similar to those of the British Liberal Democrats. Most Liberal parties would be viewed on the centre–left of the political spectrum, but some, such as the Liberal Party of Australia, are considered to inhabit the centre–right.

A helpful simplification may be to distinguish three phases in the development of liberal ideas. The earliest phase is the establishment of the idea of constitutional government based upon individual rights. The United States constitution is a good expression of this. It incorporates ideas such as government being based on the consent of the governed, the constitution as a government of laws not of men, and the entrenchment of individual rights in the constitution. These are all a systematic expression of the American colonies' inheritance of the British parliamentary constitutional tradition, and the Founding Fathers explicitly referred to the writings of Locke and to Montesquieu's [1688–1755] interpretation of the British constitution (the Separation of Powers) (see Chapter 7, pp. 182–183).

In the second phase, nineteenth-century liberal writers like Bentham and the Mills (James and his son John Stuart) developed the democratic implications of earlier statements and the experiences of earlier generations. The link with capitalism was also made explicit in a defence of doctrines of free trade and the desirability of a minimal state, building upon the writings of economists such as Adam Smith [1723–1790] and Ricardo [1772–1823]. In Britain, and on the Continent, liberals increasingly were seen as the party of the new modernising manufacturing elite opposed to the more conservative, if not 'feudal', landed gentry. In both Europe and North America liberals increasingly were the party of political reform and universal suffrage.

A distinctive feature of liberalism has been an emphasis on political freedom, both in the sense of a support of national self-determination and, particularly, in the sense of the freedom of the individual to express his or her own moral values through free speech, choice of occupation and way of life. John Stuart Mill's *Essay on Liberty* (1859) makes a memorable case against interference by the state or society in the private lives of individuals and for freedom of expression. Freedom of expression may be thought of as the classic liberal value and is encapsulated in the quotation often attributed to Voltaire: 'I disapprove of what you say, but I will defend to the death your right to say it.'

A third phase in the development of liberalism was marked in philosophical terms by the writings of the English idealists (Milne, 1962) including F. H. Bradley [1846–1924], Bernard Bosanquet [1848–1923], Josiah Royce [1855–1916] (an American writer with some similar ideas), and most notably T. H. Green [1836–1882] and Leonard Hobhouse [1864–1929]. Much of this idealist writing was a development of the theme evident in the writings of John Stuart Mill: the state exists so as to guarantee a system of rights that will enable individuals to pursue their moral development. As Green puts it: 'The state presupposes rights and rights of individuals.' 'It is a form which society takes to maintain them' (Green, 1941: 144). 'Only through the possession of rights can the power of the individual freely to make a common good of his own have reality given to it' (Green, 1941: 45). These rights include the right to private property but these must be exercised in such a way as not to prevent others exercising these rights too. The state may thus intervene to regulate property and other rights in the interests of the development of a common sense of citizenship by all. The state cannot directly promote 'habits of true citizenship' but it should actively concern itself with 'the removal of obstacles' (Green, 1941: 208, 209). He explicitly endorses state intervention to enable the mass of the population to enjoy reasonable standards of health, housing, and access to property rights (Green, 1941: 209).

Hobhouse (1964, originally published in 1911) has a more explicit statement of political liberalism. He identifies liberalism with civil, fiscal, personal, social, economic, domestic, local, racial, national and international and political liberty (Ch. II). He then goes on to make the clear assertion that 'full liberty implies full equality' and to assert the correctness of distinguishing in terms of taxation between earned and unearned income and between acquired and inherited wealth (Ch. VIII).

The third phase of 'social' liberalism is associated in Britain with the political careers, speeches and writings of Lloyd George, John Maynard Keynes and Lord Beveridge. Lloyd George, as Chancellor of the Exchequer in the pre-First World War liberal government can be seen as the practical inaugurator of social liberalism with his introduction of both old age pensions and death duties – that is both state welfare schemes and progressive taxation. Beveridge in his Second World War coalition government White Paper put forward a blueprint for the modern welfare state in which state-organised 'insurance' schemes and taxation would protect all citizens from the Five Giants of Want, Disease, Ignorance, Squalor and Idleness. Keynes as an economist and administrator successfully argued the need for government intervention to ensure the efficient working of a capitalist economy. In the United States, the inter-war Roosevelt New Deal administration rather pragmatically adopted a similar interventionist approach to the economy and welfare which has influenced the liberal left ever since. Continental European liberal and radical parties have not all adopted this third phase of liberalism . Indeed left-wing Christian democrat movements like the former French MRP (Mouvement Republicain Populaire) may be seen as in some respects having much more in common with the British Liberal Democrats than their nominal allies in the Liberal International.

CONSERVATISM

It can be argued that conservatism is more of an attitude than a doctrine. In every society many, often a majority, have been happy to conserve the existing values and institutions of that society. Naturally the more prosperous and successful members of any given society are more likely to identify with its core values and institutions than less poor and successful citizens. Conservatives in a military dictatorship in the South are likely to be committed to radically different institutions and values from those in democratic industrial Britain or the United States.

Some components of a basic conservative attitude might, however, be suggested. A pessimism about human nature is often to be discerned (see previous chapter) with an associated stress on the need for domestic 'law and order' measures and strong armed forces to repel international threats. The need to support existing spiritual as well as secular authority will also be evident. Nationalism and support for 'family values' will usually also be found.

In the aftermath of the French Revolution, Edmund Burke [1729–1797] sought to articulate a suspicion of rationalist egalitarianism and to praise instead the strength of the genius of the national constitution:

> We are afraid to put men to live and trade each on his own private stock of reason; because we suspect this stock in each man is so small, and that the individual would do better to avail themselves of the general bank and capital of nations and ages.
>
> (Burke, 1907, Vol. IV: 95)

Rather than a contract between individuals – like a trading agreement – the state is instituted as a partnership between the generations, 'between those who are living and those who are dead', to be approached with reverence.

Many of the themes presented somewhat rhetorically and unsystematically by Burke were expounded in a more philosophical, systematic and perhaps less intelligible way by nineteenth-century German idealists such as Hegel to whom we have already referred.

In Britain the Conservative Party has supported both the throne and the Established Church. In the United States the symbols of continuity are now the national and state constitutions (interpreted to stress the limitations on government), the flag, prayers in schools and the like. Historically conservatives in both countries have tended to be suspicious of grand theories of government and pragmatic in their pursuit of political support. The left has been attacked as peddlers of disunity and conflict with trade unionism regarded with distaste – in the United States its links to socialism and 'hence' the Soviet Union making it doubly unacceptable during the Cold War.

British Conservatives, however were much influenced by Disraeli's [1804–1881] doctrine of 'One Nation', popularised in his novel *Sybil* and his political practice as prime minister (1868 and 1874–1880). His idea was that national unity should be preserved through a direct appeal to the interests of the working classes on the part of benevolent Tory governments. In the nineteenth century the Conservatives were still led by a mainly aristocratic leadership who combined ideas of 'noblesse oblige' with an inclination to 'dish the

Whigs' by adopting popular social measures. The Liberals were often reluctant, because of their ideological commitment to laissez-faire (and the support of the new urban bourgeoisie) to take such measures.

Traditional conservative suspicion of grand theory may be epitomised by reference to the work of Michael Oakeshott [1901–1990]:

> To some people 'government' appears as a vast reservoir of power which inspires them to dream of what use may be made of it. They have favourite projects of various dimensions, which they sincerely believe are for the benefit of mankind. . . . They are, thus, disposed to recognise government as an instrument of passion; the art of politics is to inflame and direct desire. . . . Now the disposition of the Conservative in respect of politics reflects a quite different view . . . to inject into activities of already too passionate men an ingredient of moderation; to restrain, to deflate, to pacify and to reconcile; not to stoke the fires of desire but to damp them down.
>
> (Oakeshott, 1962: 191–192)

In a well-known and rather striking image, Oakeshott further describes the activity of politics as to

> sail a bottomless and boundless sea; there is neither harbour for shelter nor floor for anchorage, neither starting-place nor appointed destination. The enterprise is to keep afloat on an even keel; the sea is both friend and enemy; and the seamanship consists in using the resources of a traditional manner of behaviour in order to make a friend of every hostile occasion.
>
> (Oakeshott, 1962: 127)

THATCHERISM AND NEO-CONSERVATISM

Although the Conservative Party continues to attract some traditional 'One-Nation' pragmatic supporters, many MPs and party members have become committed to the idea that the political and economic system requires radical reform to allow market forces to achieve an efficient and effective allocation of resources. The doctrine which has become identified as 'Thatcherism' in Britain originated in the United States with such thinkers as Hayek (1979) and Milton

Friedman (Friedman and Friedman, 1980), and was advocated by Ronald Reagan in his Republican presidential campaigns. Its most sustained practical influence was on the Conservative administration from 1979 to 1997, led for most of that period by Margaret Thatcher.

The Thatcherites have – in distinction to usual British conservative pragmatism – insisted on applying one theoretical analysis to a wide variety of policy areas. The extent of their opposition to the growth of the 'nanny state', and insistence on the introduction of market mechanisms and privatisation, not only to social welfare areas but even to prisons, the Post Office and the armed forces, is remarkable.

'Thatcherism' can be seen as a variety of liberalism in its insistence on the importance of the free market, its individualism and support for electoral democracy on a national level. However, it retains support for the Crown, 'traditional family values' and a suspicion of internationalism (i.e. a lukewarm attitude to European Union political integration) from the conservative tradition.

More recently, in the United States, a prominent 'neo-conservative' group supporting the George W. Bush administration, and associated with the American Enterprise Institute and the Project for the New American Century, have adopted similar economic and nationalist policies. In the US context, conservatism takes paradoxical form in a belief in the compulsory export of liberal institutions to the South – including Iraq and Afghanistan. The United Nations is the focus for a suspicion of international institutions.

Conservatism by its very nature continually evolves in response to economic and social changes. Whilst neo-conservatism is still a popular strand of conservatism, it is currently being challenged by what may be referred to as 'crusty conservatism'. Probably the best known exponent of this in the UK is David Cameron, the Conservative Party leader, who stresses environmental and social issues.

CHRISTIAN DEMOCRACY

In recent years in the United States, whilst what the British might call 'Thatcherite' political attitudes have been strong, arguably the strongest organised force on the political right has been Christian fundamentalism with its emphasis on the so-called 'moral majority' issues of abortion, pornography and the like.

In continental Europe, of course, the moderate centre-right position held by the Conservatives in Britain is occupied in many countries by the Christian democrat parties whose enthusiasm for capitalism is balanced by electoral links to the countryside and by the Church's belief in co-operation and compassion in social affairs. In a number of countries links with the trade union movement reinforce Christian democrat claims to a centrist rather than conservative/right-wing classification (Michael Smart in Smith, 1989: 380). Modern Catholic encyclicals on social matters have, for instance, stressed the moral dignity of labour and the legitimacy of involving the representatives of labour in decision making in the workplace. They also endorse the idea of democratic decentralisation or 'subsidiarity' (see Chapter 6).

The strongest Christian democratic parties seem to be in those Catholic countries where the Church has adopted something of a self-denying ordinance, allowing practical politicians room for manoeuvre. For simplicity Protestant democratic parties are not considered here in detail – but they are important in the Netherlands, and of influence in Switzerland and the Nordic countries. The CDU in Germany does include Protestants but attracts more support from Catholics (Dalton, 1988: Ch. 8). Christian democracy has been defined as

> a movement of those who aim to solve – with the aid of Christian principles and 'democratic' techniques – that range of temporal problems which the Church has repeatedly and solemnly declared to lie within the 'supreme' competence of lay society, and outside direct ecclesiastical control. (Fogarty, 1957: 6).

More specifically, Irving (1979: xvii) discerns three basic principles in contemporary European Christian democracy:

> 'Christian Principles' (in the sense of a broad commitment to basic human rights, particularly those of the individual); 'democracy' (in the sense of a clear cut commitment to liberal democracy) and 'integration' (in the dual sense of a commitment to class reconciliation through the concept of the broad-based *Volkspartei* (people's party) and to transnational reconciliation through the strong Christian Democratic commitment to European integration).

As Irving argues (p. xxi), Christian democracy shares conservative values of individualism, respect for property, anti-communism and dislike of excessive state intervention. However, unlike British Thatcherites they have favoured 'concertation' – consultation between government, industry, the trade unions and other interest groups. Couple this with an enthusiasm for Europe and the similarities with the more moderate wing of the modern UK Conservative Party are evident

SOCIALISM AND SOCIAL DEMOCRACY

We have already seen that both Marxists and many anarchists regard themselves as socialists. Millions of people, however, remain committed to socialism without regarding themselves as disciples of Marx or opponents of the very concept of a state. Nor does being influenced by Marxist ideas necessarily mean an admiration for the Soviet Union. For many socialists the doctrine is the opposite of totalitarianism – it is a commitment to values of equality and justice for all. An interesting survey of British Labour MPs showed the book which had most influenced their political thinking was George Orwell's *1984* – a novel satirising the Stalinist approach to politics. In a Fabian pamphlet Tony Blair wrote of two socialist traditions: a Marxist economic determinist and collectivist tradition and another 'based on the belief that socialism is a set of values or beliefs – sometimes called ethical socialism' (Blair, 1994: 2). These values he defines as 'social justice, the equal worth of each citizen, equality of opportunity, community' (p. 4). This latter tradition he sees as predominant in 'European Social Democracy' and appropriate to the contemporary Labour Party.

Historically it does seem that a strain of indigenous radicalism often associated with the non-conformist churches and stretching back to John Ball is more important than Marxism in the British socialist tradition. The non-conformist churches trained many Labour speakers in the skills of oratory and social organisation. Apparently Tony Blair is a member of a formal Christian Socialist group. Certainly more important than Marxism has been the influence of a strong trade union and co-operative movement, which, in England, pre-date both Marx and the Labour Party. The Labour Party originated early in the twentieth century as the Labour

Representation Committee to represent organised labour in Parliament. Only in 1918 did the LRC become the Labour Party, allow individual members, and adopt a socialist statement of objectives in clause 4 of its constitution – apparently in an attempt to appeal for middle-class intellectual support (McKibbin, 1983: 97).

Clause 4 of the Labour Party's 1918 constitution stated that the objective of the party was:

> to secure for the workers by hand or by brain the full fruits of their industry and the most equitable distribution thereof that may be possible upon the basis of common ownership of the means of production, distribution and exchange, and the best obtainable system of popular administration and control of each industry or service.

There were many subsequent attempts to drop this statement by leaders of the party because it was interpreted as identifying the party too closely with the idea of nationalisation, though the phrases 'common ownership' and 'best obtainable' were surely meant to allow for at least co-operative and municipal ownership and possibly more flexible interpretation still.

For many years Labourism might have been defined in terms of a Fabian strategy to bring about the collective management of the economy through a reliance on the power of the collective might of the organised working class. As George Bernard Shaw put it in *Fabian Tract 13* (1891) socialism was a doctrine of 'gradualist Collectivism brought about by a strategy of resolute constitutionalism'. The 'revisionists' who have now succeeded in dropping the old clause 4 have argued that socialism is to be found more in a commitment to egalitarian and libertarian values than in specific measures to achieve these at any particular time. In Tony Blair's words 'the old-style collectivism of several decades ago' is no longer radicalism but 'the neo-conservatism of the left' (Blair, 1994: 7). A similar debate has taken place within many continental European socialist (and, still more, former communist) parties.

Most writers on socialism have agreed that it is about a commitment to equality, but there has been little consensus about the nature of that commitment (Vincent, 1992: 101–104). Generally speaking, however, democratic socialists have agreed on: emphasising equality of rights for all; rejecting the legitimacy of extremist coercive and violent tactics, given the presence of a liberal democratic state with opportunities for peaceful and constitutional change; and rejecting as unfair, unregulated capitalist economics. The range of opinions within these parameters has been, and remains, a very large one.

COMMUNITARIANISM AND THE 'THIRD WAY'

It will be apparent to most readers that the predominant political style in modern European and North American democracies is what we have called pragmatic rather than radical. Democratic politicians in general seem slow to relate their policy stands to explicit general principles and appear to be content to manage existing societies rather than to try to fundamentally change them. Few contemporary presidents or prime ministers would be happy to be labelled as Marxists, fascists or as radical feminists or ecologists but tend to cling to the electorally safe centre ground of politics.

Such tendencies have been described as 'The End of Ideology' (Bell, 1960), but this may be a somewhat confusing description. One should distinguish between the somewhat cavalier approach to ideas, which is typical of most practical politicians, and the absence of any ideas. Similarly a period of international confrontation between Marxist–Leninist and liberal democratic/capitalist systems may have drawn to an end, but this does not mean that new 'ideological' confrontations (for instance on religion, gender and ecology) may not occur.

The possibility of a consolidation of the centre streams of thought also seems very likely to the authors; the differences between revisionist democratic socialism, social liberalism, Christian democracy and pragmatic conservatism are surely small compared with the gulf which separates them from some of their unconstitutional radical and authoritarian alternatives.

An illustration of the possibility of such a convergence is the tendency of politicians of a wide variety of formal party backgrounds to endorse the language of 'communitarianism'. Thus Etzioni (1995: ix), suggests that several key Labour, Conservative and Liberal Democratic figures in the UK (including Tony Blair), Democrats and Republicans in the USA (including Bill Clinton) as well as Christian and Social Democrats in Germany have all endorsed such ideas.

The influential version of communitarianism propagated by Etzioni accepts the liberal legacy of individual rights and a presumption against extensive state intervention. However, he seeks to balance this with a stress on the need for individuals to accept their duties to the state and community and for the community 'to be responsive to their members and to foster participation and deliberation in social and political life' (p. 254). Sandel (1996: 5) speaks of the need to resurrect the 'Republican' tradition 'that liberty depends on sharing in self-government' which in turn requires 'a knowledge of public affairs and also a sense of belonging, a concern for the whole, a moral bond with the community whose fate is at stake'.

Communitarianism can be seen as a reaction to the extreme individualism of Thatcherism which also seeks to avoid the clumsy state collectivism of not only Soviet communism but also some versions of British socialism and American liberalism – a 'third way'. Bill Clinton popularised the 'third way' 'as a combination of small but progressive government, tight financial discipline and a programme to secure economic freedom with social cohesion – countering critics of both "tax and spend" and "permissive" liberalism' (Butler, 2000: 154).

Whilst many writers have seen New Labour and the third way as a decisive break with the past, Rubinstein (2000) emphasises that the Labour parliamentary leadership, such as Attlee, Morrison and Wilson, have often emphasised the need to appeal to the middle as well as the working class and the virtues of individualism. They also distanced themselves from organised labour when in office and adopted a pro-US foreign policy.

Bevir (2000) sees New Labour ideology as a reaction from within the Labour tradition to the three problems of how to control inflation, the existence of an underclass dependent on the welfare state and changes in the attitudes, nature and lifestyle of the working class.

The problem (or possibly advantage!) with the third way as a guide to policy is that it lacks specifics. It can be seen as a route to collaboration with liberals and progressive conservatives and European Christian democrats. More cynically, it can be viewed as a way of making Labour more electable by opening up the way for pragmatic compromise on any number of old Labour policies and values (e.g. the redistribution of wealth and unilateral nuclear disarmament as well as nationalisation).

It may be questioned, however, whether the doctrine as so far developed has been able to fully confront the economic and social problems of the new globalised economy. Indeed some have seen it as no more than a public relations fig leaf to cover a naked lack of specific remedies for current problems (Jacques, 1998). Popularised by Tony Giddens as a new form of social democracy, for a few years in the late 1990s and early 2000s, the 'third way' offered politicians such as Blair, Clinton and Schroeder a way of re-packaging left-of-centre politics. Whilst a policy legacy may last, based around the concept of a stakeholder society, as an ideology the term appears to have had a limited shelf life.

RECOMMENDED READING

Bryson, Valerie, 1992, *Feminist Political Theory: An Introduction*, *London*, Macmillan
    Useful introduction to a key issue in contemporary debate.

De Crespigny, Anthony and Minogue, Kenneth (eds), 1976, *Contemporary Political Philosophers*, London, Methuen
    Useful collection of essays on some key recent political theorists.

Dobson, Andrew, 2000, *Green Political Thought: An Introduction*, 3rd edn, London, Routledge
    Helpful exploration of a controversial area of modern political thought.

Eccleshall, Robert *et al.*, 1994, *Political Ideologies: An Introduction*, 2nd edn, London, Routledge
    Useful standard introductory text – focused on the various 'isms' including liberalism, conservatism, socialism, democracy, nationalism, fascism, ecologism and feminism.

Eickelman, Dale F. and Piscatori, James, 1996, *Muslim Politics*, Princeton, NJ, Princeton University Press
    A good introduction which emphasises the complexity of divisions in the Islamic world.

Etzioni, Amitai , 1995, *The Spirit of Community*, London, Fontana
    A somewhat polemical statement of the communitarian case.

Heywood, Andrew, 1998, *Political Ideologies: An Introduction*, 2nd edn, Basingstoke, Macmillan

Similar to the Eccleshall book above with additional chapters on religious fundamentalism and anarchism but no separate chapter on democracy.

Morgan, Michael L. (ed.), 1992, *Classics of Moral and Political Theory*, Indianapolis, IN, Hackett
Reader including the standard texts and commentary.

Plamenatz, John [Revised Plamenatz, M. E. and Wokler, Robert], 1992, *Man and Society*, 2nd edn, 3 vols, London, Longmans
Standard British text on the history of political thought concentrating on classic writers such as Machiavelli, Hobbes, Rousseau, Bentham and Marx.

WEBSITES

http://www.politicalcompass.org
Allows you to test where your political affiliations are.

http://typology.people-press.org/typology
Typology created by the American-based Pew Research Center for People and Press to assess what typology you are.

http://cpi.politics.ox.ac.uk
The Centre for Political Ideologies.

http://www.catholic.net
Catholic.net – formerly the Catholic Information Center.

http://www.islamic-world.net
Including texts of 300 Islamic books and news reports.

http://www.envirolink.org
Envirolink Network (for ecologists).

http://www.cddc.vt.edu/feminism/
Feminist theory website.

5

PROCESSES

THIS CHAPTER . . .

examines how people come to identify with particular kinds of
political groups. It analyses the variety of politically significant
groups and the nature of the divisions between them. It considers the
significance of these divisions for political stability and change and
how technological and external factors affect the nature of the balance
of power within and between societies. In considering the processes
that result in stability or change, we discuss some of the most potent
forces at work in the modern political world – those of class, religion,
ethnicity, race and national identity.

POLITICAL IDENTITY

One important clue to the ways in which people identify themselves
politically is to consider the names of political parties. Many of the
names refer to the 'ideologies' which we have already considered –
liberal, socialist, communist, conservative. What is striking, however,
is the number of names which refer specifically to sectional groups
within a state's population: national – Scottish National Party,
Inkatha ('Spear of the [Zulu] Nation'); ethnic/racial – Malaysian
Chinese Association; religious – Christian Democrat, Jan Sangh

(Hindu); or class/occupation – Labour, Peasant. Indeed, if we look behind the official name of political parties, we find that they frequently are mainly or exclusively supported by one such sectional group. For instance, the Republican Party of India was formerly called the Scheduled Castes Federation (i.e. the 'untouchables'), whilst the former grandly titled Nigerian National Democratic Party was in fact confined to a faction of the Yoruba peoples of western Nigeria. Conversely, some parties like the Congress Party of India and the Institutional Revolutionary Party of Mexico seek to unite virtually everyone in the state in the cause of nationalism.

Many studies of voting behaviour reinforce this picture of voters identifying with political parties (however abstractly described) largely as an expression of national, ethnic/racial, religious or class loyalties. Parties are seen as fighting for the interests of 'our' group, so that 'we' benefit from their success.

On the psychological level such behaviour is unsurprising. Human beings are clearly social animals loyal to the 'in'-group and suspicious of, or hostile to, 'out'-groups (see Sherif *et al.*, 1951 for a classic study of boys at a summer camp). The problem, as Tajfel and Turner (1979) point out, is that in building a positive sense of 'social identity' in-groups often resort to 'stereotyping' out-groups. That is, all members of the out-group are perceived as having a standard set of (inferior) qualities to one's own. But as students of politics we may wish to consider why the pattern of such loyalties varies from place to place. The functionalist concepts of 'political socialisation' and 'political culture' may help to describe and explain these differences, but the explanation they offer is only a partial one as we shall see.

POLITICAL SOCIALISATION AND POLITICAL CULTURE

The short answer as to why people identify themselves in different ways is to point to the political experiences that have moulded them – to the processes of 'political socialisation' (see Box 5.1). In short, they have learnt who they are. The term 'socialisation' does seem preferable to the perhaps more familiar term 'education' because it stresses the broader and more informal influences at work. In particular, home and friends have been demonstrated to be much more important influences than school or college education. The mass media are also an important source of political information and attitudes. It is also probable that influences in early adulthood, when habits of voting or other forms of political participation are established, can be crucially important: this would include influences from workmates or comrades-in-arms and key political events at this time. In short, people tend to absorb the political values and ideas of the key face-to-face social groups to which they belong (see Tables 5.1(a) and (b)).

BOX 5.1 DEFINITIONS OF POLITICAL SOCIALISATION

the personal and social origins of political outlooks.

(Dawson *et al.*, 1977: 1)

is the process of induction into political culture. Its end product is a set of attitudes, cognitions, value standards and feelings – toward the political system, its various roles, and role incumbents. It also includes knowledge of, values affecting, and feelings toward the inputs of demands and claims into the system, and its authoritative output.

(Almond, in Almond and Coleman, 1960: 26–58)

A number of studies have documented the considerable differences between countries and social groups as to their perceptions and level of knowledge of politics and their attitudes towards political power and institutions. Some of these differences in 'political culture' are summarised in Table 5.2 and clearly are important in understanding differences between political systems in different countries.

BOX 5.2 POLITICAL CULTURE

The mental and intellectual environment in which politics is shaped, interpreted and judged. The knowledge, beliefs, values and attitudes of individuals and societies towards government and politics.

(Pye and Verba, 1965)

Table 5.1(a) Typical socialisation research findings: attitudes to president

	Agreeing in school grade (%)					
	2	4	6	8	10	12
'President cares a lot' (1961)	75	56	46	43		
'President cares a lot' (1974)	79	65	32	28	22	16

Sources: Hershey and Hill (1975); Easton and Dennis (1969); Hess and Torney (1967)

Table 5.1(b) Typical socialisation research findings: most popularly used sources of information about foreign people

Nationality	USA	Bantu (sic)	Brazil	Turkey
6 year olds	TV movies (parents)	parents	parents (contact)	parents friends
10 year olds	TV movies books courses texts magazines	parents contact teachers	movies magazines contact	books texts courses magazines

Source: Lambert and Klineberg (1967)

Attitudes to democracy vary markedly in different countries. Diamond (in LeDuc *et al.*, 2002: 217–221) quotes a variety of studies showing endorsement of democratic principles varying from highs of 83 per cent in Costa Rica, 81 per cent in Nigeria and 75 per cent in the Czech Republic to much lower levels of 54 per cent in Zambia and 39 per cent in Russia and Brazil.

One explanation as to why people identify politically with distinct social groups, or adopt particular political values, is that they have been socialised into particular political cultures in which varying lines of social division and commitment are important. However, this does not explain why political cultures vary in this way. For this we have to look at the history and social structures of the specific countries concerned. It can be argued that the concepts of culture and socialisation have merely assisted us somewhat in the systematic description of the problem, rather than solved it.

Table 5.2   Typical research findings: political culture

	Agreeing (%)				
	USA	UK	Germany	Italy	Mexico
Participation/Parochialism: 'National govt. has great effect on daily life'	41	33	38	23	7
Trust/Distrust: 'Most people can be trusted'	55	49	19	7	30
Hierarchy – acceptance/ resentment: 'Expect equal consideration from bureaucracy'	48	59	53	35	14
Can affect an unjust law	75	62	38	28	38
Liberty – toleration/coercion: Against cross-party marriage	4	12+	58*		
Loyalty: Most proud of government/ political institutions	85	46	7	3	30

Source: Almond and Verba (1963)

+ = Conservative/Labour

* = Christian Democrat/Communist

LOCALISM, NATIONALISM, RELIGION AND ETHNICITY

One sort of division which seems to be almost universal in larger political systems is what Allardt and Littunen (1964) have termed vertical lines of division – those between localities, regions and, in some cases, national areas within states. It can be argued that, other things being equal, the nearer people live together, and hence the more communication and, probably, economic and social inter-dependence there is between them, the more they are likely to perceive themselves as having interests in common. Hence people in the village of Haworth may see themselves first as Haworth residents, then perhaps as people from the Bradford area or West Riding, almost certainly as Yorkshire folk, as English, as British, and possibly as Europeans too. Political (or sporting!) divisions may arise

between the interests of Yorkshire and Lancashire without eithe.
ceasing to feel loyalty to England. Divisions between England and
Scotland may not preclude common action in Europe by the British,
and so on. Similarly residents of Harlem may also feel themselves to
be citizens of New York City, and New York State, as well as of the
United States. Clearly the influence of geographical nearness will be
influenced by a host of other factors which may affect the strength of
local or regional loyalties. For example, how mobile is the population? If a resident of Haworth is commuting daily to Bradford and
was born in nearby Keighley, then the West Riding identity may be
more important than to someone born in Lancashire. How socially
and linguistically divided are the geographical communities? A
Gaelic-speaking Scot may feel a greater separation from England than
an English-speaking one. The nature of the economy may also be
important, e.g. a self-sufficient peasant agricultural community feeling much stronger local ties than a university-based one.

As the Scottish/English dimension also suggests, the influence of
historical conquests and of migration is a major factor in these sorts
of divisions. Scots have, of course, historically moved (many would
say been driven) both southwards into England and across the sea to
Northern Ireland and North America. Here they, and their descen-
dants, may retain, to a larger or smaller extent, a Scottish identity
that may cut across their 'residential' identity. In New York almost
everyone has such a secondary identity, being for example Puerto
Rican, Jewish, Irish or African-American. In Bradford a substantial
minority of inhabitants are of Bangladeshi and Pakistani origin. Such
secondary or 'ethnic' identities are often related to former nationality
(e.g. Irish-American), current religion (Jewish) or colour (African-
American). Ethnicity may also relate to tribal affiliation, way of life
and descent (e.g. Gypsies) or to a hereditary social status (caste in the
traditional Indian social system). The term covers a variety of
'horizontal' lines of division dividing geographical communities into
recognised subgroups with, to some extent, different ways of life and
prestige.

These 'ethnic' identities may be of greater or lesser social and
political importance depending upon a similar variety of factors to
those influencing localism. Major factors include their relative size
and economic and political power. Thus a small group occupying an
unimportant but useful economic role (e.g. Chinese or Indians

running takeaways and restaurants) in an otherwise undivided community may be almost invisible. A similar sized group that owns a large part of the land upon which the majority community lives and farms (e.g. 'European' farmers formerly in Zimbabwe) may be extremely visible and vulnerable to political pressure. Another factor may be the degree of linguistic, cultural and religious differences between groups – the greater the differences the less easy it may be for the groups to communicate, integrate and negotiate.

Religious and linguistic differences serve to heighten awareness of local loyalties and, indeed, lead to different perceptions of national identity. Thus in Northern Ireland, Quebec and Kosovo, some inhabitants (Protestants, English-speakers and Serb-speaking Orthodox) may see themselves as inhabitants of a locality within a currently constituted state (the United Kingdom, Canada or Serbia). Others (Catholics, French-speakers, Albanian-speaking Muslims) may feel loyalty to a different national identity – either to another state (Ireland, Albania) or to the region as an independent entity (Quebec, Kosovo).

It can be argued that many conflicts, which appear to be religious in nature, have little to do with theological considerations. Thus divisions between Catholics and Protestants in Northern Ireland appear to relate to a conflict between two social groups for economic and political opportunities. The origins of struggle can be seen historically in the British Crown allocating land to Protestant settlers from the mainland. Current differences are much more about nationality than theological concepts such as transubstantiation or papal authority.

Similarly divisions between Palestinians and Israelis may be seen as an Islamic/Jewish conflict, but more realistically may be seen as a conflict between rival national groups for land and resources. In fact many of the founders of Zionism were secular rather than Orthodox Jews, and many ultra-Orthodox Jews refuse to serve in the Israeli army. Similarly Palestinian Christians (a small minority) have generally aligned themselves with their Muslim Arab compatriots.

Another striking example of the extent to which religion may be a dependent variable in social and political conflict, is the trend in modern India for political leaders of lower caste groups to urge their followers to convert to Buddhism. This is not urged for theological reasons, but in order to escape their low prestige and influence in traditional Hindu society. However it is clear that religious, linguistic, tribal and other ethnic factors loom large in the construction of many people's political identity – but to different degrees at different times and places depending on the political environment.

RACIAL AND ETHNIC CONFLICT

An important psychological and political factor seems to be the 'racial' identity of the ethnic groups concerned. By 'racial' is meant the existence of real or assumed visible physical differences – particularly in skin colour – between the groups. Such differences are socially rather than biologically defined – existing human communities being virtually all extremely mixed genetically and not divided according to the biological definition of 'race'. For instance, most US 'blacks' would be regarded as whites in tropical Africa: most South African 'whites' probably have some 'black' ancestry. In essence the major socially defined 'racial' division is that between 'whites' and 'non-whites'.

The importance of the distinction between black and white 'races' seems to link quite clearly with our inheritance from the period of European imperialism in which a racial justification was advanced for both slavery and colonialism. For instance, British imperial prosperity was for long founded on the triangular trade, in which arms, metal tools and trinkets were exported to West Africa, these were exchanged for slaves who were transported to the Caribbean or American colonies to be used in growing tobacco, spices and cotton. These valuable commodities, in turn, could then be transported back to Liverpool, Bristol or London. Each leg of the journey was enormously profitable, but the subjection of black slaves and the conquest of the Caribbean and North America had to be justified in terms of the superiority of white Christian civilisation over the alleged barbarity of the 'natives'. As the European powers, and later the United States, continued their competitive acquisition of much of the globe, their success in subduing less well-armed and aggressive societies was, in turn, held to be an indication of this alleged superiority.

This historical legacy of racism has been accentuated by a web of cultural and literary symbolism – with black seen as the colour of evil, white the symbol of innocence – and racist pseudo-scientific findings about the inherited lower intelligence of 'non-Aryan' races.

The importance of racism is dramatically illustrated if we consider the history of ethnic relations in US cities. Waves of ethnic groups – Irish, Russian, Italian, Jewish, Puerto Rican – have arrived successively in many American cities to go through similar processes of accommodation, integration and assimilation. At first such groups have been accommodated in the worst city centre slums, in multiple occupation 'tenements'. They have taken the worst-paid lowest status jobs and usually formed isolated groups seeking help from already established members of their own community. Very often first- and even second-generation immigrants sought to maintain their own cultural, religious and linguistic traditions and planned to return to their country of origin on retirement.

However, such groups have consistently gradually assimilated to the American 'way of life'. First they have become politically organised – even if through corrupt 'bosses' (local party leaders) and trade unions. Their votes and bargaining power were sought first by others then by members of their own community. Next, second- and third-generation immigrants have sought acceptance in the wider American society by anglicising names, obtaining college education and moving out into the affluent suburbs. Integration has gradually occurred partly on the basis of the new immigrant group accepting American values and citizenship, but also on the basis of America accepting a rich kaleidoscope of cultural traditions and religious beliefs within society. The power of many 'immigrant' groups has been comfortably accepted in many respects – consider the giant St Patrick's Day parade every year in New York and the political power of the Kennedy family. Whilst Catholicism was, at first, regarded as a badge of inferior immigrant status, and, as late as the 1920s Al Smith's candidacy for the presidency may have been defeated by a Protestant backlash, it is now just one more fully acceptable denomination of Christianity (Jones, 1960).

In contrast to this, the African-American group was one of the first to arrive in what is now the United States. But this group has been the last to achieve anything near equal status with the WASP (White Anglo-Saxon Protestant) majority. For many years blacks were mainly detained as slaves on southern rural farms and plantations. But even after emancipation in 1865 they remained the victims of massive social and political discrimination. They long ago lost their specific African languages and cultures, and they have contributed

greatly to the development of a distinctive American culture an
interbred extensively with the white population. However, it was
only with the Civil Rights Act of 1965 that they can be said to have
achieved full and effective citizenship.

DOMINANCE, ASSIMILATION AND SOCIAL PLURALISM

As far as both ethnic and racial relations are concerned, three main
alternative social and political patterns seem possible. First, a
relationship of (usually racial) social and political dominance – the
South African term of 'apartheid' being appropriate. An extreme
expression of this pattern is where one group is enslaved by the other.
In more recent years, however, such a frank state of affairs has
seemed unacceptably bad public relations in a world in which the
rhetoric, at least, of democracy predominates. Therefore the language
of equality and nationalism usually prevails. In America the official
doctrine of 'separate but equal' prevailed between the landmark
Supreme Court rulings of *Plessey* v *Ferguson* (1896) and *Brown* v the
Board of Education of Topeka (1954), until it was conceded that such
a doctrine was a contradiction in terms. In Africa, white dominance in
South Africa was justified by the creation of 'homelands' in which
blacks were accorded the trappings of sovereignty – millions of blacks
being declared aliens in the land of their birth. In contemporary
Europe there is a similar tendency to declare immigrant 'guest-
workers' of unsuitable ethnic origin to be non-citizens without
rights. Similarly, in Malaysia, 'Malays' (those who speak Malay,
practise Islam and conform to Malay customs) have a special status in
citizenship and land law as opposed to others – in effect those of
Chinese and Indian origin (Suffian *et al.*, 1978: 94).

The most extreme expression of the attitudes towards racial and
ethnic difference implicit in a pattern of dominance is where the state
machinery is employed in an attempt to eliminate an ethnic, national
or racial group from a particular geographical area (or indeed totally).
This is known in international law as genocide. The best known
example is the Holocaust in which the Nazi state attempted to
eliminate the European Jewry. Unfortunately more recent examples
of 'ethnic cleansing' can be cited in the former Yugoslavia and in
Rwanda. This is usually accompanied by attempts to stereotype the

victim out-group as sub-human and inferior as discussed earlier in this chapter.

An alternative approach to the management of ethnic and racial differences is an assimilationist one in which members of 'minority' communities are granted equality and rights to the extent to which they adopt the way of life of the 'dominant' group. Thus French colonial policy was based on the doctrine of the equality of all civilised men – civilisation being equated largely with French education, language and loyalty. In effect US and British citizenship policy has had some elements of this, with requirements for fluency in English, knowledge of the constitution and the swearing of allegiance.

Another model for achieving the integration of different ethnic or racial groups in one society is the pluralist one – which, to a large extent, has predominated in the USA. In European terms one might call it the Swiss model – in which separate groups respect each other's linguistic, religious and cultural inheritances. Whilst a degree of convergence may take place in terms of values and political habits, there is no requirement that one group's values be seen as the orthodoxy for the society as a whole. Clearly tolerance and negotiated compromises must mark such a society if it is to endure.

From the point of view of political change and stability, the domination of one ethnic or racial group over others may appear to be a quite stable situation. In some cases such stability may be purchased at the price of a certain element of stagnation since intellectual and social change may be seen as threatening the ideology of the dominant group. It may well be accompanied by violent repression of dissent either by the state (as in apartheid South Africa and under colonial regimes) or by the dominant group (as with the Ku Klux Klan in the southern USA). However, repression of a majority population is a dangerous strategy and carries with it the possibility of revolutionary upheaval.

Where policies of assimilation or pluralism are adopted then the possibilities for improvement for the less-favoured groups reduce the likelihood of full-scale violent confrontation between groups. Piecemeal adjustment of conflicts between groups is possible and long-term changes resulting from immigration or industrialisation may be more easily accommodated. Paradoxically, there may be more day-to-day overt expressions of ethnic and racial conflict than in situations of dominance where frequently such conflicts are officially denied any existence.

A distinction should be drawn between social and political pluralism. What we have been describing is a model of social pluralism in an ethnically or racially mixed society. Politically this may be accompanied by explicit provision for the participation of different social groups in government. For example, in Switzerland the linguistically and religiously distinct Cantons are traditionally guaranteed participation in the Federal Cabinet (a similar arrangement has been attempted less happily in the Lebanon). In the Netherlands separate religious and political traditions are accommodated by having separate radio stations and schools. In the United States ethnic representation is accomplished through a flexible party and interest group system and a decentralised constitution.

Political pluralism, however, is a broader concept, which fits well with social pluralism in the sense we have used it, but is broader in that it suggests any group is free to pursue its interests in the political system and stands a realistic chance of exercising influence. A more sophisticated treatment of this concept requires us to consider additional kinds of social and political division.

ELITES, CLASSES AND POLITICAL PLURALISM

We have already discussed the concept of 'vertical' lines of division within society – meaning that geographical communities may come into conflict. We have also discussed 'horizontal' ethnic divisions within geographical communities. It is clear that other 'horizontal' divisions frequently divide societies so that within virtually every geographical community there are to be found rich and poor, the powerful and the powerless, those with prestige and those without. As Pareto (1976) puts it, for every desirable unevenly distributed social quality, there exists an 'elite' that possesses that quality in abundance – whether it be economic, political, social, sporting, or even 'sex appeal' – and, consequently, a usually more numerous, 'mass' that suffers from a relative lack of that quality.

As C. Wright Mills (1956) argues, the existence of elites is hardly in dispute as far as modern industrial societies are concerned. More controversial is the political significance of this observation and the causes of these differences. Simplifying somewhat, we can say that

...storically three main models have been used in discussing this ...ssue: elite theorists who see the main political division as being between the holders of political power and the rest; Marxists who see political and social divisions as reflecting economic divisions, with classes as the fundamental political entities; and pluralists who regard the divisions between elites and masses as only one of a series of non-coincidental lines of division within society.

This argument can be formulated in an alternative fashion: is there a single ruling group in modern industrial societies? If so, what are its characteristics – and is this 'class rule'?

This being a big question – perhaps the big question – in politics, it is worth considering carefully. Rather than seeking a definitive conclusion now, it may be more useful to offer some guidelines on evaluating the sort of evidence which has been put forward.

It is striking that writers supporting different models tend to discuss different types of evidence. Thus elite theorists such as Pareto (1976), Mosca (1939), Michels (1915) and Mills (1956) focus on *who rules*. They often lay great stress on alleged universal traits of human nature (e.g. the desire for power, status and wealth) and their consequences for politics. They then demonstrate the existence of hierarchies of power, wealth and status in many societies. The strategies which individuals adopt to achieve such positions are often considered with realism (even cynicism). It is shown that ruling elites tend to share a privileged lifestyle. (Michel's famous observation that two deputies, one of whom is a socialist and one of whom is not, have more in common than two socialists one of whom is a deputy and the other is not is fairly typical.) Mills is interesting in seeking to demonstrate in some detail the social, economic and educational interrelationships and common lifestyle of a number of 'separate' US elites – the businessmen, the military and top federal government appointees. (He is also unusual amongst 'elite' theorists in disliking the elite influence he portrays.) Similarly in Britain a whole literature exists analysing such interrelationships within a British 'Establishment' whose members tend to have attended the same schools, universities and clubs (e.g. Thomas, 1959; Sampson, 2004).

Marxist evidence has often concentrated on the question of *in whose interests decisions are taken*. Thus, on the basis that the proof of the pudding is in the eating, the distribution of income and of wealth in capitalist societies is shown to be still grossly uneven, despite decades of 'progressive' taxation and the welfare stat Similarly the educational and health opportunities of the working classes can be demonstrated to be much less than those of the upper classes. The argument is that the apparent opportunities for political participation by workers in a democracy are negated by continued bourgeois control of social structures such as the educational system, the mass media and the state apparatus as well as of the economy.

Pluralist writers have tended to concentrate on *how political decisions are made*. Analysts such as Dahl (1961) and most mainstream writers on British and American politics have stressed that any group of citizens is free to influence politicians in competitive party systems, and that the latter must listen to groups outside the elite if they are to remain in office. Numerous case studies have found that the same narrow group of professional politicians has not always taken decisions, but that, for instance, doctors' professional associations strongly influence decisions on health policy, neighbourhood action groups can influence planning decisions and so on.

To some extent, therefore, it can be argued that the findings of these different groups of writers are actually complementary, rather than conflicting as they often claim or imply. Consider all the propositions in Box 5.3. Are they in fact inconsistent? More sophisticated versions of each model do often concede many of these points. For instance, a neo-pluralist school of thought can be identified (Moloney, 2006). This approach refines the traditional pluralist position by suggesting that (a) not all groupings are equal, with businesses having disproportionate power and influence, and (b) that new sources of power such as pressure groups representing social movements have increased in influence since the 1960s. This is sometimes described as 'accelerated pluralism'.

BOX 5.3   PROPOSITIONS FROM PLURALIST, ELITE AND
MARXIST MODELS OF POWER

1 People in different elite groups do have a great deal of interaction and a substantially common lifestyle.
2 Politicians are often unscrupulous in search of their personal objectives.

3 Political change in democracy does not necessarily result in social and economic equality.
4 Power is conditioned by cultural and ideological assumptions that reflect those of existing dominant minorities.
5 Competitive party systems enable, but do not ensure, that groups of like-minded people can influence the policy process.

Yet important differences of perspective do remain (Table 5.3). In the end readers will need to make a personal judgement about the relative importance of the issues discussed and the strength of the empirical findings. Are the similarities between the members of the 'power elite' so great that the ideological and policy differences they profess pale into insignificance? Does the welfare state represent a triumph for popular mass influence, or is it merely a device to cloak the continuing injustice of the capitalist economic system? Does the machinery of pressure groups and elections have a real effect on the policy process? These are real and fascinating issues on which both one's own value judgements and a greater knowledge of how actual political systems work must have an influence.

POLITICAL CHANGE

An examination of past history suggests only the inevitability of political change and the likelihood that the twenty-first century will not be much like the twentieth. This in itself is worth stressing since it is all too easy to assume that the future will represent a continuation of the present. Many readers of this book will have lived all their lives in a relatively stable, prosperous and peaceful liberal

Table 5.3 Summary: critics of pluralism

	Elitist	*Marxist*
Descriptive	Elite rule not pressure groups	Capitalist manipulation subverts democracy
Prescriptive	Mob rule undesirable	Working-class revolution OK

democratic nation state. Yet it is only necessary to imagine that instead, you had been born in the former Soviet Union to realise how immensely and rapidly the political framework of your life can be transformed in a lifetime.

Political change is probably thought of most readily in terms of violent and rapid transitions such as the English Civil War and the French, American and Russian revolutions. But it is worth bearing in mind that in the English and Russian instances, at least, such violent and rapid changes were largely reversed within two generations without extensive violence. Conversely a series of piecemeal, evolutionary changes may result in a 'new' political system based on fundamentally different principles from the old.

Thus Britain in the eighteenth century was fundamentally still an oligarchic or aristocratic, if constitutional, country. It was controlled by a coalition of aristocrats and country gentlemen with limited participation by a few city businessmen. By the middle of the twentieth century, a series of limited reforms of the franchise and in the powers of the two Houses of Parliament (and a whole host of economic and social changes) meant that Britain could claim to be a democratic country.

Much the same could be said for the United States of America – whose Founding Fathers were careful to defend their new constitution against the charge of democracy (Hamilton *et al.*, 1961). Yet now the same constitution (with only a limited number of formal amendments) is seen by many as the very model of a democratic constitution. A series of piecemeal changes helped the USA to transform its political system into a democratic one. These included the change from indirect election of the president by an electoral college to, effectively, direct election through national political parties. The introduction of the direct popular election of senators was accompanied by the progressive extension of the vote to all white male, to all white women and finally to all black citizens. This was done largely through state legislation, or even changes in political practice outside of the law. (Amendments 15, 17 and 19 broadened the franchise, but 15 was ineffective and 17 and 19 mainly codified previous practice at state level (Morison and Commager, 1962).)

Returning to the three models of social and political power we introduced earlier, we can relate these to ideas about political change.

Most elite theorists have been unimpressed with the likelihood of real political change, since they see elites as holding all the best cards in the political game. Political stability is achieved by elites through ideological dominance (Mosca's political 'myths') and the superior organisation of a smaller group with greater economic resources and social prestige. However both Pareto and Mosca see the possibility of cycles of apparent change which may result in a change in the personnel of government but not in the fundamental fact of elite dominance. Thus Pareto describes cycles in which 'Lions' who rule largely by force are succeeded by 'Foxes' who attempt to rule by guile and deception. Mosca describes the possibility of popular leaders taking power in the name of democracy – but sees this process as a deception, since the new leadership will inevitably rule in its own interest.

Classic Marxist writers (including Marx, Engels and Lenin) saw key political changes as occurring through violent revolutions in which discrepancies between the political system and the underlying social and economic class system were resolved (see chapters 1 and 4). These discrepancies were the result of longer-term gradual changes in the relations of production brought about by changes in technology and trading patterns.

Pluralist writers have tended to emphasise the possibility of gradual change in response to a host of factors allowing the continuance of stable government through negotiated compromises between groups. Thus Allardt and Littunen (1964) argue that the most stable political situation is where many social divisions overlap and different groups go into political coalitions for different purposes. All groups feel that they can influence the situation and thus remain committed to the system, and are forced to stress those aspects on which they agree in order to build co-operation with others. The premium on bargaining in such situations means that as new developments arise, piecemeal adjustments to them can be made, and stability maintained.

Such a situation of healthy co-operation, competition and bargaining must be distinguished from the sort of situation characteristic of, say, the French Fourth Republic in which a kaleidoscopic variety of forces fail to agree on an effective government. In this case governments succeeded each other on average every eight months (Williams, 1964).

COUPS D'ÉTAT AND REVOLUTIONS

It should also be made clear that not every use of violence (or the threat of it) in order to change the political system can sensibly be called a revolution. The term revolution (associated with the idea of a wheel turning and hence things being turned 'upside down') may be helpfully reserved for occasions when major changes in the nature of politics and society take place. An examination of the historical record suggests that such events are relatively rare, whilst the use of force (or its threat) to change the government is much more commonplace.

In the absence of an established tradition of election or inheritance of top offices within the state, violence has been the usual way to power. In the ancient world, the Emperor of Rome was frequently the most successful general of his day, his bodyguard – the Praetorian Guard – effectively controlling succession. In much of Africa, Asia and Latin America, in the twentieth century, a similar state of affairs has been found, with the army constituting perhaps the most effective route to political power (Huntington, 1957; Finer, 1976) as we discuss in Chapter 6.

In contrast, full revolutions can be seen as rarer and more fundamental changes in the political system in which new social groups achieve power and the state carries out new tasks in a different way, perhaps with a different claim to legitimacy. Writers such as Crane Brinton (1965) and Lyford Edwards (1927) have perceptively analysed major revolutionary episodes such as the English Civil War and the French and Russian revolutions, and suggested that they tend to go through a series of distinctive phases.

Paradoxically the old regime often collapses in a relatively bloodless triumph of popular forces following a loss of legitimacy and a manifest failure to cope with the economic, political or military demands put upon it. This is followed, after a honeymoon period, by confusion and conflict amongst the revolutionary forces. In face of real or imaginary counter-revolutionary reaction, extremist forces then often take control, launching a reign of terror, not only against declared counter-revolutionaries, but also against moderate reformers. Such a situation may then be resolved by power being taken by a tyrant (Cromwell, Napoleon, Lenin/Stalin) who leads a post-revolutionary regime which may draw upon the pre-revolutionary tradition, as well as claiming descent from the revolution itself.

One might add that, in the longer term still, further compromises with the pre-revolutionary tradition are likely. This is not to deny, however, that revolutions can transform societies – they are often accompanied by a major transformation in the role and power of the state, massive changes in property ownership and in the type of legitimacy claimed by the state.

TERROR AND TERRORISM

The UK Terrorism Act (2000) defines terrorism as 'the use or threat for the purpose of advancing a political, religious or ideological cause, of action which involves serious violence against any person or property'. This is a definition that has been criticised as so wide as to include open militant actions by a variety of legitimate protest groups. It is also interesting in that, as it stands, it is not limited to conspiratorial groups seeking to overthrow a government. Arguably it could be applied to governments themselves. (See Whittaker, 2001: Ch. 1 for a discussion of rival definitions.)

In practice it is clear that the most common users of widespread politically motivated violence are governments themselves. Clausewitz [1780–1831] famously described war as 'nothing but the continuation of politics with the admixture of other means' (Clausewitz, 1967). Clearly wars involve the use of violence on an extended scale – with civilian casualties in Afghanistan and Iraq clearly exceeding the number of victims of Al Qaeda's destruction of the Twin Towers on September 11, 2001.

Whilst some wars can be defended as legitimate, widespread use of violence without due process of law against a state's own citizens is characteristic of totalitarian states such as the Soviet Union and Nazi Germany (see Chapter 6) and widely found in military and authoritarian regimes. In Argentina, for instance, a 'dirty war' was waged by the former military regime against its suspected opponents who frequently disappeared as a result of officially protected hit squads. The 'terror' may be seen as primarily a weapon of state, rather than anti-state violence.

Contemporary usage, however, tends to identify terrorism with ideologically motivated violence against states by conspiratorial opposition groups particularly where the targeting of violence appears to be indiscriminate. The difference between 'freedom fighters' and 'terrorists' is clearly somewhat subjective. However, one could argu that where no peaceful routes to political change are permitted, the cause is legitimate, and the targets are strategic ones, a guerrilla struggle is justifiable. Thus French Resistance struggles against the Nazis or ANC violence against apartheid South Africa may be distinguished from 'terrorism'. Paradoxically some contemporary US writers adopt definitions of terrorism that would condemn their own revolutionary ancestors to the category.

Terrorist groups have very different and sometimes conflicting objectives. Thus ETA (Basque Fatherland and Liberty) and the 'Real' Irish Republican Army are probably primarily nationalist organisations. Some like the former German Red Army Faction (or Baader-Meinhoff gang) and Senderoso Luminoso (Shining Path) in Peru are more concerned with Marxist revolution. Others like PAGAD (People Against Gangsterism And Drugs) in South Africa may apparently be the product of very particular local problems. The best known modern organisations like Al Qaeda and Hamas (in Palestine) are Islamic factions which may differ on questions of strategy, theology and their relations to nationalism.

The requirements of security in a violent and conspiratorial organisation mean that terrorists often adopt a similar type of organisation in which small 'cells' of activists operate in isolation from each other. Frequent sources of recruitment are educational institutions and the families of those already committed to the cause. In such cases it may be difficult for outsiders to penetrate the core activities of the group.

A key factor for success and survival is the relationship between terrorists and the 'host' population within which they operate. The terrorist group will flourish when the mass of the population support them but can survive on passive indifference or the fear of retribution if intelligence is passed to the government. A propaganda struggle for the hearts and minds of the relatively non-political mass of the population may therefore be crucial.

Schultz (1980) suggests there are three main kinds of contemporary terrorism: revolutionary, sub-revolutionary and establishment. Revolutionary terrorism involves the attempted overthrow of the state; sub-revolutionary terrorism uses political violence to change existing systems. Examples include Animal Liberation Front attacks on laboratories experimenting on animals and bomb attacks on abortion clinics in the United States. Establishment terrorism includes events like the Argentinian 'dirty war' referred to above. States may sponsor terrorism in their own territory or outside it. The United States has accused Iran, Iraq, the Lebanon, Sudan and Syria of the latter. Conversely radical critics see the US as a major sponsor of establishment terrorism in Latin America and the power whose support of the anti-Russian Mujahedin in Afghanistan helped to bring about the rise of Al Qaeda.

The rise of the Taliban in Afghanistan and of Al Qaeda and linked terrorist groups elsewhere is a fascinating case of the multiple causes of such movements. As well as the role of the USA in subsidising the armed struggle against Russian invasion in Afghanistan, the role of Saudi Wahhabists in subsidising *madrasas* or Islamic schools in Pakistan and other parts of the South may also have been highly significant. Saudi oil revenues have served to create Islamic schools in many areas where they are often the only schools available to the poor and which have served as recruiting grounds for politically and theologically extreme movements (Lewis, 2003: 99).

As we have noted, the concept of terrorism has been a political factor for many years. However, with George W. Bush's announcement of a 'war on terrorism' following the 9/11 bombing of the World Trade Center in 2001, the meaning of terrorism for many people has changed. A number of high-profile terrorist campaigns such as the Bali bombs in 2002, the Madrid train bombing in 2004 and the 7/7 London bombings in 2006 have resulted in policy makers in many countries placing a higher priority on countering what might be termed fundamentalist revolutionaries, and those who might support them. In response to this, many terrorist groups have made use of modern communication channels such as television, video and the Internet to promote their causes. Both developments represent a significant change in the global understanding of terrorism.

CLASS CONFLICT IN THE TWENTY-FIRST CENTURY

The collapse of the Soviet Union and the disintegration of the East European 'Communist Bloc' has generated the impression that Marxism is a failed ideology. Certainly many Western former communist parties have now dropped their titles and even their claims to Marxist adherence. Yet it can be argued that Marxism remains one of the more impressive political theories, particularly in relation to the explanations of political change it advances. Many 'democratic' political theories, in contrast, are oriented towards a static and idealistic analysis.

Features of Marx's theory that remain credible are its dynamic nature, and the systematic explanation it advances for political change. As we have considered, the main political actors are seen to be economic classes whose interests are in conflict. Political conflict becomes more acute as the result of both an increasing consciousness by classes of their interests and changes in their relative position as a result of what would now be termed 'economic development'. Major revolutions such as the French Revolution and the English Civil War can be seen in terms of an old dominant class (the rural feudal aristocracy) being replaced by a new dominant class (the urban capitalist bourgeoisie). Marx's prediction was that the capitalist system, in turn, would fail because of its in-built contradictions, leading to the triumph of a new dominant class, the more numerous and increasingly well-organised and militant proletariat. The logic of Marx's theory is that socialist revolution should take place in the advanced capitalist states not in a semi-feudal state on the periphery of Western capitalism (Russia).

The concept of the need for a 'fit' between the economic and political systems and the dynamic role of class structures seems well founded. A somewhat paradoxical example of this might well be the fall of East European communism. Here, one might argue, the command economy, having served its purpose in aiding the forced industrialisation of underdeveloped and war-damaged economies in conjunction with a centralised and dictatorial political system, was no longer adequate to manage a more complex affluent and consumer-oriented economy. Demands for greater political freedom thus fitted well with demands for economic reform.

More doubtful is the idea of the inevitability of a bipolar class system in which one class inevitably becomes dominant. This idea of a historical dialectic, we have seen earlier, was inherited by Marx from Hegel and, whilst politically convenient, seems far from justified by events. As we have seen, academic analysis, as well as observation, suggests that much political conflict (especially voting behaviour) particularly in Europe – but also to some extent in North America – can be explained in terms of class divisions. However, the trend would appear to be, in voting behaviour at least, away from the sort of class-based voting found in Britain in the 1950s and 1960s towards a more North American pattern in which issues, personalities and tactical voting predominate; hence an increased tendency to vote for third parties in the UK, considerable fluctuation in the socialist vote in France, the desertion of both the neo-communist and Christian democratic voters in Italy. Instead of a clear commitment to parties based upon class identification, the 'floating voter' has come to rule. However, it is worth noting that one school of thought suggests that the dominance of the 'floating voter' may be temporary until a new cleavage in voting behaviour replaces class.

Empirical studies of voting behaviour also indicate that few voters think in 'proletariat v bosses' terms. Right-wing parties (Republicans, Christian Democrats, Conservatives) have successfully appealed to a broader concept of a middle-class identity. The middle classes have been defined to include not only the self-employed and business professionals, but a whole variety of 'white-collar' occupations especially those paying higher 'salaries' (rather than 'wages') and open to growing numbers of people with higher education. Increasing levels of affluence (at least amongst those employed) and, especially, of homeownership, amongst traditional working-class voters also seem to have played a part in weakening traditional class allegiances.

Marxists may lament these trends as an example of 'false class consciousness' and also the decline in both the numbers of trade unionists and their links with socialist parties. But it seems an unjustifiable act of faith to assume that these trends are only 'blips' distorting an otherwise inevitable process.

POST-INDUSTRIAL POLITICS: THE INFORMATION POLITY?

Dahrendorf (1959) and others have argued that the trends in the class system observed above mean that Marx's analysis has been outmoded. He argues that Marx wrote in an era of lone capitalist entrepreneurs and unskilled mass production workers. This simple dichotomy is no longer adequate to a production system in which the functions of capital have become divided – for instance between shareholders and professional managers – and labour is divided between skilled professionals and unskilled labourers, between white-collar office workers and production-line operatives, and so on. Dahrendorf goes on to suggest that 'class' divisions be reinterpreted to include any politically relevant dimension; black/white, unemployed/employed, football supporters/non-supporters, etc. Further, he argues the overlapping of all these various splits has contributed to the 'floating vote' phenomena referred to above and the stability of pluralist political systems.

There is clearly some strength in these criticisms – although it can be argued that a real divergence of interests remains between 'capitalist' and labour groups, and that Dahrendorf's reinterpretation of class goes so far as to rob the term of any clear meaning.

Other writers, such as Bell (1973), have taken a rather different (perhaps 'technological determinist') line of argument: that Marx's focus on the mass production factory mode of production is fundamentally inappropriate to the emerging 'information economy'. Economic development is seen as having gone through a series of stages dominated by different occupations and technologies: hunter-gatherer with stone and wood axes, bows, coracles, etc.; agrarian with simple iron craft tools; manufacturing based on the steam engine and factory production. The main division in the economy and society is now seen as focusing on the dominant technology of the late twentieth and twenty-first centuries: information technology. The emerging dominant class are thus 'knowledge workers' who control this technology.

It is indeed difficult to underestimate the economic and social importance of scientific knowledge and its manipulation through information technology at the beginning of the twenty-first century. In the seventeenth and eighteenth centuries inventors were often practical men influenced by the experimental and innovative temper of the age, but not necessarily using the most advanced scientific theories. More recent advances such as radio, atomic energy and electronic computing were, however, all theoretically developed before increasingly large teams of scientists and technologists realised them in practical terms. Increasingly, scientific and professional expertise is being brought to bear on business and social problems. So that the ability to co-ordinate teams of highly qualified and well-informed experts becomes crucial to success – whether in developing the next generation of weapons (say anti-missile systems) or the next generation of consumer goods (e.g. digital television).

In addition to producing, recruiting and co-ordinating human expertise, information technology – the collection, storage, retrieval, analysis, presentation and communication of information using the microchip – is increasingly central to such operations. Virtually every kind of scientist and professional worker now has computing facilities on their desk. Information technology through the use of automated machinery and electronic networks can also be seen as rapidly replacing the need for the concentration of large numbers of factory production workers in urban centres (thus undermining working-class strength).

Already in the most technologically advanced economies (e.g. the USA) white-collar occupations (roughly equal to 'knowledge workers') outnumber traditional 'blue-collar' workers, whilst the information sector of Western economies appears to be the major growth sector. Some economists have gone so far as to suggest that information is a fourth major factor of production alongside the traditional trio of land, labour and capital.

Information technology can be seen to be at the core of social and economic developments in the twenty-first century because it is already transforming business, society and government. It is a pervasive technology because computers are general-purpose machines that can be used to carry out any operation that can be reduced to a series of logical steps (an 'algorithm'). These include navigating an airliner, building a car, diagnosing diseases and reading human handwriting. Computers are already doing all of these tasks. Information technology can also be predicted fairly confidently to be likely to be increasingly applied in this century given its historical tendency to reduce in price and increase in memory power and speed at ever-faster rates.

But does this mean that a post-industrial society and an information economy are likely to bring forth an 'information polity' – a society in which power rests with the group who control knowledge and its technology? This seems a much more debatable proposition than the idea that scientific ideas and information technology will be central to the development of society. If 'those who control' is interpreted to mean scientists, professionals and technologists and that these are to become the nucleus of a new dominant class, this seems a doubtful proposition for which there is, as yet, little evidence. There is no sign of such groups developing what Marx would term 'class consciousness', or, as we have earlier described it, a sense of

political identity separate from that of the middle classes as a whole
Information in the broad sense may well be a crucial source of power
in the twenty-first century, but its control is as yet predominantly
vested in the executives of corporate bodies like business corporations, government departments and universities. A 'new' source
of power, surely, only creates opportunities for power brokers to
bargain and negotiate over; it does not determine who rules.

The concept of information polity has interesting consequences for
our understanding of power. One school of thought, the normal-
isation hypothesis, associated with Margolis and Resnick (see for
example Margolis et al., 2003), suggests that the existence of the
Internet has maintained the power of existing elites. Whereas the
'level playing field' hypothesis (Rheingold, 1993) suggests that new
technologies such as the Internet provide opportunities for previously less powerful groups and organisations to build up a power base
online. The reality is that in different countries with different
political systems, cultures and use of technology either the normal-
isation or level playing field viewpoint may be more accurate.

In a different sense, however, the 'information polity' may be said
to have arrived. Taylor and Williams (1990) define it as 'a system of
governance within which the development of innovative information
systems is producing, and will continue to produce, new rationales for
the restructuring and changing focus of government'. They add that
governments have always been 'data heavy'; now they are becoming 'information rich' – able to effectively convert their data into
information for decision making.

Governments are increasingly using the new information and
communication technologies to deliver 24-hour, 365-days-a-year
online services to citizens. It has also been argued that these new
technologies are increasingly fundamentally modifying old styles of
public administration based on bureaucracy (see Chapter 8: Box 8.2)
to a new customer-focused networking one (Table 5.4).

Similar considerations to those just applied to information technology may be applied to the likely future influence of technological
developments more generally. Too great an air of inevitability may
easily be invested in predictions about both the likely development of
technology and its impact upon our environment. Research on the
development and use of energy resources, for instance, may focus
upon the employment of nuclear fission and existing fossil fuels to

Table 5.4   From public administration to information polity

1	Uniformity of provision	Targeted provision
	– the administrative principle	*– the business principle*
2	Hierarchical structure	Loose–tight structures
	– the control principle	*– the network management principle*
3	Division of work	Integration of work
	– the functional principle	*– the co-ordinative/collaborative principle*
4	Paternalistic relationships	Responsive relationships to customers and citizens
	– the professional principle	*– the 'whole person' principle*

Source: Taylor and Williams (1991)

support existing patterns of individual and government consumption – essentially a concentration of individual consumption and strategic power in the North Atlantic area. Or new technologies such as solar, wind and wave power may be developed of greater relevance to the problems of the South and to the survival of non-human species on our planet.

Clearly two major factors, which will affect the environmental future, are the balance of power between the 'North' and the 'South' and the role of multinational enterprises. The latter we considered in Chapter 2, the former deserves some more specific attention.

'NORTH' VERSUS 'SOUTH'?

Just as the confrontation between communist 'East' and capitalist 'West' dominated international relations in the second half of the twentieth century, so it seems likely that divisions between 'North' and 'South' will dominate the scene at the beginning of the twenty-first (Brandt, 1980, *passim*).

By 'South' is meant what used to be called the 'Third World', 'developing' or 'underdeveloped' countries. 'Third World' was a useful term since it suggested the geo-strategic truth that such countries were a loose block of states that could play off the capitalist 'West' against the communist 'East' at the United Nations and elsewhere. It seems hardly an appropriate term now, with the virtual disappearance of the second, communist, world. China, which professes to be communist, is of course still very much a major, but not a super, power. However, it cannot play the same sort of dominating role as the Soviet Union and has adopted many features of the capitalist economic system.

'Developing' is of course a polite euphemism for not yet developed or 'underdeveloped'. It certainly cannot be taken literally that the rate of economic growth in developing countries is greater than elsewhere. The sad truth is that the whole of Africa on average has actually stayed economically static or even retreated in terms of gross national product per head over the last three decades as World Bank statistics show.

The term 'underdeveloped' also carries something of the implication of general inferiority as against the 'developed' countries, together with an aspiration to emulate them in all respects. To assume that a subcontinent like India with its artistic and spiritual richness, diversity and long history of civilisation should aspire to emulate the United States of America is surely to adopt a somewhat limited perspective. Consider the reply attributed to Gandhi on being asked, on a trip abroad, what he thought of Western civilisation: 'I think it would be a good thing'! (Still, clean water and modern sanitation would no doubt be very welcome in many parts of the subcontinent.) The simple terms 'rich' and 'poor' states might be adopted as descriptors of the division we are making but perhaps politically and socially an oil-rich sheikhdom might have more in common with its poorer neighbours than with Sweden or Switzerland.

The 'South' then is a very loose term to describe the less industrialised countries of Africa, Asia and Latin America. Although such countries encompass an enormous variety of political, economic and social conditions, we can see they share some important similarities that may potentially place them in conflict with the 'North'. Besides the general problems inherent in a relatively low average standard of living, most of these countries share an experience of colonial subordination to the 'North' (often exacerbated by racialism) and a continuing position of economic subordination to a world market dominated by Northern interests. Although the military and economic dominance of the North seems at this date inescapable, the coexistence of the vast majority of the world's population in poverty with a relatively small minority living in secure plenty does seem to constitute a position of long-term extreme instability.

In most areas of the 'South' the institutions of a modern

independent state are relatively new (although most parts of the South contain civilised cultures dating back as far as, or further than, those of Europe). New state institutions and old social values can sometimes conflict. In other cases, rapid industrialisation and new waves of migration have created new ethnically mixed communities which can be difficult to govern – or easy to disrupt with irresponsible political agitation. Transition toward new styles of government and the lack of an established democratic tradition has helped to generate greater political instability on the whole than in the 'North'. As we shall see (chapters 6 and 7) both military governments and experiments with single-party government are much more common in the South than the North.

Having made some generalisations about the politics of the South, it is worth cautioning readers about accepting too easily general-isations put forward by Northern commentators about the nature of these systems which may appear to condemn them all to a position of permanent subordination and inferiority. Employment of huge generalisations about the 'rationality' of Western forms of political organisation (Parsons, 1957) and the prevalence of 'kleptocracy' – government by thieves – in the South (Andreski, 1968) may, on occasion, be little more than a mask for sophisticated ethnocen-trism. It is worth bearing in mind that, as we have seen, ethnic conflicts can be found in US cities, in Northern Ireland and in the former Yugoslavia as well as in Africa or the Indian subcontinent. Corruption, too, can be observed on a large scale in apparently stable and rapidly growing political and economic systems such as the nineteenth-century USA or twentieth-century Japan.

The range of social, political and economic systems to be found in the South means that the prognosis for the future of these coun-tries may well be equally varied. Already states like South Korea, Singapore and Taiwan (the 'newly industrialised countries – NICs – of South East Asia) seem to have achieved massive, if not uninter-rupted, economic growth. Japan has moved rapidly up the 'league tables' of social and political indicators. Conversely parts of the UK seem to be taking on many of the social and economic characteristics of the South – for instance acting as a reservoir of cheap labour for the assembly plants of multinational enterprises.

Rather than concentrating on the domestic political systems of the

South, it may be more relevant to a consideration of the future political stability of the planet to consider soberly the extent to which the South faces a common economic and political environment which has the potential to drive the states of the South together in an increasingly desperate and potentially aggressive alliance against the North (Box 5.4).

Box 5.4   NORTH V SOUTH: A MAJOR FAULT LINE IN INTERNATIONAL RELATIONS?

Consider such issues such as:

* Southern indebtedness to Northern banks
* adverse movements in the terms of trade for the primary products of the South
* Northern monopolisation of intellectual property rights and information resources
* activities of (Northern) multinational enterprises
* destruction of the planetary environment in the interests of Northern consumption.

Many of these issues were raised by the report of the Independent Commission on International Development Issues (Brandt, 1980) to which the reader is referred. The likelihood of such a development must depend upon the extent to which the South feels deliberately excluded from the affluent economy of the North. Conversely the degree to which it is thought possible that individual countries will gradually be able to participate in the benefits of Northern affluence will reduce instability. So far the dangers of the situation may be emphasised by a quotation from the Brandt report: 'It is a terrible irony that the most dynamic and rapid transfer of highly sophisticated equipment and technology from rich to poor countries has been in the machinery of death' (Brandt, 1980: 14).

CONCLUSION

So far in this chapter we have seen political stability or instability as arising from a number of different conflicts which can be conveniently summarised in a slightly different way from that presented so far in Box 5.5.

BOX 5.5   MAJOR POLITICAL DIVISIONS

- WHO ARE WE? Identity issues: nationalism, race, ethnicity, class, gender, religion
- WHAT DO WE DO? Distributive issues: how to deliver state services, regulate the economy
- HOW DO WE DO IT? Process issues: conservatism/radicalism, constitutional
- WHO BENEFITS? Redistributive issues: rich v poor (people, regions, states)

(After Rose, 1969)

We consider a number of these themes in other parts of the book – for instance, 'distributive' issues are discussed at more length in Chapter 8 (Policies), 'process' issues in chapters 6 (States) and 7 (Democracy) and 'redistributive' issues both in this chapter and in Chapter 8. But, in relation to all of them, it is worth emphasising that who defines what the problem is, will also tend to define what is regarded as an acceptable solution. With so many divisions between the different sections of humanity, it is unlikely that lasting 'solutions' can be found to major problems that will be acceptable to all the parties affected. This is doubly so if we consider the tendencies to change in political systems considered at length in this chapter. In the authors' view, then, a pluralist approach to the management of political differences is both desirable, and almost inevitable: groups must learn to tolerate and negotiate with those who have very different perspectives upon the issues which arise.

RECOMMENDED READING

Bottomore, T. B., 1993, *Elites and Society*, 2nd edn, London, Routledge
Excellent theoretical introduction to some of the basic concepts of political sociology.

Dawson, Richard E., Prewitt, Kenneth and Dawson, Karen S., 1977, *Political Socialization*, Boston, MA, Little, Brown
Gives a good idea of the US functionalist approach.

Enloe, Cynthia, 1986, *Ethnic Conflict and Political Development: An Analytic Study*, New York, Collier-Macmillan
A wide-ranging US study of the impact of racial and similar conflicts.

Rice, E. E. (ed.), 1991, *Revolution and Counter-Revolution*, Oxford, Basil Blackwell
Broad-ranging collection of conference papers on the politics of revolutionary change.

Smith, Anthony, 1991, *National Identity*, Harmondsworth, Middlesex, Penguin
Useful study by a leading British scholar in the area of nationalism.

Solomos, Jon and Back, Les, 1996, *Racism and Society*, Basingstoke, Macmillan
Excellent interdisciplinary approach to the problem.

Tansey, Stephen D., (2002), *Business, Information Technology and Society*, London, Routledge
Includes extended treatment of impact of IT on society and government and vice versa.

Welch, Stephen, 1993, *The Concept of Political Culture*, Basingstoke, Macmillan
More advanced and critical treatment than Dawson et al.

WEBSITES

www.incore.ulst.ac.uk
Initiative on Conflict Resolution and Ethnicity – UN University and University of Ulster.

www.terrorism.com

Terrorism Research Centre – good links section.

www.state.gov/s/ct/ris/pgtrpt

US State Department Pattern of Global Terrorism Annual Reports (official US view).

6

STATES

THIS CHAPTER . . .

considers the major types of state in the modern world starting with Crick's distinction between republican, autocratic and totalitarian states. It discusses in more detail the different forms of representative democracy; military and authoritarian government; fascist and communist government. Relationships between central, regional and local states are analysed including the likelihood of a European regional 'super state'.

TYPES OF STATE

States vary a great deal in their organisation and in their concept of the role of government. Bernard Crick has suggested a good starting point for the classification of states which brings out some of these differences. He distinguishes between republican, autocratic and totalitarian states. These categories are, however, extremely 'broad-brush' as can be seen from the variety of examples quoted in Box 6.1.

BOX 6.1 REPUBLICAN, AUTOCRATIC AND TOTALITARIAN STATES

Republican
- Government as a constitutional process in which disparate group views on the public interest are reconciled through a political process of discussion.
- Government may intervene in economic and social affairs to maintain public interest and minimum welfare standards for all.
- In 'private affairs' citizens pursue their own happiness without interference.

Examples: eighteenth-century Britain, classical Athens, modern liberal democracies.

Autocratic
- Public interest defined by government. Subjects' involvement in politics seen as suspicious/subversive.
- Government's role mainly limited to taxation, foreign policy.
- In 'private affairs' citizens pursue their own happiness without interference.

Examples: monarchic governments of the eighteenth century, military regimes.

Totalitarian
- Government defines public interest that is all-inclusive.
- Political opposition is treason.
- No private sphere – good citizens participate enthusiastically in rebuilding society. Official ideology defines happiness.

Examples: Nazi Germany, Stalin's Soviet Union.

(After Crick, 2000)

Most modern 'republican' regimes could be described as 'representative democracies' in that they are not only constitutional but also have representative institutions based on universal suffrage (one man or woman, one vote). However, historically there were many states like eighteenth-century Britain that had some respect for individual rights and a constitutional form of government, without being fully democratic. Classical Athens was not in our sense fully 'democratic' since women, slaves and resident foreigners did not vote, although all full citizens could participate directly in debate and voting on matters of public policy. The Greeks too were inclined to see the state as having more of a role in the moral sphere than we are accustomed to in modern democracies. Similarly, Renaissance city states like Venice had participative, but not fully democratic, forms of constitutional rule. As is evident from the use of eighteenth-century Britain as an example, Crick is not using 'republican' in its usual sense of 'not monarchic' but in the broader sense of a state in which affairs are public. As of 2000 around 63 per cent of modern states can be seen as representative democracies or, in this terminology, republican (Diamond in LeDuc *et al.*, 2002: 211). A more detailed analysis of the degree of democracy in contemporary states can be found on the websites of the Country Indicators for Foreign Policy project (www.carleton.ca/cifp) and the World Bank (www.worldbank.org).

Crick's emphasis on the role of an independent private sphere in 'republican' regimes has been echoed in an increasingly strong emphasis in recent years on the importance of the concept of an independent 'civil society' as a mark of a developed liberal democracy. East European writers like Vaclav Havel emphasised the moral case for self-governing social institutions in contrast to their submergence by the communist regimes they were opposing. This concept from traditional political theory has been further re-emphasised by communitarian thinkers and used extensively by policy makers in international institutions such as the World Bank (see Axtmann, 2003: 82–92).

Autocratic, or 'authoritarian' regimes were probably more common in the past than today, but they are far from extinct, particularly in the 'South'. Derbyshire and Derbyshire (1991) classified 165 states by regime type and concluded that in the mid-1980s there were 16 'nationalistic socialist', 12 'authoritarian nationalist', 14 'military authoritarian' and 11 'absolutist' regimes – a total of 53 (or 32 per cent). These regimes were mainly in Africa but with three from Asia and one each from South America and Oceania. On Diamond's figures 72 states were not democratic in 2000 (Diamond in LeDuc *et al.*, 2002: 211).

'Totalitarian' is usually used loosely to describe communist, fascist and racist regimes. But clearly the intention of such a category is to include both extreme right (fascist) and extreme left (communist) regimes. The former Soviet Bloc (eight states in the Derbyshires' study) and apartheid South Africa might have been candidates for this description in the 1980s, totalling approximately 5 per cent of states but a much higher proportion of the world's population. By 2008, however, only China, North Korea and Cuba could arguably be described as members of such a category.

We will now look in more detail at some sub-types of each of these categories – republican and totalitarian in turn. In terms of 'republican' regimes we will concentrate on the different kinds of modern representative democracies. From Crick's 'autocratic' category we will consider military government and some modern civilian despotisms – mainly in the South. Totalitarian government will be discussed both in general terms and in its communist and fascist variants.

DEMOCRACY, THE WELFARE STATE AND THE MARKET

In recent years the number of democratic states has dramatically increased, with the disintegration of the Soviet Bloc and a marked trend to democratisation in Latin America. Larry Diamond (in LeDuc et al., 2002: 211) documents the dramatic trend over recent decades (Table 6.1).

We could go further and assert that free elections along with a competitive free economy (modified by some commitment to a welfare state) have become in some sense the norm for a modern state. This combination of representative democracy and capitalism is frequently described as 'liberal democracy'. In Europe, for instance, the members of the European Union are all states of this type and for those states that aspire to join the EU, membership requires a commitment to democracy, the free market (capitalism) and a minimum standard of social policy.

Table 6.1   The trend to democracy, 1974–2000

Year	Number of democracies	Number of countries	Democracies as a percentage
1974	39	142	27.5
1988	66	167	39.5
1991	91	183	49.7
1996	118	191	61.8
2000	120	192	62.5

Source: Larry Diamond (in LeDuc *et al.*, 2002: 211)

The relationship between democracy, capitalism and the welfare state is, therefore, central to the study of politics. It is worth emphasising that this combination of characteristics is historically quite rare and has by no means always been thought to be either desirable or necessary.

Democracy is a concept with a long history, but it comes as a surprise to many modern readers to find that, until the twentieth century, it was more often a term of abuse than praise. In classical Greece, for instance, where the term originated, it was commonly understood as 'mob rule'. As described above, ancient Greek democracy did not involve elections (officials being selected by lot), and manhood suffrage (i.e. the election of parliaments by all men – but not women) only became a common institution in the nineteenth century. Even John Stuart Mill, the famous liberal philosopher, was concerned about the 'tyranny of the majority'. Britain, France and the United States have only achieved universal suffrage since the end of the Second World War. University graduates had an additional vote in the UK until 1948; women only achieved the vote in France in 1945; black voters in the southern USA were effectively disenfranchised until the implementation of the 1968 Civil Rights Act.

This is not a text on economics, but it may be useful to define briefly what is meant here by capitalism (see Box 6.2). We discuss the advantages and problems of market decision making at more length in Chapter 8.

BOX 6.2 CAPITALISM

A system of exchange based upon market prices ... in which individuals or combinations of individuals compete with each other to accumulate wealth by buying the rights to use land, labour and capital in order to produce goods and services with the intention of selling them in the market at a profit.

(Saunders, 1995: 9)

Capitalism pre-dated democracy in Britain, whilst in some parts of the world (e.g. Allende's Chile) the development of liberal democracy has been seen as a distinct menace to capitalism and resisted for this reason. Indeed, to use Greek political terminology, it might be argued that the natural form of government for a capitalist economy (allowing, as it does, the accumulation of large quantities of wealth in relatively few hands) is oligarchy (government by the – rich – few) rather than democracy (government by the – poor – many).

A wide variety of definitions of the 'welfare state' have been put forward but it is convenient to adopt Johnson's (1987) approach (see Box 6.3).

BOX 6.3   THE WELFARE STATE

A modern liberal democratic industrial state in which the state has intervened to:
1   provide a wide range of social services to the bulk of the population;
2   seek to maintain full employment;
3   nationalise or regulate a number of key industries, but in which the bulk of the economy remains in the hands of private enterprise.

(After Johnson, 1987)

One can see the welfare state as the natural consequence of the extension of democratic ideas to the social and welfare sphere. Thus President Franklin D. Roosevelt proclaimed the Allied war aims to include four freedoms (including not only freedom of worship and of speech but also the social aims of freedom from fear and freedom from want). In wartime Britain a consensus between parties was evolved on the basis of the Beveridge (1942) report on the need to conquer the 'Five Giants' of Want, Disease, Ignorance, Squalor and Idleness. We have already referred to the social dimension of the UN Declaration of Human Rights.

Despite the apparent coincidence of values between welfarism and democracy, British readers in particular may be surprised to discover that the welfare state cannot be said to have originated with the Labour victory in Britain in 1945. Many of the moves toward a welfare state in Britain took place in the early twentieth century partly as a reaction to the prior development of welfarism in Bismarck's Germany (an autocratic rather than a liberal democratic state).

FORMS OF REPRESENTATIVE DEMOCRACY

A key issue in considering the workings of modern democracies is the nature of those governments and the mechanisms for enforcing responsibility of governments to the people. The complex relationships between the elected legislature, the government and the electorate are summarised briefly in Box 6.4 and explored in more detail in succeeding sections.

BOX 6.4   FORMS OF REPRESENTATIVE DEMOCRACY

Presidential
Popularly elected head of state and government, independent legislature and judiciary, e.g. USA, Latin America.

Parliamentary
Head of state appoints head of government responsible to legislature, e.g. UK, Sweden, Italy.

Hybrid
Directly elected head of state appoints head of government responsible to legislature, e.g. France, Russia.

Consociational
Minorities have constitutional right to representation in government, e.g. Switzerland, Northern Ireland.

One-party
One party legally controls government, e.g. China, North Korea, Tanzania (before 1992).

The two major types of representative democratic constitution to be found in the world today are the parliamentary and presidential systems. The major features of these are outlined in Table 6.2, which is based on the work of Verney (1959). Parliamentary systems are found not only in Britain and the many Commonwealth countries which have retained the 'Westminster model' (Tansey and Kermode,

1967/8), but in most West European states as well (Smith, 1989: Chs. 5, 7, 8). Derbyshire and Derbyshire (1996: 40) classified fifty-five states as having parliamentary executives, most of which were Commonwealth members. Presidential systems, in this sense, are those like the United States of America with an executive president; they are the most common form of constitutional government, with seventy-seven states classified as limited presidential executives by the Derbyshires. They are found chiefly in the Americas and Africa.

The main differences between the systems may be expressed in terms of the separation and balance of powers. Following Montesquieu's interpretation of the eighteenth-century British constitution, presidential systems not only divide the powers of government into legislative (law making), executive (law enforcing) and judicial (law interpreting) institutions, but seek to separate these in terms of personnel and balance them against each other. Democratic government is seen in terms of a refusal to concentrate potentially tyrannical power so that it cannot be used to take away individual rights. Federalism is seen as a further expression of the same approach.

In parliamentary systems the main expression of democracy is seen in the enforcement of the responsibility of the executive to the people through Parliament – in practice the independence of the

Table 6.2 Parliamentary versus presidential systems

	Parliamentary system	*Presidential system*
Assembly	'Parliament'	Assembly only
Executive	Separate heads of state and government	Popularly elected president
Head of government	Appointed by head of state	Also head of state
Appointment of government	Head of government appoints ministry	President appoints departmental heads
Responsibility	Government is collectively responsible to Assembly	President is responsible to people
Personnel	Ministers usually parliamentarians	Executive/legislative separation
Dissolution of assembly	By head of state on advice of head of government	Not possible

Source: Verney (1959)

judiciary is accepted but the executive and legislative powers work in concert as a result of the government's legislative majority.

Not all systems, however, fit easily into either of the above constitutional moulds. The Derbyshires found twelve states with what they described as dual executives that we describe here as 'hybrid' systems. For instance, both contemporary (2008) France and Russia have adopted some features of each model with a directly elected president with strong powers who appoints a prime minister to head the administration who is also responsible to parliament. In both cases it seems that the drafters of the constitution anticipated a strong leader (de Gaulle, Yeltsin) faced by a scattering of weak parties. The problem with this system is that the electorate may not elect a legislature sympathetic to the political ideas of the president. In France, on several occasions legislative elections have take place after the presidential elections, and a new and different coalition of political forces has clearly been in the ascendant. The president has usually decided to 'cohabit' with the opposition forces – compromising on policy and government personnel. The alternative is to confront the opposition and cause a constitutional crisis.

Possibly a more radical institutional reinterpretation of democracy can be seen in what is sometimes called 'consociational' democracy. In all liberal democratic systems a legitimate role is allotted to minority (opposition) political forces outside of the government. In Britain this is institutionalised in the term Leader of Her Majesty's Opposition. In consociational democracy the attempt is made to ensure that all significant minorities, as well as the majority, are actually represented in government. The best known, and most successful, example of this is Switzerland where the government (the Federal Council) is composed of representatives of all the major parties in parliament in proportion to their strength.

Such an arrangement seems particularly suited to societies that are deeply divided on national, linguistic or religious lines in which important groups may be in a permanent minority. Thus in Switzerland French, German and Italian speakers, Protestants and Catholics, are all automatically represented in the government. Less successful attempts at similar arrangements in other divided societies include the Lebanon. An attempt to use such a device was in South Africa's 1994 constitution in which both the majority black (ANC) and the minority white (Nationalist) populations were guaranteed a role in government at least during a transitional period. In the 1998 Northern Ireland peace settlement the use of this device was attempted for a second time, failing at first, but reactivated once more in 2007.

Verney discusses a third major type of democratic constitution in addition to the parliamentary and presidential models: what he terms the 'convention'-style constitution modelled on the revolutionary French Assembly of 1789. The French constitutional tradition emphasised the legitimacy of the sovereign national assembly based on the popular vote. The Assembly could not be dissolved and exercised detailed control over the personnel of government drawn from its ranks. Some modern French constitutions (especially the Third Republic from 1870 to 1940) could be described in these terms, and on the letter of the constitutional instruments, the Soviet constitution – and many former Eastern Bloc constitutions influenced by it – also appeared to be based on this model.

It would be more realistic to describe Soviet-style democracy as one-party democracy, however, since the legal predominance of the assembly was clearly only a fiction that scarcely masked the monopoly of the Communist Party over government, legislature and every other social and political institution within the state. Only one party-sponsored candidate was presented in each constituency and all resolutions of parliament were passed unanimously on the initiative of the government/party. The party, in turn, was controlled from the top through the device of 'democratic centralism'. A claim to democracy could only be justified by an appeal to the top party members' superior grasp of 'scientific' socialism which enabled them to discern and represent the interests of the working masses more certainly than the workers themselves. It is perhaps surprising that such an unlikely doctrine could be taken seriously for so long not only in the Soviet Union itself – where scepticism could prove fatal in the literal sense – but even amongst intelligent commentators in the West.

Another version of one-party democracy has been put forward in a number of post-colonial regimes. Here a virtually all-encompassing political coalition has been created to fight for independence – often centred upon some 'charismatic' popular leader. Not unnaturally the national(ist) party obtains an overwhelming victory at the independence general election. Opposition to the national leader seems like treason. The national party now has a monopoly of the considerable patronage dispensed by the new state. In such circumstances it is not surprising for virtually all opposition to the party to disappear. Indeed a similar state of affairs occurred in the United States after its national revolution (Lipset, 1979). In many newly independent states ethnic and racial antagonisms constitute both a serious threat to the continued integrity of the state and the natural basis for any multi-party democratic system. In such circumstances the single-party regime may be made a legal as well as a political fact. The Soviet example serves as additional justification for such a move – particularly since communist regimes professed 'anti-imperialist' rhetoric that appealed to nationalist leaders fighting the imperial/colonialist powers.

The reality of such one-party regimes has differed greatly. In many – such as Nkrumah's Ghana – Marxist rhetoric about the importance of the party masked the reality of its virtual absorption by the government machine (Dowse, 1969). In a few states – such as Tanzania under Julius Nyerere – interesting experiments were attempted to combine the legitimacy and strength of a single national party with opportunities for popular participation and choice through contested primary elections.

It is evident that the vast majority of states in the contemporary world make some sort of constitutional claim to be 'democratic'. Hence the widespread use of elections in autocratic regimes – Golder (2005) found that dictatorships were almost as likely to use elections as democracies.

MILITARY AUTOCRACY

The major undemocratic form of government in the modern world is military government. Such is the power of the democratic myth that most such regimes represent themselves as transitional – temporary remedies for an unfortunate inadequacy in a preceding nominally democratic regime. In parts of the globe, the smartest move for an aspirant politician may well be to join the army (the navy or air force are usually less politically involved and effective). However, this is seldom openly acknowledged as a career motivation – even in areas like Africa or (until recently) Latin America where, at any one time, more heads of state may be soldiers than civilians.

Indeed a key part of the armed forces' temporary claim to power may well be that they claim to be (and may believe themselves to be) 'non-political' in the sense of both non-partisan and committed to the national interest rather than those of any narrow sections of the population. A claim is frequently made for greater efficiency and incorruptibility for officers (as opposed to civilian politicians) as part of a united, disciplined, educated and trained modern elite.

There is no doubt that many army officers do value strongly the unity, probity and capacity for effective action of the officer corps. It is therefore quite common for armies that have intervened in politics to return to the barracks after a period in power when these values come under stress. Under the pressure of being forced to make governmental decisions, which will be interpreted as favouring one section of the population or another, conflicts are frequently generated within the military which are not necessarily evident whilst the army is confined to a technical role. For instance, most Latin American officers have been recruited from white, land-owning groups, and governments dominated by them tend to be unsympathetic both to rural Indian and urban slum-dwelling populations. In Africa regional and tribal conflicts can come rapidly to the fore, as was graphically illustrated from the moment the military intervened in Nigerian politics. In the Nigerian Civil War (1966–1971) the military intervened to stop 'tribalism, nepotism and corruption' on the part of civilian democratic politicians only to preside over more bloodshed and disunity than had ever previously been experienced. Similarly there has been at least as massive an embezzlement of the oil wealth of Nigeria by politicians in uniform as there was by their predecessors and successors in civilian garb.

The mechanisms of military intervention vary greatly depending upon time and place. In countries such as Turkey and Brazil the army is often seen as having an important 'guarantor' role in relation to the constitution. In the Turkish example this is as the inheritor of the prestige of Ataturk (the founder of modern Turkish nationalism). The army sees itself as entitled to intervene to preserve Ataturk's ideas of secular modern nationalism. In such cases the army may exercise a veto on the participation of some groups in the government, rather than play a direct role. The extreme form of military intervention, in which the head of state and all cabinet posts are taken by officers, the legislature is dismissed and the courts summarily overruled, is relatively rare. More commonly a supreme military council or similar body may effectively replace the legislature whilst the day-to-day government may remain in the hands of a cabinet with civilian participants. Top civil servants may often be deputed to take over roles previously carried out by civilian politicians.

The longer the military participate in government, the more functions may be taken over by the armed forces. It is not unknown, even in civilian regimes, to deploy the army corps of engineers on major construction projects, or to use the military to keep order in cases of civil disturbance. This sort of expansion of the armed forces' role may well gather pace. The demands of individual greed and factional balance may well also lead to all sorts of government patronage posts – from nationalised industry chairmen to university chancellorships – going to military personnel.

CIVIL AUTOCRACY

Like their military equivalents, few contemporary civilian dictators (autocrats) reject the idea of democracy; most claim either to be democratic rulers or to be preparing the way for democracy when the mess created by the previous corrupt and ineffective regime has been cleared up. Finer (1970) uses the suggestive descriptions of Façade Democracies and Quasi-Democracies for regimes of this sort. As we shall see in more detail later (Chapter 7, p. 173) meaningful free elections are quite difficult to achieve so that deliberate manipulation of an ostensibly democratic system may help to confuse domestic opposition and satisfy Western aid donors, diplomatic and military allies, or investors.

A variety of devices may be used to restrict the impact of elections and opposition criticism. The most obvious devices are to postpone continually the next elections having once attained a sort of electoral victory; to ban some opposition parties as 'subversive', 'terrorists', 'communists' or 'Islamic fundamentalists' and to imprison their leading supporters; or to ban all other parties as disruptive to national unity. Slightly less obvious devices include the deployment of patronage in favour of supporters and discrimination against opponents in relation to employment by the state, public contracts and the siting of major public works. Licences and subsidies may be awarded to supporters in the media. Opponents may be prosecuted, censored or, indeed, physically eliminated. Elections can be held, but under a 'rigged' electoral system.

The constitutional basis of such autocratic regimes is quite variable. In Latin America there is often theoretically a written constitution which the president simply overrides or ignores as convenient. In Africa an original independence constitution based on that of France or of Westminster has more frequently been amended in the name of nationalism towards an explicit adoption of a single-party model. In some cases what was a military regime has ostensibly been civilianised with the original military dictator creating a civilian government party to support him. Examples include Colonel Nasser in Egypt, Colonel al-Gadhafi in Libya and Saddam Hussein in Iraq. A few regimes are more original in their form such as that of the former 'Emperor' Bokassa of the Central African Empire/Republic.

A probably more significant difference between such regimes is the basis of the political support for the regime. As we have seen, traditionally Latin American authoritarian regimes have been supported by landowners, the army and the Church. Regimes in Africa and the Middle East may represent the successors of a coalition of nationalist 'intellectuals' (i.e. a Western-educated minority) who replaced the colonial administrative elite and in some cases enriched themselves and their families through businesses benefiting from state patronage. In Haiti the Duvalier regime was supported by a private gangster army – the Tonton Macoutes.

Perhaps related to the question of the social support for the regime are questions of the degree of collegiality within the regime and its stability. To the extent that an autocratic regime is built upon one more or less charismatic leader who ruthlessly builds up a personal machine based upon patronage, terror and/or personal loyalty, it is likely to be unstable in the long run. The question of succession is clearly a difficult one in such cases, although, as with presidents Duvalier and Kim Il-sung (North Korea), the child of the dead leader may be adopted by the elements that supported the father. Where the regime is based upon a dominant coalition of social forces, it may have a wider division of power and greater stability. The best example of this is probably that of Mexico whose PRI (Partido Revolucionari Institucional) dominated Mexico for most of the twentieth century (until 1997). The PRI clung strongly to the principle that no president should serve more than one six-year term so that no faction within it could overwhelm the others. Despite the name the PRI came to represent a coalition of established local political machines often with strong bureaucratic, military, agricultural and labour links.

TOTALITARIAN GOVERNMENTS

We saw that Crick defined totalitarianism largely in terms of its all-encompassing role in contrast to modern republican (or liberal democratic) regimes which leave a much greater area to private initiative and control. The category of 'totalitarian' state has been criticised as too tightly drawn to contain, or at least usefully describe, any modern states. 'Totalitarian' state was not a term coined by Crick, nor do all authors using the term emphasise those elements of Crick's treatment which have been highlighted here.

Other writers (e.g. Arendt, 1967; Friedrich, 1964) have stressed not only the scope of the activities of the totalitarian state but the similarity of the methods employed by them to control the population. The totalitarian state is seen as one which employs modern technology and techniques of organisation to enforce total control over the lives of the population of a large modern industrialised state. Thus both Nazi Germany and the Stalinist Soviet Union employed a single mass party to generate and enforce enthusiasm on the part of the population. Modern communication methods such as newspapers, cinema and radio were monopolised by the regime and used to propagate a 'cult of personality' around the leader. The use of terror – the employment of torture, and the mass extermination of whole segments of the population – is also seen as characteristic of such regimes. Although historic dictatorships have also used such methods, this has not usually been on such a scale and so systematically. Certainly from a liberal perspective the differences in the ostensible purposes of these regimes – establishing a classless or a racially pure society – seem less significant than the horrific reality of their excesses.

Critics of such an approach to the analysis of modern states have variously argued that it seeks to tar all progressive socialist regimes with the Hitler/Stalin brush; that the post-Stalin Soviet Union was a conservative bureaucratic society rather than one based on terror; or even that the concept 'totalitarian' control is better applied to the activities of modern capitalism in creating a consumer society. Thus

Marcuse (1964: 13) argues that in modern automated consumer societies:

> the productive apparatus tends to become totalitarian to the extent to which it determines not only the socially needed occupations, skills and attitudes, but also individual needs and aspirations. ... Technology serves to institute new, more effective, and more pleasant forms of social control.

It may be worth looking in a little more detail at some actual examples before returning to an evaluation of these criticisms.

NAZI GOVERNMENT

From the point of view of political and governmental machinery, it could be argued that Hitler's Germany was less innovatory than either Soviet communism or even Italian fascism. Hitler took over the machinery of the existing German state as Chancellor and left much of it unchanged. The army functioned largely on the professional basis it had done before the Nazi victory in a democratic election. Grim additional features were grafted onto the existing state machinery in the shape of the Gestapo (the secret police) who used torture and terrorism to stamp out resistance; the SS (Black Shirt) and SA (Brown Shirt) sections of the Nazi Party were accorded state powers and recognition. Loyalty to the Führer and to the state were identified. Hitler played off one section of the party against another and confused normal lines of bureaucratic reporting.

Although there was much rhetoric about total mobilisation, American strategic bombing surveys suggest that ultimately the German economy was actually less fully mobilised in the war effort than was the British. In practice the economy was largely left in the hands of its existing owners (where they were non-Jewish). In the wartime economy, slave labourers from or in the concentration camps and from conquered areas supplemented normal labour but were a grossly inefficient resource.

Programmes of mass extermination of Jews, communists, Gypsies and the mentally deficient were a horrific feature of the regime, but seem to have affected the rest of the population to a surprisingly small degree. Their loyalty was mainly secured by propaganda appeals to national pride, massive rallies and demonstrations, early political and military victories and by the restoration of full employment rather than just by terror.

SOVIET GOVERNMENT

The Nazi Party being organised primarily as a militia for street fighting was less effective in asserting total control than the Communist Party of the Soviet Union (CPSU). The CPSU was organised on the 'cell' system based on the workplace. This reflected the factory-based organisation of the original Bolshevik faction of the Social Democratic Party. It proved ideal for asserting control not only over factories but also over government offices, army units, schools and universities. Every communist had the duty to form a cell in his or her workplace and to participate through the cell in ensuring that party policy was carried out there.

The CPSU as an anti-capitalist party also found it much easier to assert total control over economic activity through the economic planning system. Stalin's use of the secret police and of concentration camps might also be seen as a more thorough-going attempt at total control in that the ordinary Russian population, the army and even original Bolshevik party members found themselves the victims of the terror.

The institutions of government and politics were greatly transformed as a result of the revolution. The Red Army replaced the Tsarist Army. Legislative institutions were totally remodelled. Ordinary citizens were expected to participate enthusiastically in politics rather than be passively loyal to the tsar.

It is clear that in the post-Stalinist Soviet Union terror played a much smaller part in the political system, with self-interest, national pride and conservative acquiescence in a long-established system playing a much greater one.

Despite the differences, to the authors it does seem that Nazi Germany and Stalin's Soviet Union appeared to have much in common and that one can construct an extreme 'ideal type' of government – 'totalitarian' government – which encapsulates their similarities in terms of both all-encompassing scope and ruthless methods. It would not be impossible to imagine, say, an ecological or a religious totalitarian regime in the future using modern information technology and psychological and pharmaceutical discoveries for surveillance and control to a greater extent than even Hitler or Stalin achieved. What should not be done is to assume that every regime described as communist or fascist shares all these characteristics. In practice there is no clear line of division between autocratic or authoritarian regimes and the more extreme totalitarian variant. Late Soviet or present-day Chinese government could be seen as in either category – particularly as market-led economic reform reduces the direct power of the party.

Logically one can have some sympathy for Marcuse's contention that the capitalist system is moulding everyone's perceptions and behaviour – we may be being 'brainwashed' into becoming good consumers. Thus an analogy is drawn with Hitler's attempt to create pure Aryans or the Soviet Union's programme to create 'New Soviet Man'. Marcuse's use of 'totalitarian' to describe this phenomenon is however somewhat misleading in that there is no deliberate co-ordinated political direction to this process. Nor are we robbed of our freedom of choice on pain of imprisonment. Alternative lifestyles are not censored – though they may be swamped. Prisoners of war who were 'brainwashed' in Korean prison camps would surely distinguish this process from the effects of voluntarily sitting in front of (capitalist) television programmes.

ISLAMIC GOVERNMENT – BREAKING THE MOULD?

In Chapter 4 we saw that Islam is now increasingly seen as the alternative to capitalism and democracy as the way forward for the South, but the major problem is to create distinctive and effective economic and political institutions for any proposed Islamic state.

Whilst the Koranic tradition does have some positive statements to make on economic matters – the immorality of interest payments; the duty to make payments to the poor (*zakat*) – these have proved difficult to institutionalise in a modern (i.e. capitalist) economic context. Similarly the Koran makes it clear that the *umma* (community of the faithful) should be ruled by those faithful to its religious prescriptions, be united, and that rulers should listen to the voice of the community – but no concrete political and religious institutions are laid down. The two major Islamic traditions – the Shi'ite and the Sunni – differed early on the succession to the

Caliphate (political leadership) (Fischer, 1980). Other differences include the Shi'ite's greater emphasis on the importance of religious scholars and the role of martyrs. The relationship between the strongly developed traditions of Koranic law and the modern state, and the role of electoral institutions are matters of considerable debate within Islamic countries.

In practice contemporary states with a commitment to Islam differ markedly in their political and economic arrangements. For instance, Saudi Arabia, several other Sunni-dominated states around the Gulf, Brunei and, to some extent, Jordan retain a dynastic rule in which the leading family of a recently tribal society continue to rule without any great formalisation of constitutional matters. Considerable revenues derived from oil are used in a paternalistic way to ensure the loyalty of the indigenous population – many recent immigrants being denied participation in government and citizenship. Various more or less consultative assemblies have been convened, but have frequently been dissolved if they have proved overly critical. Social practices vary, but in Saudi Arabia in particular, traditional attitudes toward women, alcohol and the like are strictly enforced through religious courts interpreting the Koran in accord with the Wahhabist extreme conservative interpretation of the Sunni tradition. In Afghanistan similar beliefs culminated in the Taliban regime effectively banning female work, education and even hospital treatment, also in the destruction of world famous historic monuments.

In contrast, the Shi'ite state of Iran following a revolution against the Shah of Iran has adopted a much more original constitution. Power is divided between a government and a leader, or Council of Leaders. The government (president, prime minister and cabinet) is based upon an elected National Consultative Assembly. The Islamic Scholar or Scholars head the judicial system, act as Commander in Chief and vet the suitability of candidates for the presidency. A particular Islamic school of thought is proclaimed to be the official religion of Iran, whilst Zoroastrians, Christian and Jews are the only recognised and tolerated (non-Islamic) religious minorities. The government's responsibility to promote Islam is spelt out, and it has the power to confiscate wealth derived from 'usury, usurpation, bribery', etc. (Article 49 of the Constitution). Legislative power is divided between the National Consultative Council and a Council of Guardians – Islamic scholars who must review legislation to ensure its compatibility with Islam. In practice, since the death of the first revolutionary leader, the Ayatollah Khomeini, considerable tensions have been evident between the more pragmatic and modernising tendencies often centred on the president and the more conservative forces centred on the Leadership Council. This model of Islamic government may well be less acceptable in areas where the Sunni tradition is stronger and there is less of an established hierarchy of Islamic scholars.

In countries such as Egypt (and formerly in Iran) where Islamic forces are in opposition to a more secular government, they frequently benefit from popular support derived not only from the powerful indigenous traders of the bazaar, but also from the beneficiaries of the informal welfare system based upon the *zakat* paid to the mosques and distributed by their leaders. In opposition, intellectuals can produce more or less convincing schemes for non-capitalist economic arrangements eschewing the payment of interest. In opposition, the Islamic forces may achieve a formidable reputation for discipline and puritanism which assisted the Taliban faction in Afghanistan toward its initial victory.

So far, however, Islam has proved a useful weapon of opposition to Western influences, but has been much less effective in constructing an alternative model of political and economic management, or in uniting the faithful politically.

MULTI-LEVEL GOVERNMENT

So far in this chapter we have discussed forms of government in terms of national governments. However, it is clear that the assumption that there is only one state and one government in a given territorial area is a large and probably unjustified one. In the United States, for instance, many people live in a city with a municipal government, which may well be part of a larger county, they all reside in a state, as well as being subject to the government of the United States. Similarly in England many people are subject to three different layers of government: local, UK and European. In the rest of the UK, an additional layer of government at national or provincial level is in operation for Scotland, Wales and Northern Ireland. We have already discussed (Chapter 2) the trend for international governmental organisations to play an increasing role in the government and politics of nation states, so that the activities of the World Trade Organisation, NATO, the United Nations and its agencies must also be considered in this context. We need to analyse, therefore, the differences between levels of government, the relationships between them and what each level of government does, or should do.

In the *Social Contract* Jean Jacques Rousseau suggested that giant nation states could only really be free once every few years at general election time. He compared all such arrangements unfavourably with his native Geneva in which the citizens could be intimately involved in the sovereign government of their own community. One obvious way to minimise the degree to which state decision making is seen as remote is to try to keep the state concerned as small and consequently unbureaucratic as possible. As we have seen, anarchists advocate dividing the whole world into a network of such voluntary self-governing communities.

The disadvantages of a multitude of small-scale states may include an increased likelihood of inter-state violence. Another problem might be a failure to express larger senses of national or regional identity. Possibly, too, there would be a lack of capacity for large-scale investment necessary for complex transport systems, advanced health, education and research facilities. Manned exploration of outer space and nuclear weaponry would be unlikely in the absence of 'super-states' like the USA and EU.

The actual distribution of governmental powers between layers of government is somewhat haphazard in practice with historical influences being very important. In the UK the idea of the sovereignty of the national parliament, has contributed to a strong concentration of power at the national level. In the United States and in Switzerland, many of the component states or cantons preceded the federal governments and retain exceptionally strong powers. However, the trend in most parts of the world, however unpalatable it may be, has been toward a greater concentration of powers at the higher levels of government.

Many factors have contributed to this trend toward centralisation. One simple factor is that the central government will normally be the biggest government in the state and therefore contains the greatest concentration of expertise. The doctrine of national state sovereignty not only lends legitimacy to central government decision makers but also ensures that they are expected to co-ordinate relations with other states. Control of the major organisations capable of physical coercion (not only the armed forces but probably also some sort of internal riot squad) clearly strengthens central governments. A major factor in most systems is that the higher levels of government usually control the more effective taxing mechanisms – particularly income tax. Clearly, too, in many areas of government, as of business, 'economies of scale' mean that large, often computerised, operations can be more efficient than smaller ones.

Opposed to these centralising tendencies are not only democratic considerations but also the need to deliver policy effectively to citizens where they live. As circumstances will vary from local district to local district, a 'top down' central solution to a centrally conceived problem may well translate into an inappropriate response to local problems (see Chapter 8). In Europe, the EU has supported the development of regional institutions and makes grants available to them for economic development and other purposes.

The idea of 'subsidiarity' can be applied to decide which level of government to allocate powers to. The principle was incorporated in the Maastricht Treaty (1991) on the future of the EU (Box 6.5).

BOX 6.5   THE PRINCIPLE OF SUBSIDIARITY

Advocates that political decisions should always be made at the lowest possible level of government.

The advantages of better democratic control and the greater flexibility of response to local circumstances create a presumption in favour of the lower level. In contemporary Britain, however, governments have interpreted this principle somewhat selectively. There has not been the same emphasis on leaving to local government the maximum decision-making power as the central UK government has asserted in its relations with Europe (see Duff, 1993).

The principle of subsidiarity has been strongly endorsed in twentieth-century papal encyclicals. Thus Leo XIII in *Quadragesimo Anno* (1941) proclaimed:

It is an injustice, a grave evil and a disturbance of right order for a large and higher organization to arrogate to itself functions which can be performed efficiently by smaller and lower bodies.

Subsidiarity is therefore a principle that fits easily with the Christian democratic parties of Europe.

Two further related aspects of the division of powers between levels of government are worth exploration. First, who divides the powers between levels of government? Second, what are the relationships between levels when they are both concerned with an issue? These are summarised in Box 6.6.

BOX 6.6   RELATIONS BETWEEN LEVELS OF GOVERNMENT

In principle a FEDERAL system is one in which the allocation of powers is independent of either level of government in question. Each has its defined sphere of influence, this normally being laid down in a written constitution and interpreted independently (probably by the courts) in case of dispute.

(After Wheare, 1963)

In a system of DEVOLUTION a higher level of government creates and gives powers to a lower (elected) level of government to exercise.

In a system of DECENTRALISATION subordinate local administrative agencies are created by a central government and may be given some discretion to interpret central policy and consult local opinion.

In a CONFEDERAL system the powers of the higher-level government are granted by the lower-level governments which may withdraw them (as with most international organisations).

(Authors' definitions)

Just over a third of modern liberal democracies have a federal or semi-federal form of organisation, and just over a third have some form of devolution (Keman, 2002: 268).

One might expect the lower levels of government in a federal system to act independently of the upper layers. The lower levels in a devolved system may be expected to negotiate a local interpretation of national policies within a framework of national statutory guidance. In decentralised systems the local bureaucrats would merely interpret national policies according to local circumstances. In confederal systems the upper tier would be expected to act according to a consensus of the views of the lower tier.

In practice, in all systems, some measure of co-ordination, co-operation and negotiation between levels seems to emerge. Thus American writers on US federalism have tended to use the term 'co-operative federalism' to indicate the extent to which state authorities have tended to co-operate with federal policy initiatives partly in order to obtain access to large subsidies from the federal budget. Conversely, realistic analysis of the way government bureaucracies work suggests that even career national bureaucrats have to be motivated to implement central policies. At the extreme a part of a central bureaucracy may be so much under the influence of a local 'mafia' that national policies conflicting with local interests may be ignored, as in Italy (Banfield and Banfield, 1967). Conversely, as in the former Soviet Union, nominally independent state authorities may be under the almost total political control of a centralised political party (Schapiro, 1965). The EU is a classic example of the fuzzy relationships that can emerge between levels of government.

EUROPEAN POLITICAL INSTITUTIONS

The growing importance of European institutions for so many countries and their unusual nature, compared with the parliamentary and presidential models discussed earlier, justifies some further discussion here. By 'European institutions' is meant those associated with the European Union. However it should be noted that there are also many separate international bodies which may cover more of Europe. These include the European Court of Human Rights, the European Parliamentary Union and technical bodies such as the European Laboratory for Particle Physics based at CERN.

It is also worth relating the likely future of the European Union to some of the themes introduced earlier in this chapter and in Chapter 5 on Processes. The European Union is an interesting example of the processes of political change. Clearly a reaction to the impact of two world wars on the heartland of Europe, it has developed from an organisation to co-ordinate iron and steel production in six countries to a potential continental superpower in less than fifty years. For the most part this has been a story of building alliances around common interests, of trading advantages against disadvantages and of seeking accommodations where national interests have conflicted.

The initial creation of the European Economic Community (EEC) upon the foundations of the original Iron and Steel Community can be seen as a pragmatic bargain struck with an eye to a perhaps nobler vision. The creation of the EEC can be seen as part of a process whereby the French government accepted the rehabilitation of (Western) Germany into the democratic community of nations in return for such a measure of economic integration in basic industries and of co-operation on defence issues through NATO. Thus a German attempt to independently dominate Europe militarily and economically would not be feasible. In addition French rural voters were softened in their attitude to the EEC by a large element of agricultural subsidy and protection. Although the details of the Treaty of Rome were fairly prosaic, behind it lay the vision of Jean Monet's Action Committee for a United States of Europe.

It is significant that most of the states that 'joined Europe' between 1957 and the early 1990s shared a commitment to a vision of a united and democratic Europe – the idea of Europe as a political symbol. For instance, Spain, Portugal and Greece all joined what was by then known as the European Community (EC) after ending periods of authoritarian dictatorship, seeing this as a significant move toward joining the political mainstream of European development. Similarly, former Eastern bloc countries, such as Poland, the Czech Republic, Slovakia and Hungary, that became members in 2004 clearly wish to assert a long-term future as part of a united and democratic Europe.

In contrast the British application to join was defended domestically even by its proponents as a sensible economic move much more than a political one. Even proponents of joining the EEC asserted that Britain could still maintain its special political relationships with the United States and the Commonwealth and that parliamentary sovereignty was undiminished by the move. Long after Brussels dropped the middle 'E' in EEC, the British government retained it. In the circumstances it is understandable that France's

President de Gaulle vetoed Britain's first application to join on the grounds that Britain would be an American Trojan horse undermining European unity. Jacques Chirac, de Gaulle's successor during the Anglo-American invasion of Iraq in 2003, may well feel these fears to have been justified.

Since joining, Britain has played a somewhat ambivalent role. Under Mrs Thatcher's leadership, despite expressions of reservation on the political front, Britain did show some enthusiasm for the creation of a 'Single European Market' (1992). The removal of obstacles to trade in order to create a 'level playing field' throughout Europe fitted the free-market economic policies of the Thatcher government that permitted a temporarily strengthened legislative procedure to be introduced for the purpose. An exchange rate policy of maintaining a stable relationship with the mark and the franc eventually within the ERM (European Exchange Rate Mechanism) seemed to be the precursor of closer financial unity – despite some disavowals of any idea of dropping the pound.

The Maastricht agreement of 1991 reinforced the ambivalence of British government policies. There was a renewed nominal commitment to greater European unity and the creation of a single European currency, the strengthening of the powers of the European Parliament and of European institutions vis-à-vis domestic ones. But this was combined with a UK opt-out from the Social Chapter and single currency provisions, and the securing of general assent to the principle of subsidiarity. The New Labour government has brought about a considerable change in the tone of UK participation in Europe but a degree of scepticism and pragmatism remains in the UK's attitude to the single European currency, attempts to legislate on welfare issues and the need for a European constitution.

The most distinctive features of the European Community include the existence of a dual executive, its complicated system of legislation by delegation and the coexistence of features characteristic of both federal states and of intergovernmental organisations.

The 'dual executive' consists of the Council of Ministers and the European Commission. The Council of Ministers consists of ministers from the member states' national governments voting by votes normally weighted roughly according to the population of each state (but with smaller independent states over-represented). Ministers vote as representatives of their governments. In the end they make the final policy decisions in this way. The European Commissioners are appointed for fixed periods from member states, but are supposed to act as a single body from a European perspective. Each commissioner heads a part of the European Civil Service. Jointly they propose legislation to the European Parliament and to the Council of Ministers and are responsible for the execution of policies decided by them.

The legislative process is uniquely complicated. It starts with extensive consultation by the commissioners who may call upon formal advisory councils including employers, trade unionists and others from all over Europe. After approval by the European Parliament through an elaborate committee system and in full session, proposals go to the Council of Ministers. At present most proposals require a 'qualified majority' of votes to be approved (requiring the support of most of the larger states). Most important European legislation takes the form of 'directives' which require national parliaments to pass national legislation to implement them by a certain date, thus effectively adding a further stage to the process. Should national legislation not be sufficient to implement the directive then the Commission would have to take the national government concerned before the European Court. In the event of disagreement between Commission, Parliament and Council, then measures may shuttle between them and special majorities may be required to override recalcitrant parties.

In many, but not all, matters the Council of Ministers has the final say. In this respect the Community is like a conventional international organisation. But in having a directly elected parliament with substantial budgetary powers and a Court of Justice with authority to decide appeals from national courts on the interpretation of Community law, it is in a similar position to a federal state.

Since the Maastricht agreement of 1991, these 'Community' arrangements for co-operation on a wide range of economic matters are supplemented by the so-called second and third 'pillars' of co-operation through direct intergovernment agreements on a common foreign and security policy and on justice and home affairs (e.g. co-operation to catch international drug rings and illegal immigration). The three pillars together constitute the European Union.

In the long run, crucial technological developments are likely to require massive investments, probably by multinational companies and states with massive economic resources. Effectively the United States and, possibly, Japan are the only political and economic systems with big enough tax bases and consumer markets to develop on their own massive technological innovations such as space research, genetic engineering or super computer networks with built-in artificial intelligence. Individual European countries left to compete on their own (with the possible exception of Germany now it is united) will become (as to some extent they already are) merely important subsidiary areas for competition between US and Japanese 'multinationals'. Only if Europe is a real single market and its research and development effort is genuinely pooled can it hope to remain an area where first-rate scientific, technological and hence industrial development on a substantial scale takes place.

Politically too the existence of a directly elected European Parliament can hardly be reversed. Once constituted, given the dominant traditions of representative democracy, the European executive must, in the long term, become responsible to it (or to the people directly). A democratically constituted European executive will find itself the focus for enormous expectations for a peaceful, prosperous and united Europe. Already the EU has been expected to play a peace-making role in the former Yugoslavia – even though Yugoslavia has never been a part of the EU.

It is possible that Britain might withdraw from the 'United States of Europe'. This is, however, unlikely since the majority of its trade is with the EU and virtually all the inward investment it attracts is because Britain is inside the EU trading area. As the euro becomes better established, London may find it difficult to remain the prime European financial centre if sterling is retained.

An analogy can be drawn between European developments at the present time and American history in the period 1776–1789. Following the Declaration of Independence in 1776, the thirteen former American colonies agreed to a 'confederation'. Because of an insistence on the sovereignty of the individual states, Congress was without adequate executive, judicial or financial machinery with which to attempt to manage the security and economy of North America. Congress's failure to meet the expectations its very existence generated led to the adoption of the present constitution in 1789.

Similarly the prospect of the accession of ten additional countries to the EU and a 'democratic deficit' in existing institutions led to the formation of a European Constitutional Convention which reported in 2003 and which led to the proposal for a new constitution for Europe in 2004. This included a Declaration of Rights, a strengthened presidency of the Council of Ministers, changes in the numbers of commissioners for each state and more decision making by a qualified majority (on a modified basis) in the Council of Ministers.

The defeat of referenda on the proposed constitution in France and the Netherlands slowed the reform process but it seems likely that some of the measures proposed in the constitution – including a strengthening of the presidency and moves to include more policy areas in weighted majority decision making will be adopted piecemeal.

LOCAL GOVERNMENT

The institutions of local government often reflect, in large measure, those of central government. Thus, in well-established Western liberal democracies such as the United States and the UK, there is a long tradition of local representation and autonomy. One of the author's own town (Poole, in Dorset) has recently celebrated the 750th anniversary of the granting of a charter to its leading townsfolk by the local Lord of the Manor, establishing rights to hold markets and regulate its port. In the United States a sturdy tradition of local government was established even in the colonial era and on this was built the later development of state and national autonomy and democracy. The reverse applies in China and the former Soviet Union where the mechanisms of national one-party pseudo-democracy were reproduced at local level with large-scale participation masking central dictation of virtually all local decisions and the previously imperial bureaucracies held sway.

In some places, however, there may be conflict between national and local styles of political behaviour, which complicates the establishment of a viable local government system. To give an extreme example, the British in colonial Nigeria set up a system of 'Native Administration' designed to lead the way to a modern local government system. This was based upon the strategy of modernising and gradually democratising the administration of local 'traditional rulers'. In the north of Nigeria this had the unfortunate effect of reinforcing the power of some of the more conservative elements in a rapidly changing society. In parts of the east of the country, so-called

'Warrant Chiefs' had to be invented to attempt to impose an authoritarian (colonial) system on what was already an egalitarian society vitally receptive to change (Wraith, in Mackintosh, 1966: 212–267).

The degree to which the structure of local government is determined by central government also varies from one state to another. In parts of the United States both the boundaries and internal organisation of local government are almost entirely a matter for local decision. In France all Communes are required to have a mayor as chief executive who, whilst locally elected, also functions as an official of the central government; at departmental and regional level the chief executive is an appointed official of the national Ministry of the Interior. Communal and departmental boundaries, however, have remained relatively stable and local commitment to them is quite high. In the UK, although there is perhaps less interference in the internal organisation of authorities, there has been a great deal of change by central government in the overall structure, powers and boundaries of local authorities since the Second World War.

There is also a striking variation in the internal organisation of local authorities. The traditional UK arrangement centred around a series of only loosely co-ordinated committees of elected members, each of which supervised the work of one or more departments headed by professional specialists. In contrast many US councils have much stronger executives consisting either of professional city managers or directly elected mayors. The French pattern in which the chief executive is provided by the central government is also to be found quite widely – especially in ex-colonial areas. In recent years the British trend has been towards smaller and more tightly co-ordinated committees and a style emphasising the development of a strategic management team of professional officers. The Blair government's endorsement of experiments in the development of executive mayors was an interesting move in what might be interpreted as a more participative direction. In most cases, however, local authorities have moved toward small 'cabinets' of local councillors in parallel with the professional management teams. The New Labour administration has paid lip service to the idea of greater autonomy for local authorities, but, in practice, this usually has to be paid for by demonstrating capacity to meet Whitehall performance targets.

Just as the structure of local government frequently reflects the central government, so broadly there is a tendency for local politics to be a microcosm of national politics. Thus multi-party politics predominate in Italian and French localities, two-party politics in US communities, one-party politics in China, Cuba and in many parts of the South. However, in competitive party systems, because party differences often have a regional aspect, there is a tendency to greater variation at local level. Thus some parties – such as the Labour Party in parts of Wales and the Democrats in the US South in the days of segregation – may have a virtual monopoly in some areas so that effective politics takes place between factions within the local majority party. In other areas what are minor parties nationally may be important competitors with the established parties on a local level – as with the Liberals in New York and South West England. Furthermore some parties may have a purely local existence – as with 'Independent' groups on English councils. Thus one- or multi-party systems can be found locally even where the national system is a two-party one.

Local governments may develop distinctive constitutional conventions of their own so that, in the British context, for example, cabinets may be drawn from the parties roughly in proportion to their numbers on the council in one authority, but all from the majority group in another.

Although there is often a tendency to refer to a hypothetical past when 'politics' was absent from local government, the historical record does little to bear this out. For instance, in England before the Reform Act of 1832 each borough nominated two Members of Parliament in various ways – but usually linked in some degree to municipal government. Consequently municipalities were strongly partisan. For instance, the pre-reform council of Leicester actually bankrupted itself as a result of the legal bills incurred in creating enough freemen 'of sound constitutional principles' (i.e. Tory voters) to swing the 1830 election the 'right' way. Where local councils are not divided in a partisan way, this is often a sign of control of the area by a strong conservative elite, as in many of the old rural English counties and in some 'tribal' areas in former colonies.

Central control of local government may vary from the situation in the United States where the concept is hardly recognised, to situations in some countries in the South where the concept of independent action by local government is similarly virtually unthinkable. An important element in the relationship is the cultural one of the expectations of the parties to the relationship. Another dimension is a legal one. In the UK until recently the concept of *ultra vires* limited local authorities to those actions explicitly authorised by law (that is laws passed by the central parliament). On the other hand, the assumption in the United States is that governmental powers not explicitly granted to the centre by the constitution belong to the states or the people. In France and in many continental European countries communes are seen as having an inherent right to act on behalf of their inhabitants in the absence of legal restraints.

From a financial point of view central control over budgets obviously restricts localities. The need for French councils to have their budgets approved by the next highest level of authority used to be regarded as evidence of their relative inferiority by British writers on local government. However, the current system of financing UK local government is based effectively on the central government setting spending limits for local authorities and penalising them through the system of financial grants from the centre if they do not abide by a central civil service judgement of their needs. US local governments seldom have such limitations – although they may be required to submit large-scale borrowing to a referendum of local voters.

Related to this is the important question of the tax base allowed to local government. Again the US freedom to set effective levels of sales and property taxes might be compared favourably with the very limited powers now allowed to UK councils – which cannot even set their own rates of taxes on local business premises. Similarly in many parts of the South the major constraint on the growth of effective local government is the lack of any realistic source of independent income.

The case for more power for local governments than they achieve in most states outside of the USA is a persuasive one. The implementation of central policies by local authorities allows local people to make some independent assessment of relative local needs and priorities and allows local circumstances to be taken into account more quickly – more rational policies which suit local needs should ensue. The democratic principle of 'subsidiarity' has already been discussed – local decision making allows more participation by those affected and citizen education, training and loyalty is facilitated. 'Small is beautiful'!: the greater the autonomy accorded local authorities the less central co-ordinating machinery is required. Councils allow the expression of community identity and act as advocates for their communities to other bodies. They help preserve social diversity. They present an opportunity for policy and management experimentation, innovation and learning. Division of power in a democracy is desirable: 'Power tends to corrupt, absolute power corrupts absolutely' (Acton, 1887).

CONCLUSION

In the first decade of the twenty-first century, representative liberal democracy appears to be the globally dominant form of government. In many parts of the world, however, the institutions of liberal democracy are still either absent or so recently established that their capacity to endure in the face of economic difficulties, internal corruption, ethnic strife or international confrontation must be seriously open to doubt.

Even in those parts of the world where liberal democracy seems more securely established, there are many questions still to be settled as to the units and levels upon which it should operate. Nor have we yet examined in any depth the considerable variation in the nature of democratic institutions – this is the subject of the next chapter.

RECOMMENDED READING

Dinan, Desmond, 1998, *Ever Closer Union? An Introduction to the European Union*, 2nd. edn, Basingstoke, Macmillan
  Useful standard text on the European Union.

Hague, Rod and Harrop, Martin, 2004, *Comparative Government and Politics*, 6th edn, Basingstoke, Macmillan
  Useful text covering much of the ground in chapters 5, 6 and 7.

Peterson, John and Shackleton, Michael, 2006, *The Institutions of the European Union*, Oxford, Oxford University Press
  Discusses the individual institutions of the European Union and the process of integrating political interests through them.

Wilson, D. and Game, C., 2002, *Local Government in the United Kingdom*, 3rd edn, Basingstoke, Palgrave Macmillan
Excellent up-to-date text on UK local government experience.

Zimmerman, Joseph F., 1992, *Contemporary American Federalism: The Growth of National Power*, Leicester, Leicester University Press
An overiew of the division of power amongst different levels of government in the home of federalism.

WEBSITES

http://www.cia.gov
CIA: Central Intelligence Agency includes up-to-date statistics in the World Factbook (downloadable free).

http://new.prio.no/CSCW-Datasets/Data-on-Governance/The-Polyarchy-dataset
Measures the extent of democracy, participation and competition in 187 countries.

http://www.federalism.ch
Institute of Federalism, Fribourg, Switzerland includes working papers and online federalism games.

http://www.europa.eu.int/index-en.htm
European Union.

http://www.uta.fi/valagos/links.html
Index of local government websites.

http://www.poole.gov.uk
Poole, Dorset's local government website.

7

DEMOCRACY

THIS CHAPTER . . .

considers the meaning of democracy and examines critically some of the formal and informal institutions of liberal democracy. These include elections, constitutions and the three branches of government: executive, legislative and judicial. Informal institutions focus on the system of communication between government and people through interest groups, political parties and the instruments of mass communication.

HOW CAN GOVERNMENT BE 'DEMOCRATIC'?

It is not inevitable that the government of a state should be 'democratic'; the existence of authoritarian, fascist, military, theocratic or traditionalist regimes cannot be dismissed as impossible anachronisms even in the twenty-first century. However, for the purposes of this discussion, it is convenient to assume the desirability of popular government – what President Lincoln described in the Gettysburg address as 'Government of the People, by the People, and for the People'. We ask what values such governments may be thought to serve and the extent to which existing democratic institutions realise them.

Lincoln's memorable definition may suggest three key elements of democracy. First, that it is 'of' the people not only in the sense of being 'over' all the people but that it derives its legitimacy from their commitment to it (government by consent). Second, that it is 'by' the people in the sense that they participate extensively in governmental processes. Third, that it is 'for' the people in that it seeks to realise the common welfare and safeguard the rights of individuals.

These principles would be widely accepted not only in the liberal democracies of Western Europe, North America and Australasia, but even in communist countries and single-party nationalist regimes in the 'South'. Much controversy remains, however, about the interpretation of these principles and their relative weight where they conflict. Thus liberal democracies stress the safeguarding of individual rights, and the idea of the rule of law. Communist regimes stress popular participation and the pursuit of the interests of the common man. Populist nationalist leaders stress their legitimacy as the leaders by consent of the people and as interpreters of the national destiny (MacPherson, 1966).

PARTICIPATION AND DIRECT DEMOCRACY

The oldest recorded form of democracy is that of the Greek city states, notably Athens. Important decisions were taken by all the citizens (although excluding foreigners, women and slaves – most of the population) in a popular assembly by majority vote. Government officials ('magistrates') were chosen on a temporary basis by lot. It is worth stressing that the taking of decisions on behalf of the population by elected representatives was regarded by the Greeks as an 'aristocratic' or 'tyrannical' form of rule depending on the quality and behaviour of those elected.

Indeed, Aristotle regarded majority voting as a poor form of government because popular decisions were unrestrained by any legal protection of (rich) minorities. It is also worth considering whether, for instance, the lynching of even an obviously guilty person by the majority of the population in a small community can properly be regarded as 'democratic'. In other words, majority rule and popular participation may conflict with the ideas of justice, individual rights and efficiency and effectiveness.

In Athens, because the majority of citizens had to be convinced if the community were to act, it seems a very high standard of information and debate was often obtained alongside great commitment and loyalty to the state. In such a system individual citizens are encouraged to inform themselves, treated as moral beings with self-determination and are likely to identify with the community and its political life.

It is often thought that such direct democracies are no longer possible with the increased complexity and scale of human societies. However, decision making by the majority of citizens is still practised in Switzerland, and in several states of the United States. In Switzerland, on the initiative of a fixed proportion of the electorate or a minimum number of voters, a referendum must be held on any issue, and the result has the status of a constitutional amendment. In several US states similar arrangements apply particularly on major financial decisions. Again where decisions are made in this way there is commonly a very widespread popular debate on all the issues raised.

Such a situation should perhaps be distinguished from the much more common constitutional device of allowing or requiring the government to call a popular vote on particular issues. The problem is that such a referendum on specific issues may easily be converted into a 'plebiscite' – a vote of confidence in the government proposing the vote. Strong populist leaders, such as France's General de Gaulle or Russia's President Yeltsin, have often used such a device to strengthen themselves against parliamentary opponents.

Today the size of modern democracies is no longer a barrier to the exercise of Athenian democracy. The existence of mass communication, the Internet and the possibility of electronic polling through the telephone or other networks means that 'teledemocracy' is now a possibility (Arterton, 1987; Saward, 1993; Budge, 1996; Arblaster, 2002). In any case it is still possible to exercise this form of control in small communities on a local level (e.g. British and New England parish meetings).

The idea of involving as many citizens as possible in the governmental process remains an important element in the concept of democracy, helping to support the maintenance of the local government system and the jury in Anglo-American democracies. The former USSR attempted to support its 'democratic' credentials by the election of large numbers of citizens to Soviets (Councils), electoral commissions, factory and collective farm councils and the like.

CHOOSING RULERS

In modern liberal democracies, however, democracy is often thought of primarily in terms of the opportunity for citizens to freely choose their rulers at periodic intervals, rather than to make governmental decisions for themselves.

There seems little doubt that forcing rival groups of potential rulers to compete for popular votes is an important element in ensuring that modern democracies maintain some responsiveness to the interests and desires of their electorates. For lack of this simple device many Third World and communist regimes appear to have lost contact with their citizens and consequently have collapsed.

Free elections seem to be something which cannot be dispensed with in a democracy – and an institution which is more difficult to implement than those who take it for granted might suspect (Mckenzie, 1958). A secret ballot, freedom from blatant election bribery and corruption, parties free to campaign anywhere in the country and a reasonably unbiased electoral system seem simple and obvious devices in those countries which have achieved them. However, experience in Eastern Europe and Africa, Asia and Latin America in recent years has shown how difficult such conditions are to achieve.

More subtle factors, however, can be seen to affect the effectiveness and responsiveness of democracies; in particular the extent to which the political parties and constitutional arrangements offer a real choice to the electorate. In this respect the USA might be thought to be less 'democratic' than Britain. We should also consider the extent to which the educational and economic condition of the mass of the electorate makes effective political participation by them a real possibility.

ELECTORAL SYSTEMS

Many discussions of liberal democracy place great emphasis on the range of electoral systems used and the assessment of the merits of each. In particular the merits of 'proportional representation' versus 'first-past-the-post' systems have often been debated at length. Fascinating though the topic may be to many political scientists and armchair reformers, it seems of much less fundamental importance than many of the less discussed issues involved in achieving free elections which we have just considered.

In fact, few electoral systems are either based simply on a single-member constituency 'first-past-the post' system traditionally used in British general elections, or on a national constituency divided proportionally between the parties as in Israel. Many single-member constituency systems incorporate ways of ensuring (or increasing the likelihood of) a majority at constituency level. Thus France has a second ballot in any constituency in which no candidate gains an overall majority. The USA has a preliminary 'Primary' election within each of the two major parties so only two serious candidates are likely to emerge for the election proper. In Australia voters record preferences for candidates in order so that the votes of the weaker candidates can be transferred until one candidate obtains a majority. Most 'proportional' systems have area or regional (rather than national) constituencies, several combine single-member constituencies with a national 'pooling system' (e.g. Germany and in elections for the Scottish Parliament and Welsh Assembly). Almost all have a minimum quota of votes to obtain seats in the legislature.

It is worth echoing the conclusion of Rae's excellent (1967) study: that all existing electoral systems are less than perfectly proportional (even Israel has a minimum vote quota for a party to be represented in parliament) and that the major factor affecting proportionality is the size of the constituency employed. To achieve perfect proportionality between seats allocated in parliament and votes for each national party a single national constituency would have to be employed. However, the cost of this might well be thought too high in terms of breaking the links between individual voters and specific representatives – and the power it would give to national party organisations in determining candidates' places on the national list.

Relatively less proportional systems, like Britain's, may be defended as yielding strong or stable government. In recent years the authors have felt that 'strong' government has come to mean a government which is rather too unrepresentative and unresponsive in Britain, a criticism levelled at both the Thatcher and Blair administrations. Certainly, however, the viability of the executive produced by the system must be weighed in assessing such systems, alongside the links to constituencies and the proportionality of the legislature. To some degree the assessment of electoral systems must depend upon current political circumstances and the political preferences of the assessor.

In the abstract the preferred solution might be to achieve rough proportionality and a specific link between each voter and an elected representative with area constituencies (perhaps of four or five members) elected by single transferable vote. This is the Irish system also favoured by the British Liberal Democrats. However, it is worth stressing that a major consideration in 'electoral engineering' should be the political credibility of the system with the electorate as a whole. A simple long-established system, which is widely accepted, should only be sacrificed for an overwhelming advantage. An incomprehensible and complicated system, seen as unnecessarily favouring the political forces that recently initiated it, would be a poor exchange for such a system even if it were technically superior in the sense of being more proportional.

The electoral system is at the heart of the credibility (legitimacy) of modern democracies, so that it is important to try to establish as broad a consensus as possible about the system employed. Such situations as occurred in post-war France in which major changes of government bring about a consequent change in the electoral system are liable to breed cynicism and apathy on the part of the electorate (Campbell, 1965).

It may be helpful to clarify some of the terminology relating to political institutions which we have been employing in this and the preceding chapter. In particular some further discussion of each of three arms of government – executive, legislative and judicial – seems desirable.

THE EXECUTIVE

The executive, in the broad sense, includes the head of state, the political members of the government and the civil servants who staff the offices of state. It not only enforces the laws, but also proposes changes in them to the legislature and conducts foreign relations. Less formally the executive must often act to symbolise the unity of the country and provide leadership within the political system.

Different systems differ greatly in how roles are distributed amongst the executive, and indeed how large the executive is and, therefore, how many people control the levers of power. As we have seen, formal head of state duties such as convening and dissolving the legislature, receiving distinguished visitors, presenting honours and decorations, signing legislation into law, opening new buildings and the like may be reserved to a hereditary sovereign or a retired distinguished 'statesman'. Such kings, queens, presidents or governors customarily lead uneventful (if comfortable) lives. In times of crisis, however, they may have to arbitrate on which leading politician is most likely to command a parliamentary majority if the current prime minister loses the confidence of the legislature.

Alternatively such largely symbolic roles may be combined with the job of leading the day-to-day government of the country. Where the symbolic and real leadership are combined (as in the US presidency) this may give the head of government a boost in his or her relationships with other national politicians. However, placing a practising politician in such a powerful position may increase the possibility of misbehaviour by the head of state and disillusioning the citizenry, as the problems of presidents Nixon and Clinton suggest.

As we saw in the previous chapter, another important difference between executives is in the mechanisms whereby their responsibility to the nation is expressed and how they are selected. The presidential model with the direct selection by popular vote of the head of government increases the democratic legitimacy of the executive and helps to ensure that each head of government constructs a majority national coalition of supporters. The 'down-side' of such an arrangement is that such figures cannot be easily removed should they lose touch with their constituencies. In the USA, Congress can only impeach the president with great legal difficulty in the event of gross misconduct. In parliamentary systems the prime ministers may be less well known and supported but can only retain office for so long as they command a legislative majority. If no obvious national majority exists then a process of bargaining between parties in the legislature can produce one.

The number of political posts (that is jobs to which politicians are appointed by the head of government) in the national executive may vary from something like 5,000 posts in the United States to only a few hundred in Britain. (This excludes appointments to QUANGOs –

quasi autonomous national (or non-)governmental organisations.) Clearly the fewer the number of 'political' posts, the more top civil service jobs are likely to have a policy content. Virtually all systems have a large civil service of permanent state employees recruited on 'merit' (normally via special competitive examinations or on the basis of professional or academic qualifications). Their role will vary from country to country. The British Civil Service is relatively unusual in its degree of unity with a stress on 'generalist' administrators who may move from department to department. In France and the United States, for instance, there is a greater tendency to recruit say agronomists for the Agriculture Department, accountants for the Audit Department and so on.

It is also usual for modern executives to have some rule-making powers – 'delegated legislation' in the UK, 'decrees' in some continental European systems. These would normally cover detailed technical matters like the construction and use of regulations for motor vehicles, or the approving of by-laws by local authorities. As well as sponsoring a legislative programme, the executive often has a veto through a requirement that the head of state must sign each law for it to be valid.

THE LEGISLATURE

Legislatures in virtually all systems not only have a large formal role in making laws, but also have powers to investigate and, to some degree, control or influence the executive. A major element in this is usually the need for annual financial revenues and expenditures to be approved.

All legislatures work through a committee system – the more effective the legislature the stronger and more complex this tends to be. They usually also work through some variant of the UK system of three 'Readings' of proposed legislation ('Bills') in full session, and a committee stage. In many legislatures, but not usually in Westminster-style parliaments, the committee stage of the process is the most significant and takes place before the main debates in permanent specialised committees. In the Westminster model the committee stage usually takes place in specially set up ('ad hoc') so-called 'Standing Committees', whilst separate 'Select Committees' review areas of administration and finance.

The effectiveness of such committees and of legislators generally is also related to the number of support staff and ancillary facilities available. The US Congress has a wealth of these. Congress employs thousands of administrators, researchers and clerks as well as having a library which contains virtually all copyrighted material published in the United States and much material from overseas. The European Parliament is also well staffed – although part of the staffing is explained by the requirements of translation and operating in both Brussels and Strasbourg. In contrast MPs at Westminster until recently found it difficult to obtain even a desk for themselves, but do now have better office facilities in an expensive new building and an annual allowance sufficient to employ a handful of staff. Elected representatives have increasingly become professional politicians.

Historically the Anglo-American principle of 'no taxation without representation' has been of great importance in establishing legislative power over the executive. The need for the executive to apply for annual approval for most of its expenditure still dominates the legislative calendar in the UK with many key debates being on 'Supply Days'. However, detailed financial review now mainly takes place in Select Committees and the existence of a more or less automatic government legislative majority has weakened the effective financial power of Parliament over the executive. In the US there is a much more even struggle for control over budgetary matters, with Congress extracting political concessions on a regular basis in exchange for appropriations. It is worth remarking that the European Parliament has now achieved and asserted more control over the European Union budget than in the past – thus marking a movement toward full legislative status.

Legislative oversight and investigation of the activities of the executive varies in extent, depth and form. Parliamentary systems have the advantage that ministers as members of the legislature are in daily contact with 'backbench' MPs. In the UK particularly there is a well-developed tradition of oral questions to ministers (including the prime minister) from MPs in full sessions ('on the floor') of the House of Commons. In contrast in the United States the president normally only appears once a year to give the State of the Nation Address. However, US congressional committee investigations are probably more probing than those of Westminster (where the government has a built-in majority on each committee) and the president faces frequent media interrogation at press conferences.

Most legislatures are 'bicameral', that is they have two 'Houses'. In almost all, the 'lower' house (popularly elected by universal suffrage in geographical constituencies) is the one which has ultimate power and is the house to which (in parliamentary systems) the government is responsible. In federal systems the upper house represents the constituent states; in many other systems it is indirectly elected via panels of local government councillors. Other strange variants are to be found, however, such as the House of Lords in Britain, university representatives in Ireland and arbitrary division of elected representatives into two houses in Scandinavia.

The United States is unusual in that, if anything, the Senate (consisting of two senators from each of the fifty states) is the most important chamber. In practice the crucial decisions on legislation occur in bargaining between a joint committee of both houses and the president.

The effectiveness of legislative representation is affected by many other social and constitutional factors. Socially, for instance, most legislatures tend to over-represent men, lawyers, elite educational institutions and dwellers in the capital at the expense of women, non-lawyers, those without formal higher education and farm workers. Constitutionally there will be limits on the length of time for which legislators serve between elections and there may be formal or informal restrictions on the number of days the legislature meets.

One of the key questions asked about elected representatives is 'Who do they represent?' One school of thought suggests that elected representatives are 'mandated' to vote in line with their party's electoral pledges to the majority of their constituency. The Burkean tradition, based on the thoughts of Edmund Burke MP for Bristol in the eighteenth century, however, rejects this and suggests that elected representatives are independent and should weigh up the arguments for and against on policy issues (see Birch, 1964). The reality, as we shall see later in this chapter, is that elected representatives are influenced by a number of factors including their own party, pressure groups and constituents.

THE JUDICIARY

As was stated earlier, all liberal democracies endorse the principle of an independent judiciary but they vary as to the degree of power judges may exercise in constitutional matters. There are three main traditions in this respect.

UK judges are formally amongst the least powerful in being limited by the prerogative powers of the Crown, the doctrine of the sovereignty of Parliament, the lack of an enforceable declaration of rights (until 1998) and a tradition of deference to the executive in such matters as official secrecy and executive discretion. A further cause for concern is the secret process whereby judges are appointed by the government of the day. Such appointments are generally made from the ranks of the predominantly male and Oxbridge/public school educated, 'Queen's Counsel' who frequently represent the prosecution in criminal cases.

'Democratic' elements of the British system include the jury system, the presumption of the innocence of the accused and the principle that only activity formally proscribed by law can be illegal. In this 'common law' system highly professional lawyers interpret legislation according to the precedents set in previous cases. Despite the reservations expressed in the previous paragraph, it should be conceded that they have usually been sturdily independent within their defined limits, are only removed for gross misconduct and usually seek to interpret legislation as respecting the traditional rights of 'Englishmen'.

US (and many Commonwealth) judges, whilst still operating a common law system, however, are in a much stronger position in that they have established their powers of 'judicial review' of legislative and executive action in the light of a constitution which includes a 'Bill of Rights' for individuals. In the USA the political importance of federal judges is recognised by constitutional guarantees of independence once appointed, and an open and rigorous appointment process including endorsement by the Senate and hearings before its Judiciary Committee. At state and local level a separate judicial system operates in a similar way except that in some areas judges are elected (generally in non-partisan elections) for fixed periods.

In the continental (Napoleonic) tradition administrative courts in practice today often independently exercise a degree of control over executive action without parallel in Britain. The legal system in continental European countries is usually based upon a tradition going back to Roman law as modified by Napoleonic reforms. It places more stress on general principles (such as respect for constitutionally

recognised rights) and less on precedent. Trials are more of an inqui-
sitorial process controlled by the judge and less of a confrontation
between defence and prosecution lawyers. Separate constitutional
courts to review the constitutionality of laws or government decrees
are also to be found in a number of states. Legal education is often
much more concerned with public law and the training of public
administrators in continental European universities than is the case
in Britain and America where syllabuses are preoccupied with the law
of business contracts and crime.

CONSTITUTIONS AND CONSTITUTIONALISM

K. C. Wheare (1951) makes it clear that there are two main senses of
'constitution': first, the fundamental political institutions of a
country; second, a written document which usually defines these and
the rights of the citizens of the state. Clearly the United Kingdom
does not have the latter – although there are various legal documents
such as the Magna Carta, the Bill of Rights, and so on, which are seen
as helping to define its constitutional arrangements. The so-called
'unwritten' constitution is one of the distinctive features of only a
few democracies such as the UK, Israel and New Zealand.

As Wheare (1951) and others (e.g. Bogdanor, 1988) have shown,
liberal democratic constitutions usually have a variety of political
functions to perform. First, a symbolic and legitimising role in asserting and demonstrating the democratic credentials of the political
system concerned. Second, they are usually intended to protect and
conserve the fundamental political institutions they define and to
establish how they may be legitimately changed. Third, they are
intended to protect the fundamental rights of individual citizens.

More generally, from a broadly conservative and liberal perspective, it may be said that constitutional government means the
'government of laws, not of men' and that constitutions exist to limit
the power of the government of the day in the interests of democracy
and individual rights. Conversely, some socialist and radical interpretations would lay greater stress on the idea that constitutions
empower democratic governments to change society to achieve a
more just social order.

Where written constitutions exist, they often mark a revolutionary change in the political system, so that they may be originally

written in circumstances which emphasise a radical interpretation of constitutions. As the document ages, the emphasis may change to a conservative and legalistic interpretation of them. Britain's 'unwritten' constitution is usually defended as fulfilling the purposes of written constitutions more effectively than do these, more recent, documents. This has become a matter for considerable debate in Britain in recent years, however.

The symbolic role of the constitutional document is often of considerable importance. The US Constitution, for instance, is treated with some reverence. The first act of each president is to take an oath or affirmation that 'I will faithfully execute the Office of President of the United States, and will to the best of my ability, preserve, protect and defend the Constitution of the United States'. The French Declaration of the Rights of Man has a similar key role in French political culture.

It is often argued that Britain is unusual in embodying much of its constitution in 'conventions' – generally accepted rules that are not part of the law but whose breach may rapidly involve the breach thereof. These are seen as a more flexible way of expressing the constitution than a written legal document. However, conventions are, in fact, found in any mature constitutional system. For instance, in the USA, conventions surrounding the operation of the electoral college have effectively transformed what the founders intended as an indirect election of the president into a national popular vote.

RIGHTS AND CONSTITUTIONS

Most written constitutions incorporate some sort of declaration of the rights of citizens of the country concerned. However, there is an important distinction to be drawn between a mere declaration which is intended as a guide to politicians – and perhaps for judges to consider in their interpretation of laws – and a *justiciable* 'Bill of Rights' which is seen as a binding part of the constitution, superior in status to ordinary law and superseding it in case of conflict. A declaration may be of some symbolic political usefulness but a Bill of Rights is clearly more likely to be directly useful to ordinary citizens who consider their rights have been taken away or abused by the executive or legislature.

In the United States there is a long history of judicial use of the federal constitution to declare invalid both acts of the president and even federal legislation ('judicial review'). The main parts of the constitution which have been used in this way are the first ten amendments to the constitution (which include the rights to free speech and assembly as well as, more controversially, rights against self-incrimination and the right to bear arms). Also important are the Civil War amendments (13–15) against slavery and racial discrimination. These clauses are still more frequently invoked against state and local authorities. There are many examples of brave decisions by the Supreme Court to defend individual rights (say to free speech) in this way, but also of decisions by the court to prevent progressive social measures being implemented in the name of property rights. The political and social climate of the times has clearly influenced court decisions on many occasions: as, for instance, in 1896 (*Plessey* v *Ferguson*) when it declared that 'separate but equal' facilities for Negroes on a railway train were constitutional. Again in 1954 in *Brown* v *Board of Education of Topeka* when it declared that separate educational facilities for black students could not, in fact, be equal. In brief, a Bill of Rights takes power away from elected politicians (and bureaucrats) and transfers it to lawyers and may not always have the positive outcome its (often left-wing) British proponents anticipate.

Dicey (1959) and other traditionalist British constitutionalists, have preferred to rest their hopes for the protection of individual rights on a widespread attachment by all Britons to their ancient common law rights. These are reaffirmed in historical documents such as Magna Carta and the Bill of Rights, but not legally entrenched by them against later legislation. Asserting the responsibility of the executive to the popularly elected Commons for all its actions is seen as a major guarantee of rights for the individual. MPs have traditionally been prepared to defend the rights of their constituents of any party by interrogating ministers on their behalf in the Commons. Various features of the common law have been seen as a superior protection for individuals to either US constitutional guarantees or continental systems of special administrative courts. These features include the right to trial by jury, the right to silence in court and under police interrogation, and the writ (now judicial order) of habeus corpus ('produce the body'),

Britain does not have its own detailed Declaration of Rights (the Bill of Rights is a more limited document than its name might suggest), but it is a signatory to both the UN and European Declarations on Human Rights. The European document does have a commission and court to interpret it. It may be significant that the British government has been the subject of more actions than any other signatory (perhaps because of the relative lack of legal remedies within the UK until the 1998 Human Rights Act gave power to British courts to draw attention to such breaches). As a conventional international organisation, however, the European Court on Human Rights (which is not a part of the EU machinery) cannot enforce its judgements in Britain but must rely upon shaming the British government and legislature into action if it finds against UK authorities.

One Scandinavian institution which has been adopted in Britain to help defend individual rights against administrative error or invasion is a parliamentary Commissioner for Administration (the 'Ombudsman') who can independently investigate actions by government departments in cases of apparent 'maladministration'. (Similar ombudsmen have since been introduced in Britain for the health service, local government, banking, insurance and building societies.) This innovation was originally opposed as a breach of British parliamentary traditions but this objection was overcome by having the Ombudsman report to a parliamentary select committee.

The major limitations on the British parliamentary ombudsmen are that their jurisdiction is limited to errors of administration by a department for which a minister is responsible and that the ombudsmen can only recommend remedial action to that Minister. An 'unfair' piece of delegated legislation would be outside of the ombudsmen's jurisdiction. In Sweden, where the ombudsman originated, he or she has much stronger powers to insist on remedies and operates within a tradition of open government in which all government documents are open to inspection.

In much of continental Europe the tradition, stretching back to administrative reforms introduced by Napoleon, is for there to be a separate set of administrative courts. Whilst these were, no doubt, intended originally to be more sympathetic to the executive than ordinary local courts, they have now developed a sturdy judicial independence combined with considerable administrative expertise. In France, for instance, top graduates of the Ecole Nationale d'Administration (ENA) aspire to become members of the Council of State which is the superior administrative court. The ENA is perhaps the most prestigious postgraduate level educational institution in the country.

PLURALIST POLICY MAKING

Democratic constitutional arrangements can operate in a number of different ways in practice depending upon the use the government makes of the constitutional powers it has. Most democratic systems give numerous opportunities for the government to consult and listen to the electorate – the extent to which the government does so, and with which parts of the electorate, makes an enormous difference to the overall nature of the system. Three alternative ways of working such a system can be described as pluralism, corporatism and centralisation. We will also relate these accounts of how the constitution is being worked to the more general political theories of power introduced in Chapter 5 (pluralism, elite theories and – to some extent – Marxism).

In a politically pluralist system the legitimacy of a host of social and political interest groups is recognised. Ideally all have an equal chance to be involved in an open political process by which social decisions are reached through a process of widespread discussion, negotiation and compromise. In the last resort, where conflicts cannot be resolved into a consensus, the interests of the groups commanding majority support in the population as a whole will predominate, but strong feelings by groups most affected may count for more than weaker preferences by more numerous less affected groups. Substantial efforts will be made to facilitate tolerant compromises whereby different (for instance) religious, national or regional groups may adopt different solutions to the same problems. Authors such as Sir Ernest Barker (1961) see such pluralistic practices as intrinsic to modern democracy.

Public compromises between groups may often be struck in such systems in negotiations between different political parties within a governmental coalition (continental Europe), or in legislative bargaining or in compromises between the legislature and the executive (e.g. the USA). In the UK, a well-known constitutional authority, Sir Ivor Jennings (1957) has suggested that it is a convention of the constitution that representatives of interests affected by a Bill to be laid before Parliament should be consulted by the executive whilst it is being drafted. Groups also have the opportunity to table amendments to Bills as they go through the Commons and Lords.

Where different levels of government exist (e.g. European, British and local or federal, state and local) the pluralist principle is that of 'subsidiarity', as discussed at the end of Chapter 6. In the Netherlands such principles have become firmly entrenched with, on one interpretation, contemporary central government coalition governments being reduced to largely setting the procedural rules for local policy-making communities (Frissen, 1994).

CORPORATISM

It has been suggested that pluralism is too optimistic a description of policy making in many contemporary 'liberal democracies', and the alternative description of 'corporatism' was often thought to be appropriate in 1970s Britain. It is clear that much policy making in Britain is made behind closed doors – in Whitehall rather than at Westminster. This does not necessarily mean that no consultation takes place – an extensive network of official committees and unofficial contacts with representatives from professional, academic, managerial, trade union and other bodies does exist. It is customary, as Jennings indicated, to sound these out on policy proposals. Similarly much policy making in Brussels is made in closed negotiations between governmental delegations and by obscure discussions between the Commission and those interest groups organised on a European basis. In the United States, Congress is open to representations from any of the thousands of interest groups that exist in the country. However, only a relatively select group of interests have effective and permanent relationships with the key policy-making committees in their areas. Such interest groups often contribute heavily to the election expenses of key committee chairmen and women and exercise a virtual veto on key executive appointments in what Cater (1965) calls the 'sub-government' relating to their policy area.

'Corporatism' indicates that the consultation tends to be somewhat selective. Established bodies like the Confederation of British Industry, the American Medical Association and the French CGT

(Confédération Générale du Travail – the main trade union confederation) are regularly consulted, whilst grass-roots opinion is held to be virtually represented by these. Producer and metropolitan groups, perhaps inevitably, tend to be much more strongly represented than consumer and provincial interests. These somewhat cosy arrangements are reinforced by what some writers have called 'cooptation' whereby the favoured interest groups are even involved in administering the policies evolved, and were expected to sell them to their members. Some hostile critics have described such a system as 'fascism with a human face' (Pahl and Winkler, 1975) and suggested that all sorts of 'feather-bedding' of special interests result.

This description of liberal democracy as a corporatist system is, of course, a variety of what we earlier described as elite theory. Corporatism has been criticised for leading to cosy behind-the-scenes decision making, the so-called beer and sandwiches in smoke-filled rooms of the Harold Wilson era. Its proponents suggest that by bringing together the most powerful forces within the economy, long-lasting decisions can be made. Its opponents suggest that too many interests become alienated because their views are not given consideration.

CENTRALISATION

In Britain, Mrs Thatcher and the right wing of the Conservative Party were hostile to the idea of corporatism and denounced the growth of the QUANGOs which accompanied these practices. Rather than fascism, they saw these developments as the institutionalisation of a nanny socialist state. Their view was that too many decisions were being taken by vested interests (including the trade unions) behind closed doors at the expense of the citizen – when citizens (in the their role as consumers) could take these decisions through the market. Hence the need was seen for a radical reshaping and trimming of the state – requiring strong central political leadership to enforce budgetary control and attain efficiency through market forces.

Partly for these reasons, there was much less emphasis within the Thatcher/Major British Conservative governments on consultation, compromise and negotiation. Instead the emphasis was on the need for the government, having had its programme approved at the polls, to impress the electorate with its decisive implementation of a radical programme. Policies (such the Criminal Justice Act 1994) were pushed through against, or without the advice of, the professional groups most concerned.

Traditional British emphasis on the autonomy of local government was, as we have seen, also considerably undermined by a new stricter insistence on central financial control, the compulsory putting out to tender of many local services, taking schools out of local government control and other measures.

Of course a more hostile interpretation of these same developments is that the Conservative Party became more open in its advocacy of a straight capitalist system with its overriding of the interests of ordinary people in the interests of the capitalist 'bourgeoisie'. Miliband (1984) describes this as a slide from 'capitalist democracy' toward 'capitalist authoritarianism'. The trappings of democratic institutions can be combined with limitations which make them ineffective:

> trade unions might be allowed in such a regime providing they do not organise strikes. Parties might operate providing they were not subversive. Political activity might be possible, providing permission had been obtained for it. Newspapers would be allowed providing they did not foment 'class hatred' or 'spread disaffection'. . . . There would be censorship, but on a limited basis; on the other hand, self-censorship would be unlimited.
>
> (Miliband, 1984: 154)

Such developments do not, however, seem typical of trends in liberal democracies generally. Despite a widespread tendency towards the adoption of Thatcherite economic policies such as privatisation and monetarism, the predominant political style in Western Europe remains one of 'concertation' (see Chapter 4, p. 97) as epitomised in the Social Chapter of the Maastricht Treaty (1991) (see Chapter 6, p. 162).

In the 1990s and early twenty-first century this neo-liberal approach was challenged by what became known as the third way by centre or left-of-centre politicians such as Tony Blair in the UK, Bill Clinton in the USA and Gerhard Schröder of Germany. Such politicians critiqued the role of the state and how power is shared. For example the Labour government elected in 1997 in the UK introduced a form of devolution with the creation of national-level government in Scotland, Wales and Northern Ireland, and the potential for regional government in England. Yet at the same time the Labour government has been criticised by some commentators for centralising more power in the hands of Whitehall.

We are now witnessing a fascinating debate amongst the heirs of both the neo-liberal and third way approaches as one set of politicians is being replaced by a new set. For example what will be the attitude towards the location of power of Gordon Brown and David Cameron in the UK, the Democrat and Republican presidential candidates in the USA and Nicolas Sarkozy the president of France?

POLITICAL COMMUNICATION

We have considered democratic government in terms of the extent of popular participation in government, the extent to which the people can influence the choice of governors and the form which democratic institutions might take. Arguably more important than any of these, however, is the responsiveness of government to people's views and interests and even its capacity to leave well alone (to respect their rights).

In Chapter 1 we saw that Easton (1979) and many other writers view a political system as a mechanism for authoritative decision making linked by 'inputs' and 'outputs' to its environment. In this very simple model of politics two of the four elements (i.e. 50 per cent) are communication functions.

The responsiveness of governments involves, clearly, both governments receiving an accurate picture of the electorate's needs and the electorate having a clear picture of the government's activities. Communication between the government and the electorate and the government's monitoring of the objective effects of its policies and gathering information about policy alternatives are clearly central to a successful democratic system.

Even a very simple model of communication suggests some important questions. Who are the senders and recipients of the information? What quantity of information flows? Are the flows one way (simplex) or two way (duplex)? Are messages accurately encoded and decoded? Does 'noise' interfere with accurate reception? Does information overload prevent essential information being distinguished? In the space available only some of these points can be followed up here (but further reading can be found in *McQuail's Mass Communication Theory*).

In terms of the three models of how the constitution might work introduced earlier (centralisation, corporatism and pluralism), we can see that they involve different patterns of communication.

In a centralised pattern, most communication can consist of the government and the opposition broadcasting their views to the voters. At lengthy intervals the voters take a measured view of performance over the last four or five years and send back a simple message of acceptance or rejection at the polls (i.e. two simplex flows of information).

In the corporatist model these flows are supplemented by additional duplex flows of information between the government and selected corporate organisations. The government seeks to improve the quality of policy making by obtaining specialist advice, and negotiates some concessions with some of those most affected in return for assistance in implementing policies smoothly. The leadership of these organisations may, in turn, communicate with their members in a similar duplex flow or, alternatively, attempt to represent them 'virtually' by assuming a knowledge of their interests and views, taking a renewal of subscriptions as agreement to their interpretation of their members' interests.

In the pluralist model communication flows are most complicated and diffuse. There must be widespread knowledge not only of the government actions, but also of its intentions, so that these can be influenced before they are finalised. Elaborate duplex information flows connect not only the government and interest groups but also enable interest groups and political parties to negotiate compromises amongst each other, in order to influence events better. The government needs a good knowledge of public opinion if it is to generate a public consensus.

An examination of the activities of some of the political institutions which are usually thought of as playing a key role in political communication – political parties, pressure or interest groups, and the mass media – may suggest which model is most appropriate.

POLITICAL PARTIES

BOX 7.1   POLITICAL PARTIES

Political parties may be thought of as organised social groups that seek to wholly or partially take over the government of a country, usually by contesting elections.

(Authors' definition)

Political parties (Box 7.1) seek to take power for their leading members, either for the parties' own sake (the psychological, social and economic rewards of office), on behalf of some social group (e.g. labour, farmers, Protestants) or with some ideological objective in mind (e.g. national independence, socialism). We have seen that the names of parties are often a bad guide to their objectives; it is also worth stressing that most – probably all – parties are coalitions of people with different objectives in mind.

In most liberal democratic countries, the main obvious function of political parties is to contest elections – selecting candidates in constituencies, canvassing and organising voters, composing and delivering election addresses in local constituencies, and running local and national media campaigns. By offering voters candidates with commitments to certain policies (especially as identified by the national leadership) they make elections a choice by electors of public policies as well as the selection of councillors, legislators and (sometimes) mayors and presidents.

To understand such parties it is necessary to distinguish between the role of voluntary members in the constituencies, the activists, professionals who are employed by the local or national parties, and full-time paid and elected representatives. Most prominent of the latter are national parliamentarians but others may be elected to the state or regional legislature or be leading local councillors or mayors.

The ordinary members play only a small role in the electoral process. Even the most active do little more than pay their subscriptions or attend the odd social event. Occasionally they may act as 'tellers' at polling stations or deliver leaflets in their street. The activists who run constituency parties, act as local councillors and attend conferences or conventions, can communicate what they see as local 'grass-roots' feeling to their local legislators or at national party meetings (conventions, conferences, assemblies, etc.). In principle in Britain, Labour and Liberal Democrat Party national meetings of activists 'make' party policy, whilst the Conservative Party equivalent only advises the parliamentary leader. In practice all three are dominated by the parliamentary leadership and can be ignored by it when this is thought to be politically necessary. In the United States the only real (but very important) function of the national party conventions is the selection of presidential candidates.

In Britain, party professionals play only a small political role. On a local level they are almost exclusively concerned with keeping the party machine going (and paying their own salaries). On a national level, headquarters professionals differ in that they are officially responsible to the (parliamentary) party leader in the Conservative Party, but to the mass party executive in Labour and the Liberal Democrat parties. In the United States there are few significant party employees with each politician employing 'ad hoc' groups of image consultants, pollsters, public relations specialists ('spin doctors') and the like.

In practice, in virtually all liberal democracies, nationally elected politicians firmly control the national party machinery. In Britain, the parliamentary party (i.e. its members in the House of Commons) constitutes the core of the party and, for the government party in particular, is an important centre for duplex flows of information. Information is exchanged between MPs and government members, interest group representatives, party activists and ordinary 'constituents'. Government backbench MPs seek to increase their chances of re-election by popularising the government's message to the electorate and by alerting government 'Whips' to potential and actual problems. In the United States, incumbent Congressmen and women are at an enormous advantage in having sizeable professional staffs, free postage and travel facilities, and the opportunity to do individual constituents favours and build up good will.

In US parties, and in more conservative parties in Europe, there are often few party activists to contest control of the party machinery with elected officials and those who have, or hope to, benefit from their patronage. European socialist, Christian democratic and, to some extent, liberal parties may have larger numbers of activists, some of whom may be ideologically committed 'militants' with strong policy views. Whilst useful as enthusiastic canvassers or lickers of envelopes, such militants may be, from the professional's point of view, a source of internal conflict and resistance to the perhaps inevitable compromises of democratic politics. They may serve, however, from time to time, to inject an element of idealism and dynamic change into political systems.

'SPIN' AND POLITICAL MARKETING

In the United States the differences between parties have long been less marked than in Europe, and the system of primary elections for major party nominations encourages candidates to sell themselves as individuals rather than as party ideological standard bearers. It is not surprising that, in the home of capitalism, the use of techniques from commercial marketing and public relations should have been pioneered in politics. These techniques have now crossed the Atlantic with Britain's Labour Party 're-branding' itself as 'New Labour', and even the redoubtable former Conservative Prime Minister Mrs Thatcher consulted image consultants on how to dress and speak. More recently, the Conservative Party leader David Cameron has also been clearly trying actively to 'woo' key support by using marketing techniques.

New Labour, in opposition, imported US techniques of 'rapid rebuttal'. This involved management of the press and TV using a high-speed high-technology database of previous statements by both sides – 'Excalibur'. Rapid rebuttal means responding to your opponents' press releases/speeches/stunts, etc., in time to make the same press or broadcasting deadline so that you share the column inches or broadcasting time with them.

Some of the young advisers who helped Peter Mandelson to perfect the party organisation at Millbank Tower prior to victory in 1997 joined the new government as special advisers, and Alistair Campbell, a former tabloid newspaper political editor, was placed in charge of the prime minister's public relations efforts. New Labour MPs were given sessions advising them on how to project the right image in the television studio, and mobile telephones to which text messages containing the latest party line were transmitted. At times, the lines of demarcation between the activities of (civil servant) government information officers and those of special advisers and ministers were unclear.

Is this merely a perhaps unfortunate change of style by one party or something much more significant? Jennifer Lees-Marshment (2001) argues that Labour did much more than adopt new techniques. The party, in common with many other Western political parties, changed approach from an old-style 'product-oriented party' first to a sales-oriented party and finally to a market-oriented party (Table 7.1).

The transition from product orientation to market orientation mirrors changes made by many successful capitalist firms in recent years. This transition may also mark an era in which virtually all major democratic parties accept some form of capitalist system and attempt to work by its rules.

THE PERMANENT CAMPAIGN

The growth of spin and an increased emphasis on presentation did not just happen, it has been driven by the development of the permanent campaign. The phrase 'permanent campaign' was coined in 1980 by Blumenthal. Up to this point the orthodox view was that there was a distinction between campaigning and the business of governing. However, Ornstein and Mann (2000) have suggested that any such separation in politicians' behaviour before and after an election has been blurred, so that now *'Every day is Election Day'* (Heclo, 2000: 17). Coleman (2005) has suggested that the existence of the

Table 7.1 Political marketing and New Labour

Type of party	What they do	New Labour examples
Product oriented	Party does what it thinks is best (improving policy product)	Unilateralism and socialism
Sales oriented	Focusing on hard sell for the product	New logo, slicker party political broadcasts, rapid rebuttal
Market oriented	Giving consumers what they want	Focus groups, policy adjustment, no tax rises or sleaze

Source: Based on Lees-Marchment (2001)

permanent campaign has resulted in 'permanent communication' whereby political actors seek to dominate the political agenda every day through every available communication channel.

In order to win the media battle every day, governments, political parties and other political actors have increasingly relied on media management to dominate the news agenda. This is a competitive process where the protagonists are always looking for new techniques and technologies to gain an advantage.

The ever-increasing reliance on media management has fundamentally changed the relationship between politicians and the media. One school of thought suggests that the control of mass communication in the hands of an elite has led to a 'public relations state' (Deacon and Golding, 1994). Another view is that where journalists were deferential to politicians in the 1950s, they are now contemptuous (Barnett, 2002; McNair, 2003). A worsening relationship between journalists and politicians cannot help the transmission of political communication to citizens.

INTEREST GROUPS

BOX 7.2   PRESSURE OR INTEREST GROUPS

A pressure or interest group is a formal social group that differs from a political party in seeking only to influence the government – and not to become a formal part of it.

A pressure group can be said to be in the business of political communication. 'Interest group' may be the better term (Box 7.2) since it may well seek to influence the government more by persuasion and information than by threats of political reward or penalty. However, it would be surprising if interest groups were not listened to more closely if they represent large numbers of voters (trade unions), influential 'opinion formers' (doctors) or wealthy actual or potential contributors to party funds.

Where the interest is a professional or business one, then the group concerned may well have both specialised expertise which government policy makers may wish to draw upon and the capacity to aid the acceptance and implementation of the policy. Thus doctors' representatives (notably the American and British Medical Associations) will usually be drawn into making health policy, and will often then help to win acceptance within the health professions for an agreed policy to be implemented by their members. Most democratic governments of whatever party have tended to consult such groups and try to win them over to their policies. Although, in Britain, post-1979 Conservative administrations did on occasion seem to make a political point of not consulting groups that they regarded as having been 'feather-bedded' or over-influential in a liberal direction. It is worth pointing out, however, that consultation remains the rule. The Blair administration zealously sought business people to serve on high-profile advisory panels and appointed several business-oriented outsiders to important posts, including ministerial office.

In Britain, the links between Whitehall and such producer interest groups are institutionalised in the practice of each sector of industry having an official 'sponsoring' department. It is standard for such groups to be represented on official advisory committees and for their leaders and administrators to be on first-name terms with the corresponding higher civil servants. (So there are established unofficial communication patterns such as weekly lunches and regular telephone calls.)

Trade unions have generally speaking (i.e. post-1945) been seen within this framework – as groups that are automatically consulted, whose prominent leaders finish up in the House of Lords and are appointed to QUANGOs, etc. This was so under Conservative administrations such as those of Edward Heath and Harold Macmillan. In Labour administrations trade unions have benefited from the historic link between the various wings of the Labour 'movement'. In the past it was not unknown for trade union leaders to be appointed to Labour cabinets. Conversely some on both left and right have argued that trade union leaders have often been too pliant toward 'their' Labour governments – sacrificing their members' economic interests to the political success of the party. However, recent Conservative Thatcherite administrations were less ready to accord automatic deference to trade union leaders despite their (in some cases) nominal millions of 'followers'. Whilst the New Labour government has been more friendly to trade unions than the

Conservatives and has appointed many trade unionists to lower-level patronage posts, it has sought, for image-building purposes, to avoid the appearance of automatic deference to them, of which some previous Labour governments were accused.

In all democratic systems non-producer interest groups – residents affected by planning proposals, consumers of both private and public goods and services, housewives, carers and so-called 'cause' groups that operate more altruistically on behalf of others seem less effective than producer groups. In Britain groups such as the Royal National Institute for the Blind, Greenpeace working for the environment, the Consumers' Association and more especially the many local 'cause' groups generally have less effective and permanent communication links with Whitehall. Such groups may only hear of legislative or administrative decisions after they have been made, rather than whilst they are being considered. This then makes it much more difficult – if not downright impossible – to influence the decisions concerned. Even trying to amend a Bill in Parliament when it is still under consideration is a relatively late stage to try to affect events. By this time the prestige of the government may have been attached to the Bill and amendments may affect compromises reached between civil servants or ministers and other more established groups.

The rise to increasing prominence in the UK of professional lobbyists (Moloney, 1996) has highlighted the importance of informal links between ministers, civil servants, parties and interest groups. The more policy is made in private at the pre-legislative stage by informal coteries of political advisers, professional lobbyists retained by wealthier and established groups and small factions of politicians who are in favour with the head of government, the less responsive and democratic it will seem. If some lobby groups attain preferential access to government through financial support to parties, or by retaining well-connected professionals, then this clearly constitutes a move away from pluralism toward corporatism in the political system.

THE MASS MEDIA

Confining ourselves here to the existing conventional mass media – press, radio and television – we are mainly concerned with broadcasting: the centralised origination of simplex flows of information to large numbers of recipients whose only choice is to choose another channel, 'listen' or switch off.

In this context we might ask: what information on political life is available to be reported? How many channels of such information are available? Who controls and edits the transmission of information by these channels in whose interests? How do potential recipients of the messages react to them? Do the mass media represent the masses to the elite?

If the media do not know what the government is doing then clearly they cannot report it to the electorate. In this respect democratic countries vary greatly in the access reporters and citizens can obtain to information on government decision making. At one extreme, the Swedish tradition of 'open government' requires virtually all decision making to be publicly documented. At the other, in the past the British tradition of official secrecy has made the assumption that executive deliberations will be kept private unless a positive decision has been made to release information. The United States has adopted the opposite assumption with its Freedom of Information Act which requires federal government agencies to reveal any document at the request of any enquirer unless reasons such as national security or personal confidentiality can be plausibly advanced against this. In Britain a non-statutory Code of Practice on Access to Government Information (April 1994) rather half-heartedly moved in the open government direction. It allowed for numerous exceptions – including advice to ministers and anything that could be the subject of a public enquiry. The Blair government was pledged to introduce a stronger statutory measure, but the legislation that resulted (the Freedom of Information Act 2000) has been criticised as weaker than the Code. The Act has been implemented slowly and without enthusiasm, with new financial and administrative barriers to its use already being proposed by the government in 2006.

The extent to which journalists have a tradition of, and are rewarded for, hard-hitting investigative journalism is also of importance. In the United States there is a long tradition of such 'muck-raking' journalism culminating in the 'Watergate' investigations of Bernstein and Woodward (1974) which contributed to the ignominious resignation of President Nixon.

Another problem with political communication patterns from a democratic point of view is the relatively limited number of effective 'channels'. In Britain for instance there are only five terrestrial television channels, BBC Radio (these having only two news services between them), a largely a-political commercial radio sector, a dozen or so national daily newspapers and, effectively, one evening newspaper per city. The previous government encouraged the growth of more commercial radio channels and of cable and satellite TV, but the effectiveness of these as major independent sources of news seems fairly limited at present. In effect most citizens probably rely on, at most, four major political news channels – BBC, ITN (Independent Television News), their customary national daily and possibly a local evening paper or free weekly. In principle, of course, anyone is free to set up an alternative newspaper, or to tender for a TV franchise: in practice this means anyone with several million pounds to lose.

In the United States, of course, a much greater number of television and radio channels are available, with three major groupings of television providers and also CNN providing news services by cable and increasingly over air. Public service broadcasting is also available in many parts of the country. As a result of economic and geographical factors, however, newspapers tend to be rather parochial and uncompetitive outside of major metropolitan areas.

The digital revolution in communications technology may well be set to profoundly modify this picture. Digital technology in television and radio makes possible the broadcasting of many more programmes simultaneously, and it democratises access to them by reducing production and distribution costs as well as creating a rise in the demand for material to broadcast of all sorts. This has encouraged, in Britain, a rapid growth in the availability of digital terrestrial TV, including additional news channels and the broadcasting of parliamentary debates direct. By 2008, in the UK, and 2009 in the US, analogue TV will be switched off and only digital will be available.

In contrast to the future potential of modern technology is the prosaic reality of many countries today, particularly in the South. Here the least satisfactory arrangement from a democratic point of view obtains – the only effective mass communication channels are the state radio and television channels

The more 'channels' available the less we need to worry about the content and control of any one of them, since consumers can exercise influence over them by selecting them or not. Arguably, with so few effective major channels at present in most liberal democracies, the control and editing of those that exist becomes a matter for greater public concern. This is especially so when we consider that, in Britain for instance, satellite television and three of the major national daily newspapers are all under the control of a company grouping dominated by one man (Rupert Murdoch).

In Britain it has been accepted for many years that, because of their near monopoly situation, the BBC and ITV television channels should be carefully regulated to ensure that their output is reasonably politically balanced. This has mainly taken the form of ensuring that the views of the official opposition get exposure in replies to ministerial broadcasts, party political broadcasts, representation on discussion programmes, etc. Minor parties and minority groups such as gays, racial and religious minorities have less institutionalised exposure, but there is recognition that they should have some access to publicly financed or licensed communication channels. Further controls have been thought appropriate in the interests of children (rules about what can be broadcast before 9.00 p.m.), decency (the Broadcasting Standards Council) and, formerly, anti-terrorist measures (no live interviews with the IRA).

In contrast, the newspaper industry has, in most democratic countries, been thought to be sufficiently 'regulated' by the existence of free competition and the laws of libel. In Britain only the theoretically unofficial 'D' (Defence) notice system can be seen as attempting to regulate the distribution of politically sensitive information – and this is supposed to be restricted to matters vital to the security of the realm, not politically embarrassing information.

From the left, the present system in Britain seems most inadequate in its failure to secure political balance – with most national newspapers up to the mid-1990s clearly editorially favouring the Conservatives and only the (wavering) Mirror Group supporting Labour. Since running a national newspaper is a large financial operation, the owners and managers of such operations naturally tend to favour capitalist/Conservative values. However, the Labour government has received a level of support from most newspapers at various times since it was elected in 1997, most famously with Rupert Murdoch's News International newspapers generally encouraging a Labour vote in the 1997 and 2001 general elections. From the right, in Britain anxiety has centred upon 'irresponsible' tabloid intrusions into the private lives of both the rich and famous (including Royalty and politicians) and more ordinary people – including victims of crime and people with untypical sexual proclivities.

The Press Complaints Commission (a voluntary industry body) has been urged to introduce greater self-regulation under the threat of statutory controls. One difficulty is to find a formula for protecting the legitimate privacy of ordinary people that will not prevent the media from revealing misconduct by public figures, which affects their accountability for their deeds.

One defence which can be made for the present arrangements, in both broadcasting and national newspapers, is that the actual editing and presentation of news is done by professionals who, in order to maintain circulation/audience figures, must respect the values of a plural society and pursue 'news values'. One organisation cannot afford to neglect or distort awkward news because it will be rapidly and accurately reported elsewhere. In this respect the BBC in Britain can be seen as an important 'quality control' standard against which other organisations are judged – whilst the possibility of pro-establishment bias by the BBC is balanced by the existence of maverick organisations such as the *Sun* and *Private Eye*.

There does seem to be some strength in this argument (and it must be remembered that journalists themselves are often to the left of their managers and proprietors). But some anxieties do remain including reservations about the implications of pursuing news values (including 'scoops') in the interests of greater circulation in this way. Problems which have been raised include suggested biases against understanding (explaining events is neglected in favour of the sensational and the new) and against good news in favour of bad. The economics of capitalist journalism mean it may be a more sensible strategy to raise circulation by lotteries and price-cutting than to risk libel suits by expensive and complex investigative journalism. Many newspapers – especially local ones – do little to search out the news for themselves. Instead they rely upon a few international news agencies (Reuters, etc.), standard public sources like the courts, parliament and local council meetings, and a stream of 'press releases' from the public relations arms of government, political parties, commercial organisations and entertainers.

Another fascinating area of political and sociological research is the issue of how the potential audience chooses which messages to attend to, how they interpret the messages when they receive them, and how important these messages are in moulding political behaviour.

Evidence derived from research on party political broadcasts and newspaper circulation patterns suggests that people tend to attend to political messages which confirm their existing ways of thinking and to interpret ambivalent political messages in the same ways. There is little to suggest that people are very influenced by party political broadcasts or newspaper editorials, and much to suggest that people are influenced by face-to-face conversations with people they know.

Research suggests that political events are interpreted in terms of the recipients' own images of themselves (working class, black, housewife, etc.) and of the parties (caring, profligate, responsible, united, etc.). These must surely be continually subtly influenced by messages conveyed in the mass media (including advertising) often on a 'subliminal' (unconscious) level.

The popular press, in particular, is often keen to portray itself as the champion of its readers to the elite. To some extent this is clearly arrant nonsense – neither millionaire newspaper proprietors nor sophisticated metropolitan journalists are necessarily particularly well qualified to interpret the views of millions of provincial voters. However, letters columns and the very important modern innovation of the opinion poll – which is now a staple source of 'news' – do help to give politicians some clues on mass opinion. Still it is probable that 'informed' comment in the broadsheet newspapers and magazines is frequently misinterpreted by politicians as 'public opinion'.

THE INTERNET

The Internet uses electronic digital technology and enables ordinary users to transmit as well as receive information. Potentially every home becomes a broadcasting studio able to transmit its own political messages as well as to respond interactively to broadcasts by others. Thus flows can be described as 'multiplex' with complex networks being developed.

The Internet has been used extensively to campaign by political parties and candidates, especially through websites. It is widely believed to have helped the former professional wrestler Jesse Ventura win the governorship of Minnesota in 1998, and Roh Moo-hyun the South Korean presidential election in 2002. Early in the

2004 US presidential campaign Democrat Howard Dean's supporters mainly organised themselves through a 'meetup' Internet site (www.meetup.com) rather than waiting for professional centralised organisation. John McCain in the 2000 campaign raised 2.6 million dollars over the Internet (Parkinson, 2003). Virtually all parties and interest groups have web pages.

The Internet is also now being used to enable governments to deliver services (see Chapter 5 on the Information polity) and for electronic voting. In principle, it can be used to achieve the Athenian ideal by enabling citizens to be more regularly and extensively consulted by their elected representatives.

Potentially the Internet and similar technologies may have a still more radical impact in enabling the rapid construction of new networks of people and groups (Castells, 2002). Already, in the UK, mobile phone communication apparently played a major role in enabling more or less spontaneous protests against fuel tax rises to be effective. Similarly in the period before the invasion of Iraq in 2003, demonstrations and petitions of a size unprecedented in modern times seem to have been largely organised through ad hoc 'Stop the War' websites. More sensitively, terrorist organisations such as Al Qaeda have turned to the Internet as a powerful internal and external communication tool.

In many ways the Internet seems to be an inherently democratic and participative medium. This does not prevent the technology from being employed to great effect by governments and corporations to sell their products, services and ideas. However, the networked structure of the technology makes it more difficult for governments to control than conventional broadcast media (Tansey, 2002: Ch. 4).

Since the 2004 US presidential election, political weblogs have attracted a lot of attention. As personal individual diaries they have tended to be influential in political structures where the candidate and not the party control election campaigns. For organisations, such as political parties, a weblog creates a potential problem because an amorphous structure cannot provide a personal diary (Jackson, 2006). The strength of a political weblog is that it enables like-minded people to share ideas (Sunstein, 2004), and some act as 'focal points' (Drezner and Farrell, 2004) around which influential people congregate. Weblogs have provided an alternative to the traditional media, but are also increasingly a means by which that media communicates.

DEMOCRACY AND COMMUNICATION

In terms of our three models – centralisation, corporatism and pluralism – we can see the evidence we have reviewed provides some support for each of the patterns of communication we suggested they entailed. Centralisation seems supported by the evidence of centralised national parties and a centralised communication system mainly concerned with 'broadcasting'. Corporatism is supported by the evidence of a well-established pattern of legislative consultation with certain favoured pressure groups. Whilst we have found less evidence in the pattern of established institutions of political communication for pluralism, we saw that the legitimacy of consultation before decisions are taken and of any group to organise and protest is accepted. We might well have elaborated on this theme by emphasising a tradition of sturdy independence and well-established right to petition parliament and other decision makers in many liberal democracies. What seems inadequate to the authors are the opportunities for less well-established groups to have a real chance of influence.

RECOMMENDED READING

Arblaster, Anthony, 2002, *Democracy*, 3rd edn, Buckingham, Open University Press
Excellent short introduction to different concepts of democracy.

Bogdanor, Vernon, 1988, *Constitutions in Democratic Politics*, Aldershot, Gower
Broad survey of constitutionalism in many contemporary democracies.

Budge, Ian, 1996, *The New Challenge of Direct Democracy*, Oxford, Basil Blackwell
Considers a vision of how new technology can lead to direct democracy.

Carter, April and Stokes, Geoffrey, 2002, *Democratic Theory Today*, Cambridge, Polity Press
Review of contemporary challenges to democracy and the response of political theorists to them.

Castells, Manuel, 2002, *The Rise of the Network Society*, Oxford, Blackwell
One of the foremost thinkers on the possible effect of the Internet on the political process worldwide.

Colomer, Josep M. (ed.), 2002, *Political Institutions in Europe*, 2nd edn, London, Routledge
General description of the pattern of democratic politics in various countries of Western Europe and in the EU.

Coxall, Bill, 2001, *Pressure Groups in Britain*, Harlow, Longman
Useful basic text on interest groups.

Coxall, Bill, Robbins, Lynton and Leach, Robert, 2003, *Contemporary British Politics*, 4th edn, Basingstoke, Macmillan
One of a number of good introductory texts available on the UK.

Eldridge, John *et al.*, 1997, *The Mass Media and Power in Modern Britain*, Oxford, Oxford University Press
Mainly concerned with British media. Introduces work of Glasgow University Media Group, with strong emphasis on political issues.

Farrel, David M., 2001, *Electoral Systems: A Comparative Introduction*, Basingstoke, Palgrave
Useful introductory book.

Jackson, Nigel, 2006, 'Dipping Their Big Toe into the Blogosphere: The Use of Weblogs by the Political Parties in the 2005 General Election', *Aslib Proceedings: new information perspectives* 58(4): 292–303
Provides insight into how blogs were used in the UK during an election campaign.

Jones, Nicholas, 1996, *Soundbites and Spin Doctors*, London, Indigo
Lively account of this development.

Keman, Hans (ed.), 2002, *Comparative Democratic Politics*, London, Sage
Democracy, parties, interest groups and public policy in comparative perspective.

King, Anthony, 2001, *Does the United Kingdom Still Have a Constitution?* London, Sweet & Maxwell
Short lively perspective on the question.

LeDuc, Lawrence *et al.* (eds), 2002, *Comparing Democracies 2: New Challenges in the Study of Elections and Voting*, London, Sage
    Research on elections in democracies.

Lees-Marshment, Jennifer, 2001, *Political Marketing and British Political Parties*, Manchester University Press
    Good on 'spin' and political marketing.

McKay, David, 2005, *American Politics and Society*, 6th. edn, Oxford, Blackwell
    Well-reviewed and up-to-date text on the USA.

MacPherson, C. B., 1966, *The Real World of Democracy: The Massey Lecture*, Oxford, Clarendon Press
    Very influential essay which seeks to understand non-liberal democracy in communist and Third World Countries as well the Western liberal version.

McQuail, Denis, 2005, *McQuail's Mass Communication Theory*, 5th edn, London, Sage
    Excellent comprehensive study of communication theory.

Scott, John, 1991, *Who Rules Britain?* Cambridge, Cambridge University Press
    Some clear theoretical material as well as specific evidence on classes and elites in Britain

Wilson, Graham K, (ed.), 1990, *Interest Groups*, Oxford, Basil Blackwell
    Includes both theoretical and country-based contributions including the USA and Japan.

WEBSITES

http://www.opendemocracy.net
    An online think tank committed to promoting human rights and democracy worldwide.

http://www.constitution.org/liberlib.htm
    Liberty Library of Government Classics includes full texts of constitutions from that of Hammurabi (1780 BC) to present day.

http://www.museum.tv/archives/etv/P/htmlP/politicalpro/politicalpro.htm

Museum of Broadcast Communications looks at the impact of political processes on the development of television in the USA.

http://www.usaid.gov/our_work/democracy_and_governance/epp.html

US-based organisation which aims to help nations conduct elections.

http://www.wfd.org/pages/home.aspx?i_PageID=1811

The Westminster Foundation for Change seeks to help create sustainable political change in emerging democracies.

http://www.charter88.org.uk/

Charter 88 is committed to democratic reform in the UK.

http://www.hansardsociety.org.uk

Hansard Society is a charity which seeks to promote effective parliamentary democracy.

http://www.18doughtystreet.com

The UK's first online news service.

http://darrenlilleker.blogspot.com

Musings on political communication.

http://www.amnesty.org.uk

Amnesty International.

http://www.ucl.ac.uk/constitution-unit

The Constitution Unit (mainly UK).

http://www.jtsma.org.uk

Jennifer Trust for Spinal Muscular Atrophy (an example of an interest group).

http://www.parliament.uk

Houses of Parliament home page.

http://www.parliamentlive.tv

Live broadcasts from UK Parliament and archive of past fortnight's debates (also on UK Freeview channel).

http://www.electoralcommission.gov.uk

Electoral Commission site includes detailed statistics on recent elections.

http://www.conservative-party.org.uk
The Conservative Party.

http://www.labour.org.uk
The Labour Party.

http://www.libdems.org.uk
The Liberal Democratic Party.

http://www.whitehouse.gov
US Presidency.

http://www.aei.org
American Enterprise Institute (neo-conservative think tank).

http://www.newamericancentury.org
New American Century Project.

http://www.PoliticsOnline.com
Information on the Internet and politics.

http://www.mori.com
Leading public opinion-polling organisation.

http://www.cbi.org.uk
Confederation of British Industry.

8

POLICIES

THIS CHAPTER . . .

considers how, in liberal democracies, such as Britain, public policies should be made and implemented, how they are made, and the problems of evaluating the public policy process. Before any such discussion, however, it is important to consider the extent to which the state – especially the national government – should make decisions on behalf of the whole community. Finally we return to the extent to which it is possible and desirable for the individual to influence political policies and events.

PUBLIC POLICY PROBLEMS AND SOLUTIONS

In Chapter 1 we saw that Bachrach and Baratz (1970), writing in a US context, stress the domination of WASPs (White Anglo-Saxon Protestants) in setting the agenda of US politics. In Britain we could perhaps go further and suggest that the 'chattering classes', who dominate politics, the media, academic and professional life, and the Civil Service, are predominantly still London-resident public school/ Oxford or Cambridge arts graduates and the like. What such people define as urgent problems are not necessarily the same as what people who left school at the minimum leaving age, who are employed in manual jobs (or are unemployed) and live in Lancashire or Scotland, see as in the same category.

Similarly the 'same' problem may be understood in radically different terms from different perspectives. Thus the existence of increasing numbers of young unmarried mothers can be seen primarily as a symptom of Britain's moral decline; as a serious threat to the social security budget; as a consequence of the failure of sex education; or as a symptom of the emergence of a deprived underclass on Britain's former council estates. Alternatively it may not be regarded as a problem at all – but merely a consequence of changing individual moral choices. Indeed some would see the phenomena as a welcome sign of inevitable progress toward the extinction of the bourgeois/patriarchal family.

Hence, too, a 'solution' is an equally contentious matter. In our example, does this mean no more premarital sex; fathers supporting financially all their biological children; no more 'unprotected' pre-marital sex; full employment and community renewal in deprived areas; or abandoning the expectation that all children are brought up in two-parent families? The terminology of 'problem' and 'solution', as de Jouvenal (1963) points out, may also be introducing a mis-leading mathematical analogy – that reasoning will lead us to a unique resolution of a defined problem. One might more sensibly speak of managing a situation.

Further consideration of this 'problem' will make clear another vital point about the nature of policy making. We can see that the same problem has been seen through different ideological spectacles in the example (moral majority, 'Thatcherite', liberal, socialist, feminist). It is also clear that different perspectives are also to some extent a question of from whose eyes we are looking: the moralising detached observer, the taxpayer, a sympathetic outsider, the mothers, fathers or children concerned, fellow residents of 'sink' estates, etc. In short, political conflicts are as much about the interests of groups of people as they are about power struggles, ideas or social management.

THE CHOICE OF SOCIAL DECISION-MAKING MECHANISMS

Not every social problem is perceived as a public policy problem. Choices may be left to be resolved through the market mechanism, or informally through families and social networks. In political argument this choice of social decision-making mechanisms is often debated in terms of simple dichotomies (Box 8.1), in other cases it may be taken for granted that one mechanism is the appropriate one.

BOX 8.1 CHOICE OF SOCIAL DECISION-MAKING MECHANISM

From the right:
Individual freedom = Consumer sovereignty = Good
versus
State decision making = bureaucracy = bad

From the left:
Social decision making by welfare state = democracy = good
versus
Market decision making = capitalism = exploitation = bad

The approach we have adopted here suggests, rather, a more pragmatic approach where it is appropriate to consider the issue, the time and the place before deciding upon which way social decisions should be resolved. In addition to a pure market or a state system, it is clear that a mixed system in which the market is regulated and adjusted by the state (the so-called 'social market') is often a viable alternative to consider. This alternative combines a free market in consumer goods with a commitment to social objectives, such as equality of opportunity, and political measures to prevent the undue dominance of elites. Nor should the role of voluntary co-operation through family and neighbourhood networks or more formal organisations be neglected.

In deciding the appropriate role of the state, important considerations are: how far it is likely to reach a more rational decision than the market; how far it can effectively involve ordinary citizens in the decision-making process; and whether the increased costs of such decision making seem justified by any improvement in its quality.

THE CASE FOR THE MARKET

If the state is seeking to promote (following Bentham) 'the greatest happiness of the greatest number', it should not lose sight of the fact that only individuals can judge their own happiness.

The argument of the early economists (since endorsed by fashionable neo-liberal conservative commentators such as Milton Friedman (Friedman and Friedman, 1980) and Hayek (1979)) is that with only a finite amount of real resources, a centralised deployment of resources by the state will almost certainly result in waste. If we each have an equal amount of real resources with which to achieve satisfaction, some will achieve more satisfaction from buying fishing rods or fashionable clothes, others from the purchase of fast cars, or the consumption of malt whisky. For the state to allocate everyone equal amounts of fishing equipment, cars, clothes and whisky, and proceed on the assumption that all citizens want the same, will lead to dissatisfaction and waste. Thus fishing enthusiasts may find the concrete they wanted to be used to dam a river has been used to construct a bridge over it to somewhere they did not wish to go. Fashion enthusiasts find themselves allocated rayon pants when they aspired to a woollen kilt (or whatever is fashionable at the time). Sporting motorists may be issued with Trabant motor cars incapable of reaching the speeds they wish to attain, whilst teetotallers throw away in disgust an allocation of malt whisky which their neighbours would savour with relish. The state cannot achieve the level of information and efficiency required to satisfy individual consumer needs.

If this account of a fully centralised planned economy be dismissed as an exaggerated fantasy, an examination of the experience of the Soviet economy suggests it is not so far from the truth (Fainsod, 1963; Nove, 1980). In the Soviet model in the Stalinist era, consumers were paid in money and could dispose of their incomes largely as they pleased, while the goods available in the shops were determined by the operation of a somewhat arbitrary national plan, and prices bore little relationship to the cost of production. Since managers were rewarded for over-fulfilling their plan quotas rather than making profits, but might well not have official access to the necessary raw materials, they might resort to such expedients as making all their shoes in small sizes so as to minimise the use of raw materials. That large-footed customers could not obtain shoes, and the shops were congested with unsold small sizes, would be of no significance. Conversely housing was rented and cheap – but there was no incentive to build more housing and gross overcrowding resulted.

The argument is, therefore, that a free-market economy enables individuals to allocate resources in such a way as to maximise everyone's satisfaction. The introduction of a market economy in which all are free to spend their money income as they please enables a painless 'swap' of the whisky ration for fishing tackle. Better, factories manufacturing rayon pants when such items are out of fashion will go out of business to be replaced by weavers of kilts (or whatever is currently in demand). Further the sports car enthusiast may give up leisure to earn extra resources in (say) overtime payments in order to secure a faster car than almost anybody else, whilst the keen fisherman or woman may decide to live simply in a remote area on the proceeds of only part-time employment. As Adam Smith described, the 'invisible hand' of the market balances supply and demand to the satisfaction of all in the marketplace.

As global economic systems, capitalism and state planning have influenced international relations. These can be between systems, such as during the Cold War when the West and the Soviet Bloc argued which economic system was the more efficient and effective. But there are also subtle differences of emphasis and tone within the proponents of particular systems. For example, since the 1980s the USA and UK have taken a more 'market economy' approach to capitalism and Germany and France a more 'statist' approach. Both approaches agree on the need for a capitalist economy, but in the 'market economy' approach the state seeks to take less of a role, whereas in the 'statist' approach government tries to play a more direct management role in the operation of capitalism. One of the interesting outcomes of the 2007 French presidential election is that the winner, Nicolas Sarkozy, is committed to moving the French economy towards a more 'market economy' approach.

PROBLEMS OF MARKET DECISION MAKING

With its superior productivity and response to consumer demand, the market mechanism might appear to have justified itself. Yet the inadequacies of raw capitalism seem hardly less than those of raw centralised planning.

In terms of the justification we have so far considered, the market as a device to achieve the satisfaction of consumer demand, capitalism seems at best a doubtful device when viewed in practice rather than in terms of abstract theoretical economic models. If the theoretical assumption is made of an equal distribution of resources to everyone at the outset then, in the short term, the market mechanism seems to be a fair device for decision making. However, the engine of capitalism remains the profit motive – which is no more than each individual seeking to maximise the returns to their efforts.

The problem is that the accumulation of profit over time into the hands of successful business people ('entrepreneurs' in economic jargon) leads to a grossly unfair distribution of resources. This is particularly the case when wealth is inherited – the result being an arbitrary distribution of purchasing power and consumer satisfaction. In many cases the distribution of wealth is the consequence of obscure historical events in periods when the market system hardly functioned. Consider the English aristocrats who continue to own a totally disproportionate share of the land, or, for that matter, the superior share of the earth's resources owned by the current generation of North Americans.

Further distortions in the market mechanism, familiar to all economists, include the absence in many industries and places of the 'perfect competition' assumed in the model of the market mechanism explained by Adam Smith and usually assumed by its political proponents. That is, for consumers to obtain the goods that will maximise their satisfaction in return for their expenditure, it is necessary for them to have full knowledge of the goods and prices available. It is also required that new entrepreneurs be able to enter the market freely whenever exceptional profits are being made in an industry. The number of producers is also assumed to be so large they cannot affect the market price. In reality markets are almost always 'imperfect' in that consumers are misled by advertising; new competition faces considerable barriers to entry into the market; and governments may subsidise domestic producers and tax or obstruct foreign competition. Thus the state is often forced to intervene to re-establish a competitive environment

In a purely capitalist system the producer is responsible only for staying within the law and maximising profits for shareholders. Competitive forces are thought to ensure that individual consumer needs are met. However, it may be that the costs to the community of some productive activities will not be reflected in the costs producers (and ultimately consumers) pay. For instance, a factory may pollute its environment or workers in distant markets may be exploited. This may lead to a severe misallocation of resources, and often leads to demands for government intervention, and/or for businesses to adopt a socially responsible attitude towards all the 'stakeholders' affected by them.

VOLUNTARY ORGANISATION

So far, we have examined this question largely as if there were only two alternative modes of social action – either decisions are taken by individuals through the market mechanism or they are taken by 'the state'. This is, however, clearly an oversimplification.

In the first place it has to be emphasised that much 'individual' decision making is not market oriented, but reflects patterns of social co-operation which are more altruistic than the sort of bargaining for individual advantage which is normally associated with the market. People not only seek their own satisfaction but that of their family, their neighbours, various community groupings with which they identify and they may sacrifice immediate self-interest to causes as varied as vegetarianism, racial purity or world government.

The idea that market decision making is a form of individual choice is also an oversimplification. Individuals are generally confronted with alternatives that are the results of social processes over which they have little control. Many consumers, unlike an affluent minority in highly industrialised countries, have little 'discretionary income' with which to exercise choice. 'Consumer sovereignty' may seem like a shallow joke to many in Africa, India and China, and of limited relevance to those living on social security benefits in more affluent countries. Discretion on the supply side of the economy seems still less real for the many individuals with limited marketable skills, little or no capital and few employment opportunities.

Social co-operation on a voluntary basis, especially between relatives and neighbours, is clearly an older and more basic form of human behaviour than market behaviour. As we have seen there have been, perhaps Utopian, attempts to set up local communities on such a basis right up to the present day. In social policy, the importance of family ties and behaviour is still difficult to under-estimate even in modern communities in which work, leisure and spiritual activities that were previously family-based may now be carried on outside the family home.

In the present context, however, it is vital to consider the role of voluntary sector organisations in carrying out activities that might otherwise be the subject of market or government determination. Churches are an interesting example of voluntary organisations, since, as we have seen, in earlier times they have frequently had a legal monopoly of matters that are now seen as predominantly matters for the state or the individual. For members of these bodies their decisions may retain a greater legitimacy than those of the state. Churches retain a commitment to charitable works and to influencing government policy on 'moral' issues from contraception to debt relief to the South.

More generally a whole range of voluntary organisations carry out co-operative activities which enable their members to achieve satisfaction with little reference to either the market or state sector of the economy. Examples of this include: leisure groups such as football clubs or ramblers' groups, educational groups such as the play school and Franco-British University of the Third Age movements. Economic activities such as providing food or clothing may take place via allotment and knitting societies. Some of the oldest voluntary groups provide welfare services to their members (friendly societies, the Masons and alumni associations). The British Royal National Life-boat Institution is an interesting example of the provision of what might be expected to be a state-financed 'public good' (a free, public, emergency sea rescue service).

Most voluntary organisations, however, do relate to the state in one or both of two ways. First, they may provide services to the community in collaboration with the government – and increasingly often as contractors to it. Thus, in Britain, the Women's Royal Voluntary Service often delivers 'meals on wheels' to social services departments' clients. National Health Service hospitals are supported by Leagues of Friends who may raise additional funds for specialist equipment, visit lonely patients, or drive outpatients to the hospital. The National Society for Prevention of Cruelty to Children has special legal powers in its work of protecting children. Citizens' Advice Bureaux, staffed by volunteers, are usually financed by local councils.

Second, many voluntary organisations lobby the state to pass legislation, or spend money on causes helpful to their client group. Thus the Royal Society for Prevention of Cruelty to Animals is the major source of legislation in the UK after the government. Veterans groups and the National Rifle Association are very influential on US legislation. Some bodies, such as Mediawatch-UK, may do little other than lobby various public authorities.

A British report (Knight, 1993/4) has advocated that these two kinds of voluntary associations be formally separated with only service organisations receiving charitable status and tax exemptions. This seems to neglect the frequent interdependence of the two roles. Service provision often leads to useful expertise in an area that the government needs to listen to. Thus, Oxfam and Médecins Sans Frontières can speak from extensive experience of development work in Third World countries when lobbying governments for more official aid. The National Association of Citizens' Advice Bureaux give useful and detailed information on the effectiveness of social legislation by collecting information on the patterns of problems reported by its voluntary advisers.

The voluntary sector is viewed by some politicians as a means of combining the best features of the welfare state and the market. For example recent governments in the UK have increasingly encouraged both commercial and voluntary sectors to get involved in the provision of what were previously monopoly state social services. Whilst the state continues to fund services, actual provision services such as health and community care are increasingly delivered by the voluntary and private sectors.

RATIONAL POLICY MAKING: BUREAUCRACY

However much it may be thought appropriate to leave problems to be solved by the action of the market or through communal or individual initiatives, there will certainly be always a substantial area for centralised action through state machinery. Although many such problems will be tackled through negotiation in the sort of democratic institutions described at some length in the previous chapter, these in turn rest upon a foundation of bureaucratic state organisations, which suggest policy solutions and implement them in a more or less rational fashion. Here we seek to understand the role of such organisations and the behaviour of the bureaucrats within them.

We saw earlier how Weber used a series of models of authority to explain the range of social possibilities and to explain the internal logic of these variations (see Chapter 3). These 'ideal-type' models are often a useful analytical device – his model of 'bureaucracy' is very much of this kind.

Weber (Gerth and Mills, 1948: Ch. VIII) convincingly described some of the key characteristics of bureaucracy (literally government by offices) (Box 8.2), which he said 'compares with other organisations exactly as does the machine with non-mechanical means of production'.

BOX 8.2   WEBER'S CHARACTERISTICS OF BUREAUCRACY

(a) Fixed and Official Jurisdictional Areas – official 'duties', stable rules, methodically carried out (specialisation)
(b) Official Hierarchy – pyramid of officials each reporting up to level above (integration)
(c) Use of Files – to create an 'organisational memory'
(d) Official Activity as Full-time Work – no conflict between private and public interests (dedication)
(e) Expert Training of Officials – technical competence and *esprit de corps*
(f) Corpus of Rules – leading to predictability of behaviour

(Weber, in Gerth and Mills, 1948)

Bureaucracy may have originated in the needs of empires for the efficient administration of huge territories. However, it has flourished in recent times in meeting the needs of massive industrial populations, all of whom need to be treated alike in the name of democracy. Weber suggests such organisations are characteristic of a modern 'rational–legal' social order. They appear to be suited to making rational decisions on behalf of society. What, however, does 'rational' mean in this context, and do such organisations fulfil this role in fact?

Lindblom's 'rational–comprehensive' ideal-type model of the policy-making process may help clarify this issue. Lindblom (1959) considers how decision makers would proceed if they did so in a completely logical and rational manner (Box 8.3). This then serves as a benchmark or standard of comparison against which to compare actual processes of decision making. This model is very similar to the economists' model of individual consumer choice.

BOX 8.3 A RATIONAL–COMPREHENSIVE MODEL OF DECISION MAKING

1 Define and rank *values*.
2 Specify *objectives* compatible with these.
3 Identify all relevant *options* or means of achieving these objectives.
4 Calculate all the *consequences* of these options and compare them.
5 Choose the option or combination of options which could *maximise* the highest ranked values.

(After Lindblom, 1959)

If such an approach to decision making is treated as the paradigm for making public policy, then it is clear that few actual policy decisions are made in accordance with it. Some attempt has been made to apply such a systematic and rational method of policy decision making by employing the technique of cost benefit analysis (CBA) on, for instance, the decision as to where to build a fourth London airport. CBA, basically an attempt to put monetary figures on the costs and benefits accruing from an investment over time, is more widely used by strategic planners in business situations. As that example shows, however, there are problems in both establishing an agreed ranking of values and in measuring and predicting outcomes as far as most public policy decisions are concerned. Some of these difficulties derive from the fact that the model is implicitly based on how *one* individual decision maker would approach a problem. In practice virtually all public policy decisions are made by organisations, only some of which even claim to be 'bureaucratic' (in Weber's sense) or to be rational decision makers. Moreover, all of them are subject to pressure from influential lobbyists or interests.

PROBLEMS WITH 'RATIONAL' POLICY MAKING

The problems of interpreting organisational behaviour as if it were the product of rational decision making by its top managers are neatly illustrated by Allison's seminal book *The Essence of Decision: Explaining the Cuban Missile Crisis* (1987) to which we briefly referred in Chapter 2. He rightly suggests that most of the literature of international relations treats the behaviour of states as if it were the product of rational policy makers, behaving much as Lindblom's rational–comprehensive model suggests. This is what he calls the 'classical rational actor' model (or Model 1). In practice such assumptions seem to be a long way from empirical reality. For instance, in the Cuban missile crisis US policy makers produced a series of hypotheses about 'Russian' behaviour in installing IRBMs (intermediate-range ballistic missiles) in uncamouflaged soft silos, none of which were very convincing because they assumed the behaviour was part of a single co-ordinated and rational policy.

We can briefly summarise some reasons why any organisation is likely to diverge from the rational–comprehensive model of policy making, in Box 8.4.

BOX 8.4 WHY ORGANISATIONS ARE NOT ALWAYS RATIONAL

(a) Psychological limitations
(b) Limitations arising from multiple values
(c) Factored problems and fractionated power
(d) Information problems
(e) Cost limitations – blind rule implementation.

(Hogwood and Gunn, 1984: 50–53)

By 'psychological limitations' it is meant that organisations are composed of individuals with limited knowledge and skills and imperfectly known values.

The limitations arising from multiple values are that organisations face additional problems in determining values and objectives (compared with individuals) because they are composed of individuals with different values and objectives. Whilst this may be true of all organisations, it is arguable that it is necessarily so in organisations seeking to implement political policies on behalf of the whole community and which may have been the subject of intense debate between political parties, or which remain socially contested. For instance, the British Child Support Agency has found itself torn between rival demands from groups reflecting the interests of deserted mothers and children, those representing fathers and second families, and, not least, the demands of the Treasury that the agency make a substantial reduction in the costs of social security.

By 'factored problems and fractionated power' is meant that the division of problems amongst specialist departments helps to overcome the first (psychological) problem but creates new ones. Subunits concerned with part of the problem treat it in isolation and elevate their own sub-goals over those of the organisation as a whole, whilst their leaders seek power and influence for themselves. In *Parkinson's Law*, Parkinson (1958) amusingly documents, for instance, how the number of admirals in the British Navy increased as the number of battleships declined, deriving the 'law' that organisations grow irrespective of the amount of work they have to do.

Although organisations collectively possess much more information on problems than individuals (through filing systems, computer databases, etc.) they frequently fail to access the relevant information at the right time. Thus they lose one of the major strategic advantages they possess.

In order to achieve the cost benefits of 'mass producing' decisions, organisations tend to economise on searching out alternatives in making decisions. If a rule appears to apply, then it will be automatically operated. Subordinates can always defend an action to their superiors by referring to a rule made by those superiors. The more a bureaucracy is criticised and needs to defend itself, the worse this behaviour may get.

INCREMENTAL DECISION MAKING

Allison (1987) suggests a second 'organisational process model' of decision making which stresses that organisations normally operate without explicitly defining objectives through a *repertoire of standard operating procedures* reflecting the parochial views of its constituent departments. To put the idea more simply: departments in organisations go on dealing with standard situations in their usual set ways without relating these to overall organisational objectives.

In a non-standard situation, or if acceptable performance standards are not being met, then incremental (i.e. bit-by-bit) changes will be made. A limited search will be made for the first satisfactory solution that can be found. This is what Simon (1959) calls *satisficing* rather than *optimising* behaviour. Usually a small modification of standard operating procedures is introduced, rather than a new solution from a blank sheet.

Allison also stresses organisations' preference for avoiding the disruptive effects of uncertainty and conflict by concentrating on short-term problems rather than long-term planning (which would involve discussion of goals and values), by using 'rule of thumb' decision rules based on short-term feedback, and attempting to negotiate away uncertainties in the environment.

The various authors mentioned react to this (largely shared) perception of organisational decision making in different ways. Allison is mainly concerned to formulate a realistic descriptive model of decision making. Lindblom (1959) argues that in a pluralist society incremental decision making may not only be inevitable but also desirable. Simon (1977) made sophisticated suggestions for improving the management of organisations in the light of these observations.

Allison puts forward a third model which he describes as a 'governmental (bureaucratic) politics' one. To emphasise its generality and to avoid confusion with Weber, we shall refer to it as the political bargaining model. Briefly, this third model of Allison's stresses that social decisions may be often be more appropriately seen as *political resultants* rather than as either individual rational choices or even as organisational outputs. Essentially policy making is seen as the outcome of a *game* between *players* occupying positions. The outcome is the result of bargaining between players and is dependent on (among other things) their bargaining skill, their resources and the rules of the game. Just as in physics a resultant is the outcome of physical forces operating in different directions on a mass, a political resultant is the outcome of different social forces (players) which is unlikely to be identical to what any individual player desired.

Allison stresses among other things the importance of mutual (mis)perceptions, the variety of stakes held by the players and the number of different issues being considered. Because of the complexity of the game, players' actions are constantly focused on deadlines which have to be met by decisions – frequently on the basis of inadequate information. One important maxim Allison stresses is 'Where you stand depends on where you sit': issues look radically different to players from different organisations or from different levels of the same organisation. Each player, too, will have made prior commitments to others within or without the game and have a distinctive style of play. Another salutary emphasis in Allison's treatment of this model is on the ever-present potential for 'foul-ups'!

Although this model is formulated primarily with US foreign policy making in mind, an increasingly strong trend in the literature on organisations is to stress similar issues. In particular, writers like Ian Mangham (1979) have stressed the extent to which people in organisations pursue their own political (career, etc.) objectives, whilst others (e.g. Karpick, 1978) have stressed that every organisation has an environment composed primarily of other organisations. Thus by negotiating with representatives of other organisations a more stable organisational world can be created.

Allison's political bargaining model should also remind us that many policy decisions are not taken in a bureaucratic organisational environment. Policy decisions may be taken in a legislative assembly which characteristically works by bargaining amongst parties and factions. The resultant policy is not a clear expression of the values of any one group, but a temporary compromise reflecting the bargaining power of the parties and the state of public opinion at the time. Frequently, too, executive bodies from the cabinet down consist of representatives of departments or even outside organisations, so that policies may be modified not only to reflect experience in execution, but also to reflect changes in the political bargaining power of the parties concerned. As we have seen, many writers, like Lindblom, view such 'incrementalism' as not only inevitable, given our limited knowledge of the social effects of policy making, but as desirable in a democracy in which relationships between groups and individuals are freely re-negotiable. He also stresses that incrementalism is a safer way to adjust to events given the limitations of human knowledge in relation to the complexity of the issues facing the decision maker.

THE POLICY PROCESS

Hogwood and Gunn (1984) offer a useful and sophisticated model of the policy process (Box 8.5), which takes into account some of the points we discussed above. They offer it not as a description or prescription of what happens in every case but as a framework for understanding what does or does not happen in each particular case. Each of these stages is potentially of key importance in deciding the outcome of a policy process.

BOX 8.5   HOGWOOD AND GUNN'S MODEL OF THE
POLICY PROCESS

1   Deciding to decide (issue search or agenda setting)
2   Deciding how to decide
3   Issue definition
4   Forecasting
5   Setting objectives and priorities
6   Options analysis
7   Policy implementation, monitoring and control
8   Evaluation and review
9   Policy maintenance, succession, or termination.

In comparison with the rational–comprehensive model this formulation has some important and desirable features: it sees policy making as a more or less continuous process; it stresses political issues of agenda setting, decision process and definition; and it does not take the implementation of the decision for granted.

Items (1) and (9), in particular, in the model rightly suggest that policy making is an extended process in which certain issues are picked out for attention (Bachrach and Baratz, 1970, again) and may be approached in different ways during the process of decision and implementation, and then be subsumed into debates on other issues as time goes by.

Rather than a one-off decision on values, we have already stressed the extent to which policy making often reflects compromises on values between different groups. These groups, in turn, may define 'the problem' in different ways. As we saw earlier, the question of whether a problem should be dealt with by the state, the market, voluntary action or whatever, is a crucial part of many contemporary policy discussions.

Partly as a consequence of the extended time policy making takes and the partial nature of the consensus built up behind many policies, it cannot be assumed that decisions once made will automatically be implemented. Many agencies, firms and individuals and levels of government may be involved in realising a decision initially taken at one level of the state machinery. The outcome may not be recognisable to the initial policy makers. The consequences of the policies adopted may not, in fact, be as predicted by the original analysis upon which the policy was based. For these reasons it is sensible that policy makers set up mechanisms to monitor the success or failure of their policies so that they may be adapted, refined or indeed abandoned as appropriate.

IMPLEMENTING PUBLIC POLICY

Public policy is often discussed almost entirely from a central government perspective. A problem is identified, a 'solution' propounded, after which the solution to the problem is assumed to be the effective and efficient implementation of the policy at local level. Indeed many commentators on public policy – especially in the national press – scarcely consider the possibility of a gap between policy prescription and its implementation. Yet, most public policies are implemented by local agencies at various distances from the central government.

Hood (1976) introduced the concept of 'perfect implementation' for a state of affairs in which central policy makers' prescriptions were perfectly realised. The likelihood of such an eventuality in the real world is remote. For instance, studies by the National Audit Office show that social security payments, being paid through local branches of a central ministry on the basis of relatively clear and unambiguous rules enforced through a single bureaucracy, suffer from a 35 per cent error rate. In the case of the Child Support Agency, its first Annual Report referred to a study by its Chief Child Support Officer who found, of 1,380 assessments checked, only 25 per cent were judged correct, 39 per cent were found to be incorrect, whilst in 35 per cent of cases insufficient information was recorded to tell if the assessment was right or wrong. When policies are implemented through a series of agencies, each of which expects to have some influence on the nature and interpretation of the policy, then clearly 'perfect implementation' becomes still less likely. Inter-organisational bargaining will doubtless affect the outcomes of policies, and with different agencies in different parts of the country considerably different outcomes may result (see Figure 8.1).

Pressman and Wildavsky (1973) in an American study graphically entitled *Implementation: How Great Expectations in Washington Are Dashed in Oakland or Why It's Amazing that Federal Programs Work at All* demonstrates that if a series of administrative agreements or clearance stages are necessary for implementation, even with 99 per cent of agreement at each 'clearance', overall probability of perfect implementation falls below 50 per cent after 68 clearances.

Is 'perfect implementation' always desirable? Local conditions may differ radically from those central policy makers had in mind in formulating their response to 'the' problem. Barrett and Fudge (1981) attack the traditional British 'top/down' approach to public problem solving, arguing that local communities can deploy scarce resources much more effectively to meet their real need rather than the centrally perceived 'problem'. Lindblom (1959), as we have seen, defended incrementalism as a policy-making procedure in cases where it is difficult to define a clear consensus on policy goals and circumstances are rapidly changing – as is the case with much public policy. If the central policy is a radical one then the analysis of Bachrach and Baratz (1970) referred to earlier may well help to explain its non-implementation. Equally any central government may find local areas (particularly those controlled by a different political party) will stonewall on the implementation of economic and fiscal policies with a severe local economic impact.

In some cases it may even be the case that policies are not even intended to be implemented. Edelman's (1977) study of political

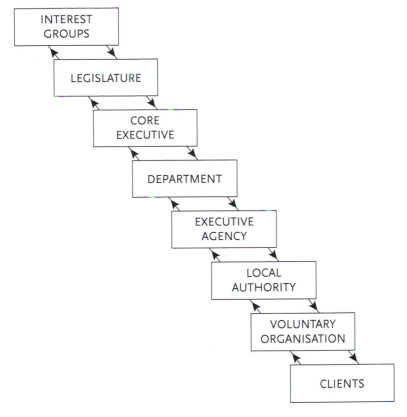

Figure 8.1 Levels of inter-organisational bargaining

language has emphasised the symbolic function of many policy declarations. A fine-sounding policy may have its origins in a political compromise at central level which was acceptable because it was too vague to be implemented unambiguously.

'Perfect implementation', then, is not necessarily desirable – and certainly is not inevitable. To overcome the barriers to implementation may well be costly in both communication effort and need to offer sanctions/inducements to the implementer. Following Neustadt (1960), the requirements for implementation seem to include:

(i) unambiguous signal of required behaviour must reach local implementer and be understood;

(ii) either (a) they must want to conform to new policy and have power
to implement it, or (b) costs of non-implementation must be made
to clearly exceed benefits of inertia.

MANAGING LOCAL PUBLIC POLICY

It may be helpful to expand upon the previous section by looking
briefly at the implementation of public policy from the point of the
local managers of such a service. This may help to add a realistic
perspective to the problems of implementing policy prescriptions.
Although such managers are in very varied circumstances we can
point to some likely common characteristics: they are in a multiple
series of bargaining relationships as suggested by the diagram in
Figure 8.2; they have limited time and information sources, many
tasks and limited resources.

A minor example of this would be one of the author's research on
the Youth Training Scheme (Tansey, 1989) in which training officers
within organisations were seen as having to negotiate with:

personnel and finance directors for permission to run/finance the
scheme;

departmental heads to offer worthwhile placements for trainees;

Manpower Service Commission (a QUANGO) representatives to
approve the scheme;

Careers Service (local government) officials to publicise and recruit for
the scheme;

technical college course tutors on the content of off-the-job training;

industrial training boards (more QUANGOs) on the acceptability of the
training for apprenticeship purposes;

the trainees themselves in respect of their behaviour;

and so on.

Some major variables which may affect managers' capacity to take an
independent view of how policy should be implemented will include
their relationship to, and distance from, clients, their relationship to
local authorities/central departments, and the degree of their dependence on firms/voluntary organisations, etc. for resources.

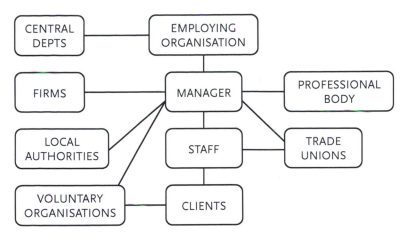

Figure 8.2 Managing local public service provision

MULTI-LEVEL GOVERNANCE

Two major factors have helped extend and complicate the chain of relationships involved in policy implementation in recent years. One is the trend towards multi-level government (see Chapter 6). The second is the trend away from monolithic government departments that both decide policy and manage the nationwide delivery of public services towards a reliance on a network of agencies – public, voluntary and private – for local delivery.

Neo-conservative thinkers have influenced many democratic governments toward attempting to slim the institutions of government into a role of regulating and co-ordinating the delivery of public services rather than undertaking their supply directly. Coupling these factors together, the phrase, 'multi-level governance' may help to encapsulate recent trends (see Pierre and Stoker, 2002).

'Governance' is a fashionable but tricky term that can be used in a variety of different ways. Rhodes (1996: 653) suggests at least six major uses of the term. Strictly one might argue it refers broadly to 'the process of making collective decisions in a more or less binding way' (Keman, 2002: 260). Hence it could encompass decision making through the market, by networks of voluntary co-operation and bargaining and by government. In practice it is often used to emphasise that public policies are increasingly implemented in a pragmatic way through a network of organisations which must then be managed professionally: 'Governance is about managing networks' (Rhodes, 1996: 658).

A moderate and extremely influential version of this approach is to be found in the work of the US writers Osborne and Gaebler (1992) who argued that approaches to the delivery of public services should be rethought along the lines of ten principles (Box 8.6).

BOX 8.6 TEN PRINCIPLES FOR REINVENTING GOVERNMENT

Entrepreneurial public organisations should:

i   steer more than they row
ii   empower communities rather than simply deliver services
iii   encourage competition rather than monopoly
iv   be driven by their missions not rules
v   fund outcomes not inputs
vi   meets customer, not bureaucratic, needs
vii   earn as well as spend
viii prevent rather than cure
ix   decentralise authority
x   lever the marketplace rather than spend on public programmes.

(Osborne and Gaebler, 1992)

In the UK Mrs Thatcher was successful in cutting the size of the Civil Service, privatised many nationalised industries, introduced requirements for contracting out as many central and local government functions as possible, and began the process of subdividing existing departments of state into business units ('executive agencies'). The overwhelming majority of public servants in the UK are now either in executive agencies, national or local QUANGOs such as National Health Service Trusts, or working for local government.

Additionally, many posts which were formerly in the Civil Service or part of a nationalised industry are now in the private sector.

Although Labour in opposition opposed many of these developments, New Labour governments have endorsed 'public private partnerships' as being a pragmatic way of ensuring the efficient delivery of public services. In the White Paper 'Modernising Government' (1999) and reforms of the NHS, they have placed more emphasis on achieving user-centred targets and less on cut-throat competition and financial economy. The mechanism of contractual delivery of public services by private companies in collaboration with public sector commissioning agencies has remained prominent. Gordon Brown continued the project of reducing the size of the Civil Service, announcing a reduction of 104,000 posts in July 2004.

Recent agreements by the World Trade Organisation require all signatory states to open up the market for government services to international tender. This, and the accession of the former Eastern Bloc countries to the EU, has meant that privatisation and public private partnerships have become a worldwide trend.

EVALUATING PUBLIC POLICY

Evaluation of the effect of decision-making processes on public policy can concentrate on either procedural or substantive issues. From a *procedural* point of view, we can ask whether the process of making the decision accords with the evaluative criteria to be applied (e.g. was the decision taken in a democratic manner, or did the decision maker consider all rational alternatives and cost them?). From a *substantive* point of view we can ask was the result 'correct', set against appropriate criteria in terms of its outcome? The criteria employed may be many and various – ethical, economic, ecological, egalitarian, etc. (e.g. Were the decision makers' objectives achieved? Did the decision promote justice?).

Assuming we have defined our values and specifying objectives, using Lindblom's terminology, it may be possible to assess decision making in a less controversial way. Here we may offer some more 'managerial' concepts for evaluating policy making (Box 8.7)

BOX 8.7   THE 3 'E'S: EFFICIENCY; ECONOMY;
           EFFECTIVENESS

Efficiency can be seen as something like the physicists' definition of 'the ratio of useful work to energy expended' (*Shorter Oxford English Dictionary*: Addenda). Thus given fixed resources and a fixed objective, efficiency can be seen as achieving the maximum effect in the desired direction. The emphasis is often on implementing planned actions to specification.

Economy is clearly closely related to efficiency, but is more likely to be expressed in financial terms. It can be seen as employing minimum resources to achieve a fixed objective. It is more likely to encompass costing of alternative ways to achieve an objective.

Effectiveness can then be seen as including the choice of objectives in order to realise the values desired. The emphasis here is not on the volume of work done, but the overall impact of the work done. In economists' terms has utility been maximised?

The three concepts can thus be seen as occupying a hierarchical relationship with efficiency the most limited concept, economy a somewhat broader one and effectiveness the most comprehensive. Economy in public administration (and more generally) may be interpreted irrationally merely as minimising financial expenditure on a particular budget. If, however, a reduction in expenditure means that the department or organisation fails to achieve its objective, or if, for instance, refusal to buy capital equipment means that expensive staff time is not made good use of, then such behaviour is far from economical in the true sense.

MONITORING PERFORMANCE IN PUBLIC POLICY

Any rational monitoring and evaluation of public policy needs to measure as precisely as possible how far objectives are being achieved. In the absence of a general-purpose measure of efficiency, such as profitability in the private sector, then the output of public sector organisations can only be measured in more specific terms related to their objectives. In principle the establishment of performance indicators' seems unexceptionable. The attempt to define performance indicators has, however, become more controversial and central to the political process in Britain in the light of a number of political developments. These developments include the role of such indicators as part of the privatisation process; their use in the context of 'Citizen's Charters'; and their role in public sector pay bargaining.

In the privatisation process, performance indicators are important in defining the standard of service to be expected from the privatised service provider. Merely specifying a maximum level of profits or prices could encourage the provider to produce a substandard service (perhaps with minimal investment) allowing exploitation of a monopoly position. Thus an electricity company is required to restore any interruptions to supply to at least 85 per cent of domestic customers within three hours (Southern Electric, 1994: 7). Such indicators can then be policed by an independent regulator (in this case the director-general of electricity supply) with 'league tables' of the efficiency of each supplier being compilable and the possibility of the removal of franchises from non-performing companies.

In a series of 'Citizen's Charters' the Conservative Major government in Britain established publicly known standards of performance to which consumers/citizens are entitled. In some cases compensation is payable for underperformance (e.g. refunds on rail season tickets if trains run persistently late). In some cases these standards have been criticised as unacceptably anodyne (e.g. 'you will get a reply within seven days' – but the letter may merely say, 'We are looking into it').

Such standards may be linked to the appraisal of the performance of individual public servants, which, in turn, may be linked ultimately to some sort of payment by results. Such moves have been opposed by most public sector trade unions as a move away from nationally negotiated common standards of pay and service toward individual contracts and as failing to recognise environmental factors that affect individual performance.

One of the major problems may be that those aspects of performance which are most easily quantified are not necessarily the most significant parts of the public sector organisation or individuals' work. Yet, particularly where managers' pay or career success are felt to be crucially affected by them, such performance indicators may come to be 'the tail that wags the corporate dog'. Thus if police officers and forces are judged by the crime clear-up rate, crime prevention and developing good community relations may be neglected. Such statistics may also be subject to manipulation – in our example criminals may be induced to confess to a string of unsolved crimes they did not commit, or 'unsolvable' crimes may not be recorded.

Another example of the problems inherent in the use of such performance indicators can be seen in the publication of school league tables of examination and test performances. The problem here is that the environmental differences between schools are neglected – together with the starting points from which their pupils begin. Some attempts have been made to assess the 'added value' by schools but these have received much less attention than the misleading crude headline figures.

EVALUATING POLICY OUTCOMES: THE DISTRIBUTION OF WEALTH AND INCOME

We shall discuss briefly here the outcomes of public policies in modern welfare states such as Britain in terms of equality and justice.

Consider, by way of example, the distribution of wealth and income. In contemporary Britain, the official statistics on the distribution of marketable wealth are given in Table 8.1.

Whilst the distribution of income is not quite so dramatically unequal, 2005/6 UK Official Figures (Office for National Statistics, 2007) still show the bottom 20 per cent of the population receive only about 25 per cent of the income of the top 20 per cent *after* tax and cash benefits (£13,500 versus £49,300).

In other developed countries published statistics suggest a similar distribution of both income and wealth. The most striking inequalities however can be seen if the figures from less developed economies are taken into account as Table 8.2 shows.

Table 8.1 Marketable wealth in Britain

	1976 (%)	1986 (%)	1996 (%)	2003 (%)
Most wealthy 1 per cent	21	18	20	21
Most wealthy 10 per cent	50	50	52	53
Least wealthy 50 per cent	8	10	7	7

Source: Office for National Statistics (2006)

Table 8.2 World population below international poverty line (2001)

	Population (%)	Millions
All developing countries	21.1	1,089
South Asia	31.3	431
Sub-Saharan Africa	46.4	313
China	16.6	212

Source: World Bank estimate based on population living on below $1.00 per day in *Global Economic Prospects* (2005, Table 1.5)

From a socialist point of view, such statistics suggest that policies attempting equity between individuals in the UK (and similar economies such as those of the EU and the USA) will have to abandon the market mechanism altogether and distribute benefits direct without regard to ability to pay. It is in this context, also, that some radical socialist critiques of piecemeal welfare reforms become intelligible. Such massive inequalities are felt to be incompatible with equal rights for all in a democratic society.

A liberal approach might be to adopt some form of means testing, or redistribute income on a large scale, perhaps through a 'negative income tax' scheme instead of social security and means-tested benefits. In such a scheme a minimum standard of living is guaranteed to all, with a minimum of stigmatising special treatment for the poor, by paying out income through the same machinery which collects taxes on the basis of one declaration of income and circumstances for everyone. Solutions are sought which preserve the individual freedom associated with market mechanisms, whilst treating all citizens by consistent rules.

From a conservative point of view, an uneven distribution of capital may merely be seen as enabling worthwhile investments to be made and as the result of rewards of previous risk taking and effort. Providing the income of the bottom 20 per cent of the population is judged to be above an adequate 'safety net' level, the existence of unequal incomes is not seen as a problem for social and economic policy.

It is often thought that the 'welfare state', both through progressive taxation and the redistributive effect of its 'universal' social services, has radically affected the distribution of income and wealth (especially the former after tax and benefits). A considerable academic literature exists on this (which concentrates, however, on the tax element of the equation). Summarising this brutally, the overall conclusion seems to be that taxation has had surprisingly little effect – other than to redistribute within social classes. Perhaps surprisingly, it seems that the social services have also had virtually no redistributive effect between classes as LeGrand (1982) clearly shows. In Britain working-class gains from unemployment benefits have been counterbalanced by middle-class gains from post-school-leaving age educational benefits – with the middle classes showing a greater capacity to benefit from the National Health Service.

The global inequalities referred to seem difficult to address in a world divided into sovereign states and employing a capitalist economic trading system. As we briefly considered in Chapter 2, the rules governing finance, trade and aid are clearly less than ideal in terms of promoting equality. More important still, it might be argued, is the lack of any real commitment by either ordinary people or politicians in richer states to make extensive sacrifices to achieve greater justice and equality across the globe. The reluctance of US voters to give up gas-guzzling automobiles which help to create global warming – thus ruining the environment of Bangladeshi coastal farmers and flooding low-lying Pacific islands – seems to support this. On the other hand, the partially successful movement for a moratorium on the public debts of the poorest countries gives cause to hope that a sense of a global community is emerging. Colas (2002) highlighted the need for a sense of international civil society to be developed in a globalised world. Social movements of ordinary citizens must develop to balance the power of multinational enterprises and governmental organisations.

Thus, in the end, any discussion of public policy is likely to return to the ideological differences explored in more depth in Chapter 4. Individual choices on political values cannot be avoided in evaluating public policy. However, the potential for consensus can be underestimated since many enlightened social policies (e.g. effective health and educational services) are good for the individuals they benefit as well as contributing to the efficiency of the overall economy.

THE POLITICAL POLICY-MAKING PROCESS

This chapter has largely focused on what might be termed 'macro'-level policy making in terms of how governments make and implement policy. But this can be shaped by 'micro'-level policy decisions made by individual politicians (in weak party systems) or political parties (in strong party systems). These political actors develop and present the suite of policies they believe will be electorally successful.

The 'micro' policy process is not just about the end result of producing the policies, but also the process itself and what that says about the political organisation. After four successive election defeats (1979, 1983, 1987 and 1992) the Labour Party in the mid-1990s felt it had to change both how it decided party policy as well as the actual policies themselves. Under Tony Blair's guidance the Labour Party streamlined the policy process by significantly reducing the number of people who were consulted in the process. At the same time Labour made use of political marketing techniques such as focus groups (Wring, 2007) to obtain feedback from voters.

The effect of these changes was to strengthen the position of the Labour Party leadership on policy making. Once elected Tony Blair's government was adjudged to have continued this centralised approach.

A CRISIS IN DEMOCRATIC POLITICS?

Civic engagement is where citizens participate in civil society, such as being a trade union member, organising a youth group or belonging to a charity. Together such disparate activities comprise social capital in terms of the overall well-being of society and so act as a social bond (Norris and Curtice, 2004). Putnam (2000) suggests that civic engagement is the invisible cement which brings together different communities within one overall social infrastructure. Although civic activity may be non-political, it does imply an interest in public affairs, the very basis upon which politics is founded.

The widely accepted view amongst sociologists and political scientists is that over the past thirty years there has been a general decline in civic engagement in liberal democracies (Norris and Curtice, 2004). It is suggested that this decline has been especially acute amongst younger people and the better educated (Putnam, 2000). One clear manifestation of this, it is argued, has been a general fall in voting turnout in many Western countries. It is suggested that this decline represents either a political apathy towards liberal democracy or a sense of alienation, especially amongst young people.

A number of different explanations for a growing sense of civic disillusionment or alienation have been put forward. One view is that a crisis in liberalism has created the growth of individualism which undermines the connective nature of civic engagement (Mazzoleni, 2000). An alternative view suggests that it is the communication process, in the form of political marketing, which has led to a focus on the individual at the expense of society (Turow, 1997; Putnam, 2000). Focusing specifically on Britain, Pattie *et al.* (2004) suggest that there are a number of factors which are reducing the willingness of citizens to co-operate: increased geographical mobility; the decline of religion; the weakening of class solidarity; and the growth of a 'market state'.

Not all commentators, however, believe that these developments suggest civic engagement is in decline. Rather, one school of thought suggests that one type of civic engagement is being replaced by another. In this new form of civic engagement citizenship is increasingly based around consumption (Giddens, 1991; Bennett, 1998; Scammell, 2001). Consumer behaviour is increasingly adding to civic participation through its focus on environmental and ethical concerns, and the consequent growth of 'accelerated pluralism' (Moloney, 2006). Communication by politicians, therefore, needs to reflect that the recipient is the citizen-consumer not the citizen-voter.

TAKING POLITICAL ACTION

Every reader of this book about politics will, after reading it, go on to practise politics in the all-encompassing sense we defined it in Chapter 1. Even the most private of individuals will inevitably need to work with, and on occasion come into conflict with, others in social situations. At every point upon the globe some state will claim jurisdiction over your actions. It is hoped that this book will, at a minimum, have given some sense of the processes at work and have suggested some sources of further information when they are required (for more see the Recommended reading sections at the end of chapters and the Appendix). It is hoped that some readers not already enrolled on politics courses may have been inspired to do so. A section of the Appendix gives further details on courses available in Britain.

Politics is not only a spare-time or academic activity, however. There is truth in the feminist slogan 'the personal is the political'. It is worth reviewing your personal relationships and professional activities and plans to see if they are in accord with political principles you profess (although this can be rather sobering).

No sensible author would urge all their readers to go out and become professional politicians, but the authors share Aristotle's conviction that it is a mark of civilisation to wish to join in the political life of the community. There is great satisfaction to be had in not only discussing political issues in the abstract but in helping to build a better world through membership of voluntary organisations which attempt to influence events – from Greenpeace through to Unidentified Flying Object enthusiasts. Almost everywhere local party organisations tend to fall over themselves with eagerness in welcoming new members. Independently readers may actually exercise real influence through writing to newspapers and to their elected representatives.

If politics is thought of only in terms of the activities of the nation state, then the scope for ordinary citizens is necessarily a limited one. But the argument of this book has been that important political decisions can be made at the level of work, educational and leisure organisations, by local and regional authorities, voluntary interest groups and by international co-operation. The scope for individual action is already large and should, in the authors' view, be made larger.

RECOMMENDED READING

Allison, Graham T., 1987, *The Essence of Decision: Explaining the Cuban Missile Crisis*, New York, Harper College
    Develops three theoretical models of decision making from a study of the Cuban missile crisis. Influential in management schools as well as amongst political scientists.

Friedman, Milton and Friedman, Rose, 1980, *Free To Choose*, Harmondsworth, Middlesex, Penguin
    A popular exposition of the fashionable market-oriented view of the relationship between government and the economy.

Hill, Michael, 1997, *The Policy Process in the Modern State*, London, Prentice Hall
    A standard UK public administration text with welcome emphasis on more general themes.

Hogwood, Brian W. and Gunn, Lewis A., 1984, *Policy Analysis for the Real World*, Oxford, Oxford University Press
A general model of the policy process which can be applied in any country.

Lewis, Gail *et al.*, 2000, *Rethinking Social Policy*, London, Sage for the Open University
Useful introduction to social policy analysis.

Stevens, Joe B., 1993, *The Economics of Collective Choice*, Oxford, Westview
A more challenging and academic treatment of attempts to apply market-oriented models to understanding society.

Young, Michael, 1961, *The Rise of the Meritocracy 1870–2033*, Harmondsworth, Middlesex, Penguin
Thoughtful, well-written and amusing discussion of the political implications of equality of opportunity in the form of a social history of Britain written in 2033.

WEBSITES

http://www.ukonline.gov.uk
UK Government information portal.

http://www.official-documents.co.uk/document
UK official documents.

http://thomas.loc.gov/
THOMAS: US Legislative Information, with link to Library of Congress, etc.

http://lib.umich.edu/govdocs
University of Michigan Documents Center – government resources on the Web.

http://www.gpoaccess.gov/index.html
GPO Access – US Government Printing Office – full text of many US Government documents.

APPENDIX:
SOURCES ON POLITICS

This guide is mainly intended for use by British students on under-graduate courses with access to a university library and the Internet. Some of the obscurer sources mentioned would perhaps only be likely to be used by students writing dissertations – but could earn extra credit if used in ordinary assignments. Large city libraries may also provide many of the same resources and increasingly owners of personal computers with modems can gain access via the Internet to much of the world's knowledge. Non-university readers may not realise that many academic libraries will give reference access to non-members of the university with very little formality (although you are less likely to be able to borrow directly). Most public libraries can also obtain items not in stock on inter-library loan at minimal cost to the reader. Schools and public libraries also usually provide access to the Internet.

BOOKS

Too many students search for material by going to what they think is the right shelf in the loan section of the library, finding little or nothing and then reporting back to their tutor in all seriousness, 'There is nothing on it in the library'. If you have some authors and titles in mind (for instance references from this book) look these up in the catalogue – they may not be where you think – and view adjacent entries in the catalogue and on the shelves. The catalogue may lead you to restricted loan collections, reserve stacks or departmental collections, which may not always be obvious. You should also check the subject catalogue, trying to think of related terms ('Socialism' as well as 'Labour Party', 'Soviet Union' as well as 'Russia', etc.).

Consider also the possibility of using the Reference shelves. Much valuable material can be found in sources like the *Encyclopaedia of Social Sciences*, Kogan and Hawkesworth (1992), and various specialised dictionaries especially McLean and McMillan (2003) and Jay (2006). Most useful statistical sources will probably also be in the reference section including many published by the Office for National Statistics.

An important part of the reference section will be a collection of specialised bibliographies, which will give you further ideas for books and journals to look for – for example Royal Commission on Historical Monuments (1982); Shaw and Sklar (1977).

NEWSPAPERS

Much valuable and (especially) recent material is to be found in newspapers and magazines. The problem is to find it. When, for instance, did the last election in France take place? If you do not know, you cannot easily find reports on it in quality daily newspapers such as *The Times*, the *Guardian*, *The New York Times* or *Le Monde*. *Keesings Contemporary Archives* is a valuable and clearly indexed summary of contemporary events which can help you with this as well as providing much useful information in its own right. Several newspapers such as *The Times* also print quarterly or annual indexes. (See also below for electronic versions/searching.)

JOURNALS

University libraries also contain extensive collections of (usually quarterly) academic and professional journals. They often cover the points you are looking for in a pithier and more up-to-date fashion than do textbooks. Key British academic journals include *Talking Politics*, *Political Studies*, *Politics*, *Political Quarterly* and the *British Journal of Political Science*. Other important journals include the *American Political Science Review* and the *Revue Français de Science Politique*. In addition to articles, these journals usually carry very useful book reviews – excellent for supplying telling critical points about books recommended by your tutor. The greatest volume of reviews is to be found in the *Political Studies Review* (these are available online).

The same problem applies to journals as to newspapers – finding the relevant article. To some extent their titles may help – public administration in *Public Administration*, etc., but serious use of journals requires you to master the bibliographical tools available. Examples of these are the *International Political Science Abstracts* (six per annum) which index and summarise most relevant academic journals and the annual *International Bibliography of Political Science*.

OFFICIAL SOURCES

British government publications may be kept in a separate sequence from other publications and may not be individually catalogued alongside the book collection. This can lead students to miss very valuable information. Most important central government publications are published by Her Majesty's Stationery Office (was HMSO now TSO, The Stationery Office) and their catalogues are a valuable way to track down recent publications in this category.

TSO publications come in four main categories. First, Hansard the daily record of parliamentary debates which are subsequently bound and indexed. References to Hansard will normally refer to which House (Commons or Lords), the Parliamentary Session (e.g. 2008/9), possibly the date of the debate, and certainly to the 'Column' in which the remark quoted is reported (each page being divided into two columns). Debates often read better than they sounded, because MPs can 'correct' Hansard's reporting. Second, 'Parliamentary Papers' which are numbered in order of publication during a session (e.g. HC 213 2008/9) and include the reports of select committees – these often contain interesting interviews with ministers, civil servants, industrialists, academics and others about the workings of government policy. Third, a series of Command Papers (i.e. issued theoretically by command of Her Majesty), the most important of which are White Papers stating government policy in a particular area. Others are consultative 'Green Papers'. Finally, the TSO issues a host of more specialised publications by government bodies.

Unfortunately for scholars, many government publications are not published by TSO, but by the departments or agencies concerned, and are therefore more difficult to track down. Some useful documents may be lodged only in the library of the House of Commons or the department concerned (e.g. reports on the tendering out of parts of their work). All publications by local government bodies and nearly all by QUANGOs are also naturally published by the individual bodies concerned in an uncoordinated manner. For local government see Nurcombe (1992) and Snape (1969).

EU documentation is as complex as that of the British government (see Thomson, 1989; Thomson and Mitchell, 1993 onwards), US government publications more so (see Morehead, 1996).

An important point to note is that most official documents are now available on the World Wide Web (see below).

OTHER PRINTED SOURCES

Politically relevant bodies like the Confederation of British Industry and the Trades Union Congress, major pressure groups and the political parties all publish numerous reports and papers which can often only be obtained by writing to them direct.

Unpublished student theses and conference papers may also contain valuable information. Some of these are catalogued by the British Library and may be obtained from them on inter-library loan.

VIDEOS/TELEVISION/RADIO

Electronic mass media sources can be valuable but are difficult to identify, capture and use. The BBC monitoring service provides some bibliographical assistance to academics. For undergraduates the most useful source is your own library's catalogue. The single most useful source of video material in UK higher education is the Open University, which publishes catalogues and provides broadcasting calendars to the general public. Archives of news television programmes are increasingly available on TV station websites, but there does not appear to be a separate systematic index of this material.

CD-ROM

All major libraries now have collections of material on CD-ROM (compact disk – read-only memory) and facilities to view them. Most of these so far are either bibliographic databases, or electronic versions of reference works such as encyclopedias, dictionaries, company information, etc.

The big advantage of CD-ROM sources is that they can be searched far more easily and in far more sophisticated ways than conventional printed versions of the same material. For instance a set of academic journal articles or abstracts can be searched for any mention of both say 'information' and 'politics' in the same article or abstract – or within so many words of each other.

In principle CD-ROM as well as DVD format material can be used to present exciting interactive multimedia teaching materials. Unfortunately only a limited amount of relevant materials are yet available. An instance is Boynton (1996) on *The Art of Campaign Advertising*, which includes samples of US political advertising. Two articles which review political CD-ROM material are Ludlam (1997) and Luna and McKenzie (1997).

ONLINE DATABASES

Just as there are so many journals that no library is likely to have all the relevant journals, there are now so many bibliographic databases that no library is likely to have all of them either in printed or CD-ROM versions. Fortunately most academic libraries now have access via SuperJANET to literally hundreds of databases held at computer centres like Dialog in California. These online systems are somewhat less user-friendly than the CD-ROM versions mentioned earlier so that you may have to ask a librarian to search for you, but this does mean that, in a sense, the resources of most of the world's major libraries can be searched from any one of them.

Not only bibliographic databases are accessible in this form, but also a number of 'full-text' databases are available, including for instance the full text of the *Harvard Business Review* and recent issues of the *Guardian* and other quality newspapers. Thus a required article can be downloaded onto your own computer and quotations from it pasted into the assignment you are writing. Where the full text is not available a fax of any article indexed can usually be sent.

THE INTERNET

Computer-literate students can use direct access to the Internet to search campus information systems and libraries almost anywhere in the world for relevant information. Some information facilities, like Dialog, are commercial operations to which you must pay a subscription, but many are open access. For instance you can access the Library of Congress and British Library catalogues direct and free of charge.

A word of warning should be issued on using Web sources 'it's on the Web' is even less a reliable guide to truth than 'it's in print'. It is essential to assess the reliability of the source and the credibility of the information. The conclusions of an academic article in a refereed e-journal; a statement made in a government policy document; a claim made on an interest group website; a news report in a popular newspaper or a revelation in an anonymous blog all have very different status as evidence for an argument. Of course, wherever your evidence or argument comes from it needs to be properly acknowledged.

Some of the most useful World Wide Web addresses from a political point of view have been listed at the end of each chapter. Note especially the general political science references after Chapter 1 and the official government sources noted after Chapter 8. A few more general sources are listed here:

http://www.loc.gov
  Library of Congress catalogue – US copyright library.

http://catalogue.bl.org
  British Library catalogue – UK copyright library.

http://scholar.google.com
  Google Scholar – indexes articles in learned journals.

http://www.wikipedia.org
  Wikipedia – comprehensive but not entirely reliable encyclopedia.

http://www.internetworld.com
  Internet news service.

http://www.washingtonpost.com
  Washington Post.

http://www.guardian.co.uk
  Guardian *newspaper.*

http://www.mori.com
Leading public opinion poll organisation.

http://www.Yougov.com
Internet polls.

http://library.ukc.ac.uk/cartoons
University of Kent Cartoon Centre (many political cartoons).

http://www.stansey.com
The principal author's home page including a feedback facility.

COURSES ON POLITICS

Any reader not already enrolled on a politics course who is now contemplating doing so is recommended to look at an informative pamphlet – *Study Politics* – produced by the Political Studies Association (PSA) (Fisher and Arthurs, 2003 – downloadable from http://www.psa.ac.uk) which outlines the nature and implications of choosing an undergraduate politics course. The career development organisation CRAC produces biannually a more detailed booklet that outlines all full-time degree courses available in Britain. There is also an annual supplement to the *New Statesman* produced in collaboration with the PSA. Most further education colleges and university extramural departments provide part-time courses suitable for the beginning student, as does the Open University. Increasingly even full-time courses have a fair proportion of 'mature' students, so that older readers should not dismiss the possibility of pursuing their interest in this way.

Courses in Britain are very diverse but there is now an agreed specification for first degrees in political science agreed by the European Conference of National Political Science Associations. This includes the following core subject areas:

Political Theory/History of Political Thought
Methodology including Statistics
Political System of one's own country and of the European Union
Comparative Politics
International Relations
Public Administration and Policy Analysis
Political Economy/Political Sociology

(*Political Studies Association News*, 14(3): 3)

However, this is a set of recommendations that has not been fully implemented. Students who wish to explore in-depth international relations, public policy and administration, the politics of a particular area (e.g. the South), or even the history of political thought, should ensure that these options are available on the course they are contemplating.

ASSOCIATIONS FOR POLITICS STUDENTS

Readers already enrolled on politics courses will find it helpful to join an appropriate association. For sixth formers and undergraduates in Britain, the Politics Association Resources Centre (Studio 16, I-Mex Business Park, Hamilton Road, Manchester, M13 0PD) offers a bargain rate subscription entitling them to a very useful journal (*Talking Politics*) and access to various revision conferences and learning resources. For postgraduate students, the Political Studies Association of the UK, Department of Politics, University of Newcastle, NE1 7RU, organises an excellent Annual Postgraduate Conference and offers discounted membership, which includes four journals and a newsletter. The addresses of corresponding groups in other countries can be had from the International Political Science Association Secretariat at SB-331, 1590 Avenue Docteur Penfield, Montreal, Quebec, H3G 1C5, Canada (http:///www.ipsa-aisp.org).

RECOMMENDED READING

CRAC, 2007, *Degree Course Guide to Politics Including European Studies*, Cambridge, Hobsons
   These pamphlets are often found bound in two-volume sets of Degree Course Guides *covering all subjects in reference libraries.*

Englefield, D. and Drewry, G. (eds), 1984, *Information Sources in Politics and Political Science World Wide*, London, Butterworth

Levine, John R. *et al.*, 2005, *The Internet for Dummies*, Hoboken, NJ, Wiley

Mardall, B., 1976, *How To Find Out in Politics and Government*, London, LLRS Publications

REFERENCES

Acton, Lord, 1887, 'Letter to Bishop Mandell Creighton', in Jay, Anthony (ed.), 1996, *Oxford Dictionary of Political Quotations*, Oxford, Oxford University Press

Allardt, E. and Littunen, Y. (eds), 1964, *Cleavages, Ideologies and Party Systems*, Helsinki, The Westermarck Society

Allison, Graham T., 1987, *The Essence of Decision: Explaining the Cuban Missile Crisis*, New York, Harper College

Almond, Gabriel and Coleman, James (eds), 1960, *The Politics of Developing Areas*, Princeton, NJ, Princeton University Press

Almond, Gabriel and Verba, Sidney, 1963, *The Civic Culture*, Princeton, NJ, Princeton University Press

Andreski, Stanislav, 1968, *The African Predicament: A Study in the Pathology of Modernisation*, London, Michael Joseph

Arblaster, Anthony, 2002, *Democracy*, 3rd edn, Buckingham, Open University Press

Arendt, Hannah, 1967, *The Origins of Totalitarianism*, 2nd edn, London, Allen & Unwin

Aristotle, 1946, *The Politics of Aristotle*, ed. Ernest Barker, Oxford, Clarendon Press

Arterton, C. F., 1987, *Teledemocracy*, London, Sage

Axtmann, Roland, 2003, *Understanding Democratic Politics*, London, Sage

Bachrach, Peter and Baratz, Morton S., 1970, *Power and Poverty*, New York, Oxford University Press

Banfield, Edward C. and Banfield, L. F., 1967, *The Moral Basis of a Backward Society*, Glencoe, IL, Free Press

Barker, Sir Ernest, 1961, *Principles of Social and Political Theory*, Oxford, Oxford University Press

Barnett, S., 2002, 'Will a Crisis in Journalism Provoke a Crisis in Democracy?' *Political Quarterly* 4: 400–408

Barrett, Susan and Fudge, C., 1981, Policy and Action, London, Methuen

Baylis, John and Smith, Steve (eds), 2005, *The Globalization of World Politics*, 3rd edn, Oxford, Oxford University Press

Bell, Daniel, 1960, *The End of Ideology*, New York, Basic Books

—— 1973, *The Coming of Post Industrial Society*, New York, Basic Books

Benedict, Ruth, 1935, *Patterns of Culture*, London, Routledge & Kegan Paul

Benn, Stanley I. and Peters, Richard S., 1959, *Social Principles and the Democratic State*, London, George Allen & Unwin

Bennett, W., 1998, 'The Uncivic Culture: Communication, Identity and the Rise of Lifestyle Politics', *PS: Political Science and Politics* 31: 741–761

Bentham, Jeremy, 1948, *Introduction to the Principles of Morals and Legislation*, ed. W. Harrison, Oxford, Blackwell

Berlin, Isaiah, 1958, *Two Concepts of Liberty: An Inaugural Lecture*, Oxford, Clarendon Press

—— 1969, *Four Essays on Liberty*, Oxford, Clarendon Press

Bernstein, Carl and Woodward, Bob, 1974, *All the President's Men*, New York, Simon & Schuster

Bevir, Mark, 2000, 'New Labour: A Study in Ideology', *British Journal of Politics and International Relations* 2(3): 277–301

Birch, A. H., 1964, *Representative and Responsible Government*, London, George Allen & Unwin

Blair, Tony, 1994, *Socialism*, London, Fabian Society

Bloch, M., 1961, *Feudal Society*, London, Routledge & Kegan Paul

Blumenthal, S., 1980, *The Permanent Campaign: Inside the World of Elite Political Operatives*, Boston, MA, Beacon

Bogdanor, Vernon, 1988, *Constitutions in Democratic Politics*, Aldershot, Gower

Bohannan, Paul, 1965, 'Social and Political Organisation of the Tiv', in Gibbs, J. L. (ed.), *The Peoples of Africa*, New York, Holt, Rinehart & Winston

Boynton, G. R., 1996, *The Art of Campaign Advertising*, Chatham, NJ, Chatham House

Brandt, Willy (Chairman), 1980, *North–South: A Programme for Survival*, London, Pan

Brinton, Crane, 1965, *The Anatomy of Revolution*, London, Jonathan Cape

Budge, Ian, 1996, *The New Challenge of Direct Democracy*, Oxford, Basil Blackwell

Burke, Edmund, 1907, *The Works*, 6 vols, Oxford, Oxford University Press (World's Classics)

Butler, Anthony, 2000, 'The Third Way Project in Britain: The Role of the Prime Minister's Policy Unit', *Politics* 20(3): 153–160

Campbell, Peter, 1965, *French Electoral Systems and Elections Since 1789*, rev. edn, London, Faber & Faber

Castells, Manuel, 2002, *The Rise of the Network Society*, Oxford, Blackwell

Cater, Douglas, 1965, *Power in Washington: A Critical Look at Today's Struggle to Govern in the USA*, London, Collins

Clausewitz, Karl Von, 1967, *A Short Guide to Clausewitz On War*, ed. Roger Ashley Leonard, London, Weidenfeld & Nicolson

Colas, Alejandro, 2002, *International Civil Society: Social Movements in World Politics*, Cambridge, Polity

Coleman, S., 2005, 'New Mediation and Direct Representation: Reconceptualising Representation in the Digital Age', *New Media and Society* 7(2): 177–198

Cranston, Maurice, 1954, *Freedom: A New Analysis*, 2nd edn, London, Longmans Green & Co

—— 1962, *Human Rights Today*, London, Ampersand Books

Crick, Bernard, 2000, *In Defence of Politics*, 5th edn, London, Continuum International

Dahl, Robert A., 1961, *Who Governs?* New Haven, CT, Yale University Press

—— 1971, *Polyarchy*, New Haven, CT, Yale University Press

Dahrendorf, Rolf, 1959, *Class and Class Conflict in Industrial Societies*, London, Routledge & Kegan Paul

Dalton, Russell J., 1988, *Citizen Politics in Western Democracies*, Chatham, NJ, Chatham House

Dawson, Richard E. *et al.*, 1977, *Political Socialization*, Boston, MA, Little, Brown

De Jouvenal, Bertrand, 1963, *The Pure Theory of Politics*, Cambridge, Cambridge University Press

Deacon, D. and Golding, P., 1994, *Taxation and Representation*, London, John Libbey

Derbyshire, J. Denis and Derbyshire, Ian, 1991, *World Political Systems: An Introduction to Comparative Government*, Edinburgh, Chambers Political Spotlights

—— 1996, *Political Systems of the World*, New York, St Martin's Press

Deutsch, Karl, 1963, *Nerves of Government*, Glencoe, IL, Free Press

Devine, Fiona, 2002, 'Qualitative Methods', in Marsh, D. and Stoker, G. (eds), *Theory and Methods in Political Science*, 2nd edn, Basingstoke, Palgrave

Dicey, A. V., 1941, *Law of the Constitution*, 9th edn, ed. E. C. S. Wade, London, Macmillan

Djilas, Milovan, 1966, *The New Class*, London, Allen & Unwin

Downs, Anthony, 1957, *An Economic Theory of Democracy*, New York, Harper & Row

Dowse, Robert E., 1969, *Modernization in Ghana and the USSR*, London, Routledge & Kegan Paul

—— 1972, 'Functionalism in Political Science', *World Politics* 18(4): 607–622

Drezner, Daniel and Farrell, Henry, 2004, 'The Power and Politics of Blogs', paper presented to the Annual Meeting of the American Political Science Association, Chicago, IL

Duff, Andrew (ed.), 1993, *Subsidiarity Within the European Community*, London, Federal Trust for Education and Research

Duverger, Maurice, 1972, *The Study of Politics*, London, Nelson

Easton, David, 1979, *A Framework for Political Analysis*, Chicago, IL, University of Chicago Press

Easton, David and Dennis, Jack, 1969, *Children in the Political System*, New York, McGraw-Hill

Eberhard, Wolfram, 1977, *A History of China*, 4th edn, London, Routledge

Edelman, M., 1977, *Political Language*, London, Academic Press

Edwards, Lyford, 1927, *The Natural History of Revolution*, Chicago, IL, University of Chicago (reprinted 1970)

Encyclopaedia of Social Sciences, 1963, ed. Edward R. A. Seligman, New York, Macmillan

Etzioni, Amitai, 1995, *The Spirit of Community*, London, Fontana

Eysenck, Hans J. and Kamin, L. J., 1981, *Intelligence: The Battle for the Mind*, London, Pan Books

Fainsod, Merle, 1963, *How Russia is Ruled*, Cambridge, MA, Harvard University Press

Finer, Samuel E., 1970, *Comparative Government*, London, Allen Lane/The Penguin Press

—— 1976, *The Man on Horseback*, 2nd edn, London, Pall Mall Press

Firestone, Shulamith, 1971, *The Dialectic of Sex*, New York, Bantam Books

Fischer, Michael, 1980, *Iran: From Religious Dispute to Revolution*, Cambridge, MA, Harvard University Press

Fisher, Justin and Arthurs, Jack, 2003, *Study Politics at Universities in the United Kingdom*, Newcastle, Political Studies Association

Fogarty, M. P., 1957, *Christian Democracy in Western Europe*, London, Routledge & Kegan Paul

Friedman, Milton and Friedman, Rose, 1980, *Free To Choose*, Harmondsworth, Middlesex, Penguin

Friedrich, Carl J. (ed.), 1964, *Totalitarianism*, New York, Grosset & Dunlop

Frissen, Paul, 1994, 'The Virtual Reality of Informatization in Public Administration', Conference on ICTs in Public Administration, London, 30 September

Gbadamosi, T. G. O., 1978, *The Growth of Islam Among the Yoruba, 1841–1908*, London, Longman

Gerth, H. and Mills, C. Wright (eds), 1948, *From Max Weber: Essays in Sociology*, London, Routledge & Kegan Paul

Gibbins, John R. and Reiner, Bo, 1999, *The Politics of Postmodernity*, London, Sage

Giddens, A., 1991, *Modernity and Self-identity: Self and Society in the Late Modern Age*, Stanford, CA, Stanford University Press.

Gluckman, Max, 1965, *Custom and Conflict in Africa*, Oxford, Blackwell

Golder, Matt, 2005, 'Democratic Electoral Systems around the World, 1946–2000', *Electoral Studies* 24: 103–121

Goldman, Emma, 1915, *Anarchism and Other Essays*, New York, Mother Earth Publishing Association

Gorovitz, S., 1976, 'John Rawls: A Theory of Justice', in de Crespigny, Anthony and Minogue, Kenneth (eds), *Contemporary Political Philosophers*, London, Methuen, 272–289

Gramsci, A., 1969, *The Prince*, New York

Green, Thomas H., 1941, 'Lectures on the Principles of Political Obligation', quoted in Milne, A. J. M., 1962, *The Social Philosophy of English Idealism*, London, George Allen & Unwin

Greenleaf, W. H., 1983, *The British Political Tradition*, London, Methuen

Hamilton, A., Jay, J. and Madison, J., 1961, *The Federalist Papers*, ed. Jacob E. Cooke, Middletown, CT, Wesleyan University Press

Hayek, F. A., 1979, *Law, Legislation and Liberty*, London, Routledge & Kegan Paul

Heclo, H., 2000, 'Campaigns and Governing: A Conspectus', in Ornstein, N. and Mann, T. (eds), *The Permanent Campaign and Its Future*, Washington, DC, American Enterprise Institute and the Brookings Institution

Hershey, Marjorie R. and Hill, David B., 1975, *Watergate and the Benevolent Leader*, Chicago, IL, Midwest Political Science Association Proceedings

Hess, Robert D. and Torney, Judith V., 1967, *The Development of Political Attitudes in Children*, Chicago, IL, Aldine Press

Himmelweit, Hilde, Humphrey, Patrick and Jaeger, Marianne, 1985, *How Voters Decide*, Milton Keynes, Open University Press

Hobhouse, Leonard, 1964, *Liberalism*, New York, Oxford University Press (reprint of 1911 edn, with new intro.)

Hogwood, Brian W. and Gunn, Lewis A., 1984, *Policy Analysis for the Real World*, Oxford, Oxford University Press

Hood, C., 1976, *The Limits of Administration*, London, Wiley

Horowitz, Irving, 1964, *The Anarchists*, New York, Dell Publishing Co.

Huntington, Samuel P., 1957, *The Soldier and the State*, Cambridge, MA, Harvard University Press

Irving, R. E. M., 1979, *The Christian Democratic Parties of Western Europe*, London, George Allen & Unwin

Jackson, Nigel, 2006, 'Dipping Their Big Toe into the Blogosphere: The Use of Weblogs by the Political Parties in the 2005 General Election', *Aslib Proceedings: New Information Perspectives* 58(4): 292–303

Jacques, Martin (ed.), 1998, *Marxism Today*, Special Issue, London

Jay, Anthony (ed.), 2006, *Oxford Dictionary of Political Quotations*, 3rd edn, Oxford, Oxford University Press

Jennings, Sir Ivor, 1957, *Parliament*, Cambridge, Cambridge University Press

John, Peter, 2002, 'Quantitative Methods', in Marsh, D. and Stoker, G. (eds), *Theory and Methods in Political Science*, 2nd edn, Basingstoke, Palgrave

Johnson, Norman, 1987, *The Welfare State in Transition*, Brighton, Wheatsheaf

Jones, Maldwyn A., 1960, *American Immigration*, Chicago, IL, University of Chicago Press

Karpik, Lucien, 1978, *Organisation and Environment*, London, Sage

Keman, Hans (ed.), 2002, *Comparative Democratic Politics*, London, Sage

Knight, Barry, 1993/4, *Voluntary Action*, London, Home Office/ Centris

Kogan, Maurice and Hawkesworth, Mary (eds), 1992, *Encyclopaedia of Government and Politics*, London, Routledge

Kuhn, T., 1970, *The Structure of Scientific Revolutions*, Chicago, IL, University of Chicago Press.

Lambert, Wallace E. and Klineberg, Otto, 1967, *Children's Views of Foreign Peoples*, New York, Irvington

Lasswell, Harold, 1936, *Politics: Who Gets What, When, How?*, London, Peter Smith (Reprinted)

LeDuc, Lawrence, Nienú, Richard G. and Norris, Pippa (eds), 2002, *Comparing Democracies 2: New Challenges in the Study of Elections and Voting*, London, Sage

Lees-Marshment, Jennifer, 2001, *Political Marketing and British Political Parties*, Manchester, Manchester University Press

LeGrand, Julian, 1982, *The Strategy of Equality: Redistribution and the Social Services*, London, Allen & Unwin

Lemarchand, Rene (ed.), 1977, *African Kingdoms in Perspective*, London, Frank Cass

Lenin, N., 1917, 'The State and the Revolution: Marxist Teaching on the State . . .', in Marx, K., Engels, F. and Lenin, V. I., 1960, *The Essential Left: Four Classic Texts on the Principles of Socialism*, London, Unwin

Lewis, Bernard, 2003, *The Crisis of Islam: Holy War and Unholy Terror*, London, Weidenfeld & Nicolson

Lindblom, C. E., 1959, 'The Science of Muddling Through', *Administrative Review* 19: 79–88

Lipset, Seymour Martin, 1979, *The First New Nation: The USA in Comparative and Historical Perspective*, New York, Norton

Lovelock, James, 1979, *Gaia*, Oxford, Oxford University Press

Luard, Evan, 1990, *The Globalization of Politics: The Changed Focus of Political Action in the Modern World*, New York, New York University Press

Ludlam, Steve, 1997, 'CD-ROM Reviews', *Political Studies* 45 (4): 784–789

Luna, C. J. and McKenzie, J. M., 1997, 'Beyond the Chalkboard: Multimedia Sources for Instruction in Political Science', *PS: Political Science and Politics* 30(1): 60–68

McClellan, D., 1986, *Ideology*, Milton Keynes, Open University Press

McGrew, Tony G. and Lewis, Paul G., 1992, *Global Politics*, Cambridge, Cambridge University Press

Mckenzie, W. J. M., 1958, *Free Elections*, London, Allen & Unwin

McKibbin, R., 1983, *The Evolution of the Labour Party 1910–1924*, Oxford, Oxford University Press

Mackintosh, John P., 1966, *Nigerian Government and Politics*, London, George Allen & Unwin

McLean, Ian and McMillan, Alistair (eds), 2003, *Oxford Concise Dictionary of Politics*, 2nd edn, Oxford, Oxford University Press.

McLuhan, Marshall, 1964, *Understanding the Media: The Extension of Man*, London, Routledge & Kegan Paul

McNair, B., 2003, *An Introduction to Political Communication*, London, Routledge

MacPherson, C. B., 1966, *The Real World of Democracy: The Massey Lecture*, Oxford, Clarendon Press

McQuail, Denis, 2005, *McQuail's Mass Communication Theory*, 5th edn, London, Sage

Mangham, Ian, 1979, *The Politics of Organisational Change*, London, Associated Business Press

Marcuse, Herbert, 1964, *One Dimensional Man*, London, Routledge & Kegan Paul

Margolis, M., Resnick, D. and Levy, J., 2003, 'Major Parties Dominate, Minor Parties Struggle: US Elections and the Internet', in Gibson, R. *et al.* (eds), *Political Parties and the Internet*, London, Routledge

Marsh, David and Stoker, Gerry (eds), 2002, *Theory and Methods in Political Science*, 2nd edn, Basingstoke, Palgrave

Marshall, L., 1961, 'Sharing, Talking and Giving: Relief of Social Tensions Among the !Kung Bushmen', *Africa* 31(3): 231–249

Marx, Karl and Engels, Frederick, 1962, *Selected Works*, 2 vols, Moscow, Foreign Languages Publishing House

Mazzoleni, G., 2000, 'A Return to Civic and Political Engagement

Prompted by Personalised Political Leadership?', *Political Communication* 17: 325–328

Michels, Robert, 1915, *Political Parties*, New York, Constable (reprinted 1959)

Milgram, Stanley, 1965, 'Some Conditions for Obedience and Disobedience to Authority', *Human Relations* 18: 57–74

Miliband, Ralph, 1969, *The State in Capitalist Society*, London, Weidenfeld & Nicolson

—— 1984, *Capitalist Democracy in Britain*, Oxford, Oxford University Press

Mills, C. Wright, 1956, *The Power Elite*, New York, Oxford University Press

Milne, A. J. M., 1962, *The Social Philosophy of English Idealism*, London, George Allen & Unwin

Mitchell, Duncan, 1959, *Sociology: The Study of Social Systems*, London, University Tutorial Press

Moloney, Kevin, 1996, *Lobbyists for Hire*, Aldershot, Dartmouth

—— 2006, *Rethinking Public Relations*, London, Routledge

Morehead, Joe, 1996, *Introduction to United States Government Information Sources*, Englewood, CO, Libraries Unlimited

Morgan, Michael L. (ed.), 1992, *Classics of Moral and Political Theory*, Indianapolis, IN, Hackett

Morison, Samuel Eliot, and Commager, Henry Steele, 1962, *The Growth of the American Republic*, 5th edn, 2 vols, New York, Oxford University Press

Mosca, Gaetano, 1939, *The Ruling Class*, ed. A. Livingston, New York, McGraw-Hill

Nettl, Peter, 1966, 'The Concept of System in Political Science', *Political Studies* 14: 305–338

Neustadt, R. E., 1960, *Presidential Power: The Politics of Leadership*, New York, Wiley

Norris, Pippa, 1994, 'Political Science in Britain and America: The Decline of a Special Relationship?', *PSA News* Autumn: 15–17

Norris, P. and Curtice, J., 2004, 'If You Build a Political Website, Will They Come? The Supply and Demand Model of New Technology, Social Capital and Civic Engagement in Britain', paper delivered to the Annual Meeting of the American Political Science Association, Chicago, IL, September

Nove, Alec, 1980, *The Soviet Economic System*, London, Allen & Unwin

Nurcombe, Valerie, 1992, *Local Authority Information Services: A Guide to Publications, Databases and Services*, London, SCOOP (The Library Association Standing Committee on Official Publications)

Oakeshott, Michael, 1962, *Rationalism in Politics, and Other Essays*, London, Methuen

Office for National Statistics, 2006 and 2007, National Statistics website, http://www.statistics.gov.uk

Ornstein, N. and Mann, T., 2000, *The Permanent Campaign and Its Future*, Washington, DC, American Enterprise Institute and the Brookings Institution.

Orwell, George, 1949, *1984*, London, Secker & Warburg

—— 1968, 'Politics and the English Language', in *Collected Essays*, etc., Vol. 4, Harmondsworth, Middlesex, Penguin

Osborne, David and Gaebler, Ted, 1992, *Reinventing Government: How the Entrepreneurial Spirit is Transforming the Public Sector*, Harmondsworth, Middlesex, Penguin

Pahl, R. E. and Winkler, A. M., 1975, 'The Coming Corporatism', *Challenge* March/April: 28–35

Pareto, Vilfredo, 1976, *Sociological Writings*, ed. S. E. Finer, Oxford, Blackwell

Parkinson, C. Northcote, 1958, *Parkinson's Law: Or the Pursuit of Progress*, London, Murray

Parkinson, Derek, 2003, 'The Message Not the Medium', *VoxPolitics Bulletin*, reproduced in *Netpulse* 7(15): October 16 (www.Politics Online.com)

Parsons, Talcott, 1957, 'The Distribution of Power in American Society', *World Politics* 10: 123–143

Pattie, C., Seyd, P. and Whiteley, P., 2004, *Citizenship in Britain: Values, Participation and Democracy*, Cambridge: Cambridge University Press

Pennock, J. Roland and Chapman, John W. (eds), 1978, *Anarchism* (Nomos 19), New York, New York University Press

Peters, G., 1999, *Institutional Theory in Political Science: The 'New Institutionalism'*, London, Pitman

Pierre, Jon and Stoker, Gerry, 2002, 'Towards Multi-Level Governance', in Dunleavy, Patrick *et al.* (eds), *Developments in British Politics 6*, Basingstoke, Palgrave

Plato, 1866, *The Republic of Plato*, ed. John Llewelyn Davies and David James Vaughan, London, Macmillan

Popper, Karl, 1960, *The Poverty of Historicism*, 2nd edn, London, Routledge & Kegan Paul

—— 1962, *The Open Society and Its Enemies*, London, Routledge

Poulantzas, Nicos, 1973, *Political Power and Social Classes*, London, New Left Review Books

Prawer, J. and Eisenstadt, S. N., 1968, 'Feudalism', in Sills, David L. (ed.), *International Encyclopaedia of Social Sciences*, New York, Macmillan, Vol. 5: 393–403

Pressman, J. I. and Wildavsky, Aron, 1973, *Implementation: How Great Expectations in Washington Are Dashed in Oakland or Why It's Amazing that Federal Programs Work at All*, Berkeley and Los Angeles, University of California Press

Putnam, R., 2000, *Bowling Alone: The Collapse and Revival of American Community*, New York: Simon & Schuster.

Pye, Lucian and Verba, Sidney, 1965, *Political Culture and Political Development*, Princeton, NJ, Princeton University Press

Rae, D. W., 1967, *The Political Consequences of Electoral Laws*, New Haven, CT, Yale University Press

Rawls, John, 1971, *The Theory of Justice*, London, Oxford University Press

Reischaur, Edwin, 1956, 'Japanese Feudalism', in Coulborne, Rushton (ed.), *Feudalism in History*, Princeton, NJ, Princeton University Press

Rheingold, H., 1993, *The Virtual Community: Homesteading on the Electronic Frontier*, Reading, MA, Addison-Wesley

Rhodes, R. A. W., 1996, 'The New Governance: Governing without Government', *Political Studies* 44(4): 652–667

Rhodes, R., 1997, *Understanding Governance*, Buckingham, Open University Press

Ridley, F. F., 1975, *The Study of Government: Political Science and Public Administration, London*, Allen & Unwin

Rose, Richard (ed.), 1969, *Policy Making in Britain*, London, Macmillan

Rousseau, Jean Jacques, 1913, *The Social Contract and Discourses*, ed. G. D. H. Coles, London, J.M. Dent

Rowbotham, Sheila, 1972, *Women, Resistance and Revolution: A History of Women in the Modern World*, New York, Random House

Royal Commission on Historical Monuments, 1982, *Papers of the British Cabinet Ministers 1782–1900*, London, HMSO

Rubinstein, David, 2000, 'A New Look at New Labour', *Politics* 20(3): 16–18

Runciman, W. G., 1969, *Social Science and Political Theory*, Cambridge, Cambridge University Press

Russell, Bertrand, 1938, *Power: A New Analysis*, London, George Allen & Unwin

Rutter, M. and Madge, N., 1976, *Cycles of Disadvantage: A Review of Research*, London, Heinemann

Sabine, George, 1951, *A History of Political Theory*, 3rd edn, London, George G. Harrap

Said, Edward, 1987, *Orientalism*, Harmondsworth, Middlesex, Penguin

Sampson, Anthony, 2004, *Who Runs This Place? The Anatomy of Britain in the 21st Century*, London, John Murray

Sandel, Michael, 1996, *Democracy's Discontent: America in Search of a Public Philosophy*, Cambridge, MA, Belknap Press

Sartori, Giovanni, 1970, 'Concept Misinformation in Comparative Politics', *American Political Science Review* 54: 1033–1053 (reprinted in Lewis, Paul G. *et al.*, 1975, *The Practice of Comparative Politics: A Reader*, 2nd edn, London, Longmans)

Saunders, Peter, 1995, *Capitalism: A Social Audit*, Buckingham, Open University Press

Saward, Michael, 1993, 'Direct Democracy Revisited', *Politics* 13(2): 18–24

Scammell, M., 2001, 'The Internet and Civic Engagement in the Age of the Citizen-consumer', *Political Communication* 17: 351–355.

Schapiro, Leonard, 1965, *The Government and Politics of the Soviet Union*, London, Hutchinson

Schattschneider, E. E., 1960, *The Semisovereign People*, New York, Holt, Rinehart & Winston

Scholte, J. A. 2000, *Globalization: A Critical Introduction*, London, Macmillan

Schultz, Richard, 1980, *Responding to the Terrorist Threat: Security and Crisis Management*, New York, Pergamon

Seale, Patrick and McConville, Maureen, 1968, *French Revolution*, Harmondsworth, Middlesex, Penguin

Seckinelgin, Hakan, 2007, *The International Politics of HIV/AIDS*, London, Routledge

Sell, Susan K., 2003, *Private Power, Public Law: The Globalization of Intellectual Property Rights*, Cambridge, Cambridge University Press

Shaw, R. and Sklar, R. L., 1977, *A Bibliography for the Study of African Politics*, Walthon, MA, Cross Roads Press

Sherif, M. *et al.*, 1951, 'A Preliminary Study of Intergroup Relations', in Rohrer, J. H. and Sherif, M. (eds), *Social Psychology at the Crossroads*, New York, Harper, 388–524

Simon, Herbert A., 1959, 'Theories of Decision Making in Economics and Behavioural Science', *American Economic Review* 49(3): 253–283

—— 1977, *The New Science of Management*, Englewood Cliffs, NJ, Prentice Hall

Singer, Peter, 1973, *Democracy and Disobedience*, Oxford, Clarendon Press

Sklar, Richard L, 1963, *Nigerian Political Parties: Power in an Emergent Nation*, Princeton, NJ, Princeton University Press

Smith, Gordon, 1989, *Politics in Western Europe: A Comparative Analysis*, Aldershot, Gower

Snape, Wilfred E., 1969, *How to Find Out About Local Government*, Oxford, Pergamon Press

Southern Electric, 1994, *Caring for Customers*, Maidenhead, Southern Electric

Stiglitz, Joseph, 2002, *Globalization and Its Discontents*, London, Penguin

Stoker, Gerry, 2006, *Why Politics Matters*, Basingstoke, Palgrave Macmillan

Suffian, Tun Mohamed *et al.*, 1978, *The Constitution of Malaysia: Its Development 1957–1977*, Kuala Lumpur, Oxford University Press

Sunstein, Cass, 2004, 'Democracy and Filtering', *Communications of ACM* 47(12): 57–59

Tajfel, H. and Turner, J., 1979, 'An Integrative Theory of Inter-group Conflict', in Austin, G. and Worschel, S. (eds), *The Social Psychology of Inter-group Relations*, Montery, CA, Brooks/Cole

Tansey, Stephen D., 1973, 'Political Analysis: A Report on a Project of Syllabus Development', MSc report, Birkbeck College, London

—— 1989, 'Employers' Reactions to the Youth Training Scheme', MPhil thesis, University of Bath

—— 2002, *Business, Information Technology and Society*, London, Routledge

Tansey, Stephen D. and Kermode, David G., 1967/8, 'The Westminster Model in Nigeria', *Parliamentary Affairs* Winter: 19–37

Tawney, R. H., 1938, *Religion and the Rise of Capitalism*, Harmondsworth, Middlesex, Penguin

Taylor, C. L. and Jodice, D. A. A., 1983, *World Handbook of Political and Social Indicators*, 3rd edn, New Haven, CT, Yale University Press

Taylor, John and Williams, H., 1990, 'Themes and Issues in an Information Polity', *Journal of Information Technology* 5(3): 151–160

Taylor, John and Williams, H., 1991, 'From Public Administration to the Information Polity', *Public Administration* 69(2): 171–190

Thomas, Hugh (ed.), 1959, *The Establishment*, London, Anthony Blond

Thomson, Ian, 1989, *The Documentation of the European Communities: A Guide*, London, Mansell

Thomson, Ian and Mitchell, Duncan, 1993 onwards, 'The Documentation of the European Communities: Annual Review of Activities', *Journal of Common Market Studies*

Trotsky, Leon, 1945, *The Revolution Betrayed*, New York, Pioneer Publishers

Tullock, Gordon, 1965, *The Politics of Bureaucracy*, Washington, DC, Public Affairs Press

Turow, J., 1997, *Breaking Up America: Advertisers and the New Media World*, Chicago, IL, University of Chicago Press

Verney, Douglas, 1959, *The Analysis of Political Systems*, Glencoe, IL, Free Press

Vincent, Andrew, 1992, *Modern Political Ideologies*, Oxford, Blackwell

Voltaire, 1756, 'Essai sur l'histoire générale et sur les moeurs et l'esprit des nations', Paris

Weiner, Myron, 1962, *The Politics of Scarcity: Party Politics in India*, Princeton, NJ, Princeton University Press

Weldon, T. D., 1953, *The Vocabulary of Politics*, Harmondsworth, Middlesex, Penguin

Wheare, K. C., 1951, *Modern Constitutions*, Oxford, Oxford University Press

—— 1963, *Federal Government*, 4th edn, London, Oxford University Press

Whittaker, David (ed.), 2001, *The Terrorism Reader*, London, Routledge

Williams, Gavin (ed.), 1976, *Nigeria: Economy and Society*, London, Rex Collings

Williams, Philip, 1964, *Crisis and Compromise*, Harlow, Longmans

Wittfogel, K., 1957, *Oriental Despotism*, New Haven, CT, Yale University Press

Wollstonecraft, Mary, 1985, *A Vindication of the Rights of Women*, Harmondsworth, Middlesex, Penguin

World Bank, 2006, *Global Economic Prospects 2005*, Washington DC, online at http://www.worldbank.org

Woodcock, George, 1975, *Anarchism*, Harmondsworth, Middlesex, Penguin

Wring, D., 2007, 'Focus Group Follies? Qualitative Research and British Labour Party Strategy', *Journal of Political Marketing* 5(4): 71–97

INDEX